BOXING PANDORA

TIMOTHY WILLIAM WATERS

Boxing Pandora

RETHINKING BORDERS, STATES, AND

SECESSION IN A DEMOCRATIC WORLD

Yale

UNIVERSITY PRESS

NEW HAVEN & LONDON

Yale University Press books may be purchased in quantity for educational,
business, or promotional use. For information, please e-mail sales.press@yale.
edu (U.S. office) or sales@yaleup.co.uk (U.K. office).

Set in Times Roman type by Integrated Publishing Solutions,
Grand Rapids, Michigan
Printed in the United States of America.

Library of Congress Control Number: 2019936842
ISBN 978-0-300-23589-0 (hardcover : alk. paper)

A catalogue record for this book is available from the British Library.

This paper meets the requirements of ANSI/NISO Z39.48-1992
(Permanence of Paper).

10 9 8 7 6 5 4 3 2 1

Quod petis, hic est: Est Ulubris, anima si ti non deficit aequus

*B*ecause I found, writing a book about

*L*eaving, I couldn't stay:

To you.

CONTENTS

PREFACE: WHY WRITE A BOOK ABOUT SECESSION? WHY READ ONE?

THIS BOOK IS ABOUT MAKING new states, letting people secede from the states they live in and form new ones. This is either a good idea or a very dangerous one—deciding which is what this book is about—but we should deal with one concern right away: Why write such a book at all? Borders matter less and less, supposedly, and states are increasingly irrelevant in a globalizing world, unable to respond to challenges that demand transnational cooperation. It might seem retrograde to be making more divisions—doubling down on the troubled model of the national state, talking about walls—rather than breaking down borders and getting beyond the state. Aren't borders passé? Why add deck chairs while the ship of states steers toward the iceberg of a new global age?

There are many things in this book that are politically implausible in the short term, but they are quite realistic compared to a stateless world of global citizens. Such a world does not exist, and there's good reason to think it won't for a long time, if ever. Anyone who has ever worked abroad or just visited another place will have noticed that things are done quite differently. And not only over there: *Within* most societies, it's obvious both that things vary from place to place and that the state exercises considerable power—sometimes all-consuming, sometimes marginal, sometimes for good, sometimes evil. Where you live matters, and rarely is the state you live in an irrelevance.

There are places where borders barely exist, whole regions in which local authorities and folkways are far more consequential.[1] Even where the state is powerful, it's not the sum of society, and we miss a great deal of the richness of human experience if we only look at its formal structures—constitutions and laws but not social practices; rules but not their transgression; the border but not the crossings. Focusing only on the lines on the map or the colors of the fill blinds us to the diversity and hybridity of the world. People are forever passing over boundaries, mixing identities and cultural practices. That richness is lost if we imagine states as hermetically sealed monoliths.

But we are not compelled to such extremes. In much of the world the state exercises considerable power, shaping social, economic and political life. Sometimes borders matter a great deal: In Berlin, the Wall is gone, but crosses mark the killings of those who tried to get through it. In many places, life is radically different in the space governed by one state rather than by another—sometimes for good, sometimes not. People do transgress borders, but borders have to be transgressed; they are there, shaping behavior even while being overcome or evaded. Smuggling exists because the state has (imperfect) power to shape laws and markets; without the state, smuggling is trade. Even problems that seem to emblemize states' fecklessness show the state's continued relevance and power. Millions of migrants entering Europe look like a tide overwhelming hapless states, but harsh border regimes diverted the flow. And those migrants keep trying because, behind Schengenia's walls, Europe's societies are different from the ones they're fleeing. Migration isn't only a challenge to the Westphalian state but a confirmation of its enduring, consequential power—and a reminder that when we talk about borders, we're really talking about the territory beyond and the people within. Borders are just the limits of places people live—the end of one, the beginning of another, and the way of crossing.

If states are weakening in some ways, in others they are becoming stronger—the bureaucratic state, the surveillance state. By most measures, over the last two centuries states have become vastly more powerful. States change, and changing, they will still be here. The state's persistence suggests we ought to come to grips with it, rather than fantasize about it withering away. Perhaps someday we will arrive at disaggregated networks, global governance, even a single world government. But perhaps not, and until we do, we must be concerned with the states we have, which shape much of life for better or worse. States are persistent social facts. For as long as they matter, to the degree they do, we should be concerned with their qualities.

People are persistent facts, too. They are why a book about secession matters: States aren't going away, so neither are the problems states create nor the challenges people mount to them. A glance at the headlines shows as much: Scotland

(and Brexit), the annexation of Crimea, ISIS' caliphate, South Sudan, Kosovo, East Timor, separatists in Aceh, Kurdistan, Congo, Kashmir, Tibet, Bougain-ville, and a dozen other places that don't make the news but matter to those living there. After the election of Donald Trump, there was even talk of 'Calexit.' These things are happening—we live in a world in which, *because* countries matter, they are challenged by people convinced that the states we have aren't the ones we ought to—and so we need law and politics to address that reality. People are physical beings; governing ourselves in shared space is the very essence of politics. Place matters, and so units do, too. This book doesn't take *existing* states as givens, but it does assume states are a persistent feature of our global society and asks how best to shape the units that shape our shared life.

But, since you've already picked up this book, perhaps you already know that question is worth asking.

A NOTE ON READING THIS BOOK

SINCE YOU ARE ABOUT TO READ this book, a word about how: This is a practical, politically relevant approach to secession. It may not be a beach read, but it's meant to be accessible to well-informed readers—and academic audiences, although they may have to adjust their expectations. The appendix discusses scholarship, but I've kept notes to a minimum and avoided making particular works or scholars the grammatical subjects of my sentences; this book is about ideas, not their authors. The general reader will hardly miss such things, but specialists shouldn't mistake these departures from usual practice for a lack of seriousness: This book is informed by an engaged reading of scholarship and the broader political conversation of which that scholarship is a part. Indeed, *Boxing Pandora* is a contribution to that conversation—my contribution: No one thinks or writes in a vacuum, but I am the author of this book, and its argument—original, worthwhile, worthless or otherwise—is my own.

BOXING PANDORA

Introduction: The Boxes We Live in, the Beliefs We Have

We believe fixed borders increase stability and reduce violence. But do they? Have we gotten the equation between states and human beings backward?

THIS BOOK PROPOSES A NEW RIGHT to secession, and here it is:

Groups of people may form a *new* state by holding a referendum on part of an *existing* state's territory. If the group wins the vote, the existing state must negotiate independence in good faith. The group's members don't need to share ethnicity, language, or culture; they just have to live in the same place.

That is the short version. The fuller expression of the right is more complicated and nuanced; you'll find it at the start of part II, and it's the subject of this book. But even in abbreviated form, you might think this is a terrible idea—a formula for chaos, instability, and violence—and you can already think of many objections. Surely the *current* rule—a legal and political system of states with fixed borders—is a much safer and better way to organize the planet and the people living on it.

I'm not so sure, and exploring that doubt is what this book is about. In writing it, my purpose is to consider why this intuition about fixed borders—which, as we'll see, is the conventional wisdom and the commonest sense, even though borders have only been fixed since 1945—may well be wrong, why the objections to secession prove less obvious than they seem, and why it is actually very hard to be so very, very sure that the rule we have now does what we think it does.

In recent years, the international order established at the end of the Second World War has been subjected to critical scrutiny. The state—the basic unit of our global system—has been seen as increasingly unresponsive and irrelevant, an anachronism unable to deal with the challenges of a post-Westphalian world: climate change, pandemics, migration, terrorism, global trade. Instead, all kinds of transnational and subnational alternatives are flourishing—networks of environmental activists, the Occupy movement, tech giants, ISIS—to supplant or bypass the hoary old territorial state.

Yet in all this ferment, the most fundamental pillar of our global order has been almost universally and uncritically accepted as moral and necessary: that preserving states in their existing borders—maintaining their territorial integrity— contributes to stability and reduces violence. This intuition remains as easily assumed as it is hard to test, and is shared across a variety of ideologies and political persuasions. Those who continue to believe in the importance of states are almost uniformly convinced that it is dangerous to tinker with borders. But equally, those convinced that the territorial state is outdated rarely want to multiply an anachronism—states should wither away or unite, not divide. Individual cases might deserve special treatment—places like Kosovo or East Timor—but the idea that *in general* states' borders might change is thought to invite chaos: to open Pandora's box.

But what if borders *are* the problem? What if borders don't do what we think they do—what if changing borders could increase stability, cause less violence, and make societies more just? That's the possibility this book explores: challenging the assumption that fixed borders are necessary and good, showing how that assumption is untested and unfounded, and proposing an alternative that could better serve our common goals. That alternative is a right to secession.

The legal and political order established at the end of the Second World War, under which we still live, has confined questions about the shape of states—and changes to their shape—to a very limited space. Rules protecting territorial integrity ensure that states can maintain their historical borders, while the rules for creating new states—especially the right of self-determination—mostly involve liberating colonies. The rise of human rights has eroded the notion that what happens inside the state is no one else's business—as if there was ever a time when states didn't interfere in each other's affairs!—but this rise has had little effect on the fixity of frontiers; whether in Iraq or Myanmar, Afghanistan or Bosnia, we demand improvement in rights *and* expect it to happen within the states we already have. When, sometimes, borders change, politicians and lawyers alike struggle to call it something, anything other than 'secession,' denying any precedent for other people who might not like the state they live in.

Fixing borders supposedly does several good things: increases stability, reduces violence, and discourages illiberal nationalism's dangerous progeny—intolerance, revanchism, ethnic cleansing. Fixed borders create an expectation of permanence and, with it, of community:

> [T]he "locking in" of different groups within a single polity provides the state with relative permanence and stability and conveys to the different ethnic groups within the state the idea that, from an international perspective, they share a single national identity and, perhaps, a common destiny.[1]

And perhaps that really is true, though "true" is a tricky word: This intuition mixes assumptions about how humans behave, with preferences for how they ought to. As we'll see, the *belief* that fixed borders do these things and the *desire* that they should are curiously, dangerously conflated. For although we believe giving states permanent territory stabilizes politics, it's not clear that's what has actually happened. (That quote about 'locking in' groups is about Jews and Arabs in Israel.)

Meanwhile, new understandings of what states ought to look like—claims to form new states—have repeatedly intruded into this supposedly fixed system, challenging the comfortable notion that the states we already have are actually the right ones. Much of this book looks at self-determination, and how this powerful yet inchoate concept interacts with secession. Self-determination has an old and rich history of justifications for why human communities ought to govern themselves. But in our postwar era, self-determination was put to work as an engine of decolonization, justifying states for 'peoples' defined as the populations of *existing* territories. Perhaps you already see the problem.

The idea that the right to a state shouldn't be limited to those who already have one has persisted, and self-determination's supposedly settled meaning has remained open to challenge. But international law has proven curiously unable to respond effectively. Not that it hasn't changed: Beginning in the 1960s,

self-determination was mobilized to support democratization, autonomy, federalism, and the rights of minorities and indigenous peoples. These claims about
the *internal* working of states have been described as internal self-determination.
And in recent years, debates about humanitarian intervention and regime change
have raised questions about the legitimacy of governments ruling their people
in the ways they do, and about the rights or obligations of outsiders—the international community—to intervene to protect populations at risk. But even these
debates have assumed that the states we intervene in and repair are the default
units; we try to fix the states we have.

Yet alongside these debates, human beings continue to claim a right of self-
determination as *they* understand it: a right to form their own states. Territorially concentrated communities—often ethnic or national, but sometimes representing regional identities or political persuasions, or just structural losers in a
state's internal governance—have continued to see the creation of new states as
self-determination's real value. They have not been content with self-determination's often-frustrated promise to humanize the states in which they happen
to live; "colonial groups and oppressed minorities have put more faith in obtaining a state of their own than in the protection of international human rights
regimes."[2]

Since the end of the Cold War, these claims have become increasingly visible. One 2008 estimate, for example, found about seventy secession movements, including two dozen active ones and seven involving significant violence.[3] Some are entirely peaceful, like the one in Scotland; others have shifted
between violent and peaceful phases, like the Basque or Kashmiri movements;
or began peacefully and then radicalized, like Kosovo's. Some have changed
their goals, shifting between demands for greater participation in the state, internal autonomy, or full independence. These protests, rebellions, and civil wars
suggest not everyone has gotten the message about how the world order works—
at least, not everyone agrees. States' responses—repression, marginalization,
discrimination, persecution, genocide—suggest our present system, whatever its
virtues, does not react well to collective expressions of political identity or
produce outcomes to match the desires of real human communities.

Because for all their diversity, these movements mostly share another feature: They have failed. Few secessionists achieve independence, and fewer are
recognized by other states. As a political matter, these voices have seldom been
listened to, and their claims have not been matched by changes in the canon of

agreed rules about how new states form. Instead, law and politics continue to marginalize external self-determination in the moribund category of decolonization, with very few exceptions, while focusing on internal democratization. We will succeed, or fail, with the states we have.

Law and policy have come to favor integrative solutions and demonstrate a distrust of, even an animus against, changing borders. (When I talk to groups about secession, I am often asked, "But why not focus on autonomy?" as if that is intuitively better and secession would be a kind of failure.) A historical narrative about self-determination has developed, which consigns its radically disruptive—and generative—qualities to a failed period of idealistic Wilsonianism, whose endpoint was Munich, *Lebensraum,* and the ovens. We certainly don't want that again, if that's what making new states means.

Of course, it isn't. Many new states have been created in recent decades, and although some have been colossal failures, others have done fine, and refreshingly few people have put on jackboots as a result. In 1945, there were about 70 widely recognized states; today, 194. Some two-thirds of today's states have come into existence during the period when, notionally, borders had already been fixed. Many were colonies, which meant they already had identified frontiers. But many were formed by the division of existing states; the Soviet Union and Yugoslavia divided into 22 states, more than a tenth of the world total. So perhaps we actually have a flexible enough system?

New states do get created, but the process has been curiously limited. Decolonization was treated as a special category, a one-off often not even seen as secession. For units other than colonies, claims of self-determination or secession are generally avoided. Instead, the focus is on voluntary consent (Czechoslovakia, Bangladesh), constitutional arrangements allowing division (Eritrea, the Soviet Union), or 'dissolution' (Yugoslavia). In the rare cases when a state appears and there is no other way to explain it, states fiercely resist recognizing the new country or the implications: even states favoring Kosovo's independence vehemently insisted the case was sui generis, a precedent for absolutely nothing.

These explanations preserve doctrinal purity—they allow us to *say* states are not being created by means we don't want to accept—but also remove us from political realities. This has not only been a problem of law, but of practice: Existing states don't simply hide behind doctrine, they seem to take it seriously, actively resisting the creation of new states almost regardless of circumstance.

Think about how rarely states support secession. States frequently intervene in the internal problems of other states. When they do, they may insist on human rights protections or new governance arrangements—federalism, autonomy, a new constitution—but they almost never change the shape of the state. Even states that back guerrilla movements rarely support secession. When states have reluctantly acquiesced in creating new states, they default to internal boundaries, as happened in Yugoslavia. It's commonly supposed this reflects political realism, but it is its own form of idealized policy.

Consider a thought experiment: If the United States were motivated solely by self-interest, it would sometimes favor preserving states and sometimes favor dismantling them. Yet in the postwar period, the United States has almost never supported a unilateral secession; Kosovo is really the only example, and there, US policy defaulted to existing provincial boundaries for the new frontier and denied the case was a precedent. In defining its interests, the United States has internalized a highly rarified normative principle:[4] a commitment to the status quo of existing states in almost all circumstances. This is a principle almost all states have embraced, regardless of their position in the global order.

Law and politics have placed a bet on a model that favors the permanence of borders and relies on internal accommodations to manage conflict within states. Often this works—federalism or autonomy or human rights can mitigate strife and provide a decent life for all. Yet relying on internal approaches will sometimes fail, because sometimes the shape of the state is part of the problem. A model that insists all solutions must be found within existing states ensures that some changes, however desirable they might be to people within, are never going to happen.

A broad range of actors has recognized these rigidities and sought to challenge or defend them. (Secessionists obviously contest the system's limits, though sometimes only for themselves). Some scholars, especially in law, try to shore up formalist doctrine, dismissing claims for statehood as morally unacceptable "postmodern tribalism."[5] Others try to deconstruct self-determination into distinct solutions, like autonomy, federalism, or minority protection, or try to embed it in states' constitutional order, in hopes of coming up with solutions that avoid the moment, or the danger, of secession.

This approach has real merit in specific cases but doesn't provide a general solution. By insisting that change preclude supposedly radical solutions, it fails to harness self-determination's potential. Part of the problem today is that the options are all shaped by the shadow of a rigid global rule. Focused on redesigning highly variable constitutional systems or local autonomies, they forgo the power of a single global rule to make those particular solutions less likely to underperform or fail.

Others, understanding that the current system's rigidity might be a problem rather than a positive quality, have criticized that model for failing in specific places—in Yugoslavia or Africa—or by critically examining the provenance of self-determination, and this book will do that, too. Yet with rare exceptions, what such criticisms lack is a comprehensive attempt to synthesize those aspirations and the law that governs them in a robust new model: a practical pathway for societies to change their borders peacefully when the humans living within them wish to.

This book attempts just that. I examine our current rule, the assumptions underlying it, and its effects. I propose an alternative: an international right of secession realized through plebiscites. I consider the new rule's likely effects, as well as some important objections to it. The goal is not a new rule for its own sake, but a means to help change the real prospects human beings have to challenge the states they live in and shape their own governance. By examining the assumptions underlying the current rule, we will see that the real danger to global stability is not the attempt to form new states—it is the capacity of existing states to resist those attempts, even with violence. Chaos and death are not consequences of opening Pandora's box—they *are* the box.

How This Book Is Organized

This introduction sets up the basic questions: Do fixed borders provide stability and reduce violence? Have we gotten the equation between states and the people who live in them backward? The rest of the book answers those questions. Part I lays out the present rule—our assumptions about what it does and the difficulties we have even figuring out what its effects are. Part II introduces a new rule and suggests a practical pathway to it, both because it might be a better alternative—flexible borders could prove more stabilizing and more just—and to give us some way of testing the rule we have.

Chapter 1, "The Failure of a Flourishing Idea," lays out a history of self-determination: What are the origins of our system for organizing territory? How did self-determination move from making new states to focusing on democratization within existing states? As we'll see, the earlier, preclassical model had serious problems but also offered a substantive approach to the problem of political community that the current rule can't. Chapter 2, "The Map of Our World," surveys current law and politics, revealing a period of ferment and stagnation: the postwar order in its late, classical decadence. Chapter 3, "The Measure of Nations," examines what we think the prevailing model actually does. Observing that the current system is untested, it examines the assumptions we make about the rule, and how we might test them. We'll see that much of what we think the current rule does may not be true—and as for the rest, we don't know. But one thing will become clear: It is possible to do better.

So part II introduces "The New Rule." Drawing on a modified, democratized Wilsonianism, chapter 4 describes a right of secession by self-identified communities through plebiscites—a truly self-determined process. The rule, allowing local majorities within states to vote for independence, is outlined in general terms, then chapters 5 ("People, Territory, Plebiscite") and 6 ("Broader Implications") examine how it differs from the existing rule and looks at the more important concerns the new rule raises. This new rule is by no means perfect—but it only has to be better than the one we have now. The real purpose isn't to create implausible rights and feckless institutions, but to improve people's ability to negotiate with their own states. Chapter 7, "The Hardest Part," considers strategies to achieve acceptance of a right to secede, whether as a legal rule or as a model for individual states.

Finally, the conclusion returns to the value of critically assessing the basic rules we live under: Persistent violence and instability suggest there must be a better rule, and it is only by challenging the current order's hidden assumptions that we will find it.

Three Assumptions

I make three assumptions of my own. First, human beings have diverse identities. Almost everyone is a citizen of some state, but many people have connections to more than one. People also belong to other communities—tribes, social classes, associations, churches, ethnic groups, nations, gender and sexual orientations, ideological communities—that may matter more to their daily lives and worldview. This diversity is both mutable and irreducible: Its content changes

Five Ways of Thinking about Secession

There are four basic ways to justify secession: as property, nationalism, justice, or democratic choice.* These overlap: Nationalists assert an inherent right but often also believe they were the original occupants (a property claim) and have unjustly suffered; and if they are a majority, they claim a democratic basis, too.

But property, nationalism, and justice have real limitations and real problems. Property theories analogize the state to private property, which is very different, and don't say much about the interests of people who don't own property. Nationalist theories can be exclusivist, even racist (although liberal versions also exist), and often assume identity rather than acknowledging its constructed nature. Justice-based logics tend to allow secession only under limited, often horrendous circumstances, which reinforce states' authority so long as they meet minimum standards. Most problematically, nationalist and justice claims rest on 'thick,' irreducibly contestable claims about identity, morality, and history.

By contrast, democratic choice theories can be 'thin' and procedural, in the same way we can agree on who won an election. Democratic claims have problems, too—much of this book is about them—and my purpose isn't to argue against the other justifications. I think they are important *in politics*—as the reasons people give for making decisions. But this book advances a democratic choice model as the most defensible basis that evades or minimizes the traps of contestation and actually has practical traction.

Because there is a fifth way to think about secession: hostility, which is the most common approach in politics. That's the view against which any argument for a right to secession must contend.

*See Dietrich, "Changing Borders by Secession," 81–93. This book's appendix also discusses broader scholarship.

as identities are created, altered, and destroyed, but the pluralism and richness of identity is a permanent part of our humanity.

Second, states won't disappear: Something like the modern state is the default for much of political and social life on the planet. Its qualities change, as they always have, but there is a predictable minimum of functions and influences we can expect most states to exhibit, which relate to territory. This is because of another irreducible quality of human beings: their physical nature—their biological existence in space and their consequent need to organize their physical environment. In current material conditions, we can expect the *physical* nature of human beings to manifest itself *politically* in territorial states.

Third, those physical beings expect to govern themselves—a recent trend, but one likely to continue. States don't always behave democratically, but they do so more than in the past; even those that don't often pay lip service to the idea, and this is not trivial. We can assume that democracy—the expectation of it, if not always the reality (or the rationality of voters)—will be a part of the normative order.

These three assumptions help frame our question: If states aren't going away, and democratic processes increasingly displace other principles, and humans have diverse identities, what can we expect? How should we structure the rules to govern ourselves in a global system of diverse, democratic states? (By rules, I mean norms we choose, not sociological 'laws' describing how humans interact. Such 'laws' should inform our choices, because there is little sense prescribing the impossible.)

The new rule in this book is likely a better answer to that question than the rule we have, and I will try to show why. But my purpose isn't just to prove that my alternative is better: It's also to show the lack of reasons for believing the current rule does what we want it to do, and to find a way—since we can't directly test our current rule—to evaluate it. The new rule is therefore an alternative and a provocation: It encourages us to be skeptical about our too easy confidence in the rightness of the system we have and our ability to answer fundamental questions about the global order. This book proposes a new rule but equally aims to convince you we shouldn't be so confident in the rules we have.

The argument is framed in terms of law—I am a law professor—but nothing in it supposes law exists in some pristine vacuum apart from politics. On the contrary, I assume politics and law dynamically interact, and politics' priority is at its greatest and law at its thinnest in the international realm. This book emphasizes the practical and empirical whenever they contradict the formal or doctrinal; I am not interested in law for its own sake. But it so happens the law we currently have closely tracks the assumptions of our politics, and because my proposal itself has a normative purpose—it proposes a change—law is a valuable framework. The question of 'should,' of what humans ought to do, is one properly discussed in politics, morality, and law, informed by the insights of the social sciences. So this book is organized on that basis: a normative proposal grounded on empirical considerations, using the language of international relations and politics as well as law and justice.

This book argues that secession might be a solution, rather than a problem. If that intuition seems plausible, even compelling, then there is a great deal of work to be done to figure out how the new rule ought to be structured. And because I don't want to leave things in the realm of pure abstraction, I propose a concrete solution—an international legal right to secession based on plebiscites. But although the rule I propose is pretty specific, I'm not going to work out every detail. For example, what should happen with individuals who want to retain the citizenship of the old state—should they have that right, and under what conditions? There are several plausible answers, both under the law we currently have and under a humane and functional new rule. While I note major alternatives, I won't choose one right answer; I only intend to propose the outlines, the minimal elements so we can assess the basic idea. Even so, as soon as one proposes concrete solutions, concrete objections arise. I will sometimes get into the weeds and suggest a preferred model, if the answer to an objection lies in a particular variant; objections to the very real failings of Wilsonian self-determination can be answered by specific design choices, for example. But this isn't only about adding up costs and benefits. As we'll repeatedly see, the fallback defense of the current system is that it is the system—a status quo we fear to disrupt even if there are better alternatives. I try to answer this important if very disturbing objection, because the purpose of this book is to show that this new idea is worth considering.

If you are convinced that it is, or might be, you will naturally wonder what form it should take, and that means a practical conversation about how this might actually be done. That's why the last chapter lays out pathways by which this idea might become established law and practice. It considers the politics and strategies for getting this new rule adopted—should it be part of a treaty, or should certain states adopt it in their constitutions?—drawing lessons from other improbable projects that have become orthodoxies, such as decolonization and human rights.

But that's the last thing this book gets to. First I want to show that this implausible, counterintuitive idea is actually a good one, because unless you believe that, there's little point in discussing how to make this right a reality. First the devil, then the details.

PART ONE

THE CURRENT RULE

1

The Failure of a Flourishing Idea:
The Decadence of Self-Determination

How did we arrive at a world of fixed borders? How did self-determination move from its disruptive origins to the current rule, which reinforces existing states' territorial integrity?

The Origins of Our Commitments about Territory and Peoples

THE RULES AND ASSUMPTIONS governing how we think about territory and political community are not immutable; in fact they are quite recent in origin. Their history, like that of many ideas, is full of reversals of meaning, which are themselves significant for our story. So let's look briefly at how the legal doctrines and political commitments developed historically, to see how we have arrived at the particular system of rules about territory, states, and people that we have today.

At the center of this system is the idea of self-determination, but the broader frame concerns rules and justifications for forming and preserving states. It's possible to talk about new states or even secession without invoking self-determination. The term will prove useful, however, when we consider the reasons for making new states: We will find that self-determination provides the underlying logic for why we might want to make new states at all.

Popular and Nationalist Conceptions

Our contemporary understanding of self-determination is rooted in the Enlightenment and in eighteenth- and nineteenth-century theories of political participation and nationalism,[1] though those roots have borne curious fruit. The question of how people should take part in their own governance is much older than the eighteenth century, of course, as is the phenomenon of unwilling and unhappy subjects; peasants have been revolting, and nobles rebelling, for as long as we have records, and equally old are attempts to justify or constrain the exercise of power, one over another.

So even before anyone ever uttered the word "self-determination," we find attempts in the early modern period to give the ruled options in relation to their rulers. The Peace of Augsburg in 1555 and the treaties making up the Peace of Westphalia in 1648 affirm the *jus emigrandi,* the right of religious minorities to migrate to more congenially Catholic or Protestant lands. But a right of emigration avoids rather than answers the question of what an individual's relationship to the ruler in a given place is—whether people are properly governed, where they live, only by their consent.[2]

The most consequential expressions of that idea, and the direct antecedents of self-determination, appear in the two great revolutions of the late eighteenth century—the first of which, the American, was not a revolution but a secession. The American Declaration of Independence of 1776 advances a clear claim that an aggrieved political community—"one people"—has a right unilaterally to "dissolve the political bands which have connected them with another, and to assume among the powers of the earth, the separate and equal station to which the Laws of Nature and of Nature's God entitle them[.]"[3] A people deserves a separate and equal station—it deserves statehood. The American rebels' assertion was initially just that—an assertion, vindicated only through victory in war. And why exactly those thirteen colonies constituted a people—after all, Britain had adjacent colonies that didn't rebel, and there were many loyalists in those thirteen—was equally a question best answered by the outcome. The idea, however, has exhibited considerable traction.

The French Revolution, beginning thirteen years later in 1789, produced claims about individual liberty and popular sovereignty—the promulgation of the Declaration of the Rights of Man and of the Citizen—and an extensive if imperfect practice of democratic consultation. This was evident in how the French Republic decided the status of territories its armies had conquered. War remained a valid instrument of policy, but revolutionary France forswore the sovereign's traditional right of conquest; instead, in areas it wished to annex, plebiscites were conducted, with the question addressed to the populations directly affected rather than the notional sovereign. Thus, French forces held a plebiscite in the papal enclave at Avignon, before its annexation; the people, not the pope, were asked. And this from a proclamation to the population of Savoy, issued in 1792 after France's victory there:

> Proud of the success of our arms, we could give you orders, but the French Republic has effaced from its annals the words king, master and subjects . . . we only give you advice. . . . Hence, we exhort the free people of Savoy to gather today, peaceably, without weapons, under the guidance of the French arms, in each commune, in order to nominate a deputy charged to express in a general assembly their wish for a new government.[4]

These democratic exercises were not free and fair, to apply the current standard anachronistically—"the guidance of the French arms" tells us what we need to know—but they were a radical departure from prevailing practice: A plebiscite suggested that the relevant source for deciding who and how that place should be governed was the people of a territory—that people made the law for their own land.

A few decades later, in the early nineteenth century, the Latin American independence movements—influenced by the French and American Revolutions—developed a conservative principle to limit the effects of radical changes in territorial sovereignty when new states formed: the doctrine of *uti possidetis.*

Uti possidetis—from the Latin *uti possidetis ita possideatis* ("may you have what you have had"), a holding action in Roman property disputes—was adapted into international law in the early modern era. Relying on a questionable analogy between sovereignty and private property, at first it operated in Europe as a legal justification for states' taking title to territories they had conquered in war. It was a way to assimilate military control to the legal order—or, more accurately, the other way round.

In the wave of Latin American independence, the doctrine was repurposed, no longer for the post hoc justification of war but as a means to avoid it: The newly independent states, all derived from Spanish provinces, agreed to treat the provincial and administrative boundaries as of 1810 or 1821—the accepted start of the general independence movements in South and Central America respectively—as their mutual international frontiers. This effectively divided up all territory between them: Everything Spain (and Portugal) had claimed had belonged to some administrative unit, and everything devolved to those units at independence. This also excluded interference both from external actors, since there was no *terra nullius* to claim, and internal challengers, such as indigenous populations.

The mechanism of *uti possidetis* was separate from succession. The new states agreed they were each heirs to Spain but applied *uti possidetis* to determine which would hold title to exactly what territory, based on what they actually administered.[5] The new states were therefore not a perfect match to the imperial divisions (which had changed frequently over the centuries), and *uti possidetis*—applied in various, conflicting interpretations—did not resolve all disputes over where to draw the borders. Nor did the newly independent states actually avoid warfare. Indeed, where factual control during or after the revolutionary period differed from "any line of Spanish origin or making in the last monarchical hour[,]"[6] the ultimate outcome generally bore little resemblance to the doctrine's predictions.[7]

But the doctrine provided, at the least, a framework—and unlike the earlier Roman maxim, this was no provisional placeholder but a means of fixing a permanent frontier. This was not as yet clearly identified as a mandatory rule of international law: The new Latin American states had adopted the practice of *uti possidetis,* but not out of a sense of legal obligation; that would come more than a century later, when the principle was repurposed yet again for African decolonization.

From these instances—especially the American and French Revolutions—we can see that both the historical development of what we came to call self-determination and its normative logic began with the individual but quickly moved to the collective: individual dignity and liberty, but also collective claims about the basis for governance. The innovations of both revolutions reflect the radical intuition that individuals ought to govern themselves; but equally they offer the cautionary observation that this is impossible in practice, indeed not even necessarily desirable, since individuals require societies to flourish and prosper. The individual is radically free and can only be truly free in society with his fellows. The interesting and difficult question, therefore, is how to determine who those fellows are.

In answering that challenge, early philosophical treatments of self-determination—now using the term explicitly—drew upon and wove together both strands. Each individual had a right to self-determination, but in turn, the individual right provided the basis for collective claims, including democracy and nationalism, twins who grew together through the late eighteenth and nineteenth centuries. Rising theories of popular sovereignty gave impetus to democratic politics, on the one hand, and a concern with the proper shape of the polity, on the other, often conceived as an organic community of ethnically or linguistically connected individuals—a nation. Thus, German philosophers after Immanuel Kant, such as Johann Gottlieb Fichte and Johann Gottfried Herder, identified an organic, national community as the locus for moral reasoning beyond the individual, and thus for politics. Likewise, John Stuart Mill stressed the affinity between individuals as the basis for their political connection:

> A portion of mankind may be said to constitute a Nationality if they are united among themselves by common sympathies which do not exist between them and any others—which make them cooperate with each other more willingly than with other people, desire to be under the same government, and desire that it should be government by themselves or a portion of themselves exclusively.[8]

Nowadays, we don't assume any essential connection between democracy and nationalism—we don't need some organic or primeval relationship to explain and legitimize popular rule, and we positively distrust the idea that identities are exclusive—but historically there is clearly a relationship. The concurrent rise of democracy and nationalism was no coincidence: They are entwined aspects of a complex effort to identify some rational or moral basis to substitute popular sovereignty for divine decree or royal hierarchy. Subjects must simply know their sovereign and the reasons for their servitude. But if the people rule, it matters, as it had not before, who the people are.

Of these two concepts, it was nationalism that proved the greater challenge to existing territorial arrangements. Democracy was potentially consistent with existing states (assuming they could shift the benefits of governance to broader groups, first the bourgeoisie, then the working class, racial groups, and women), but a concern with the identity of the polity proved disruptive. Many movements exhibited both democratic and national aspects—a reminder that these are not antithetical but complementary processes, whatever we think now—and both presented challenges to the multiethnic empires of Europe. Although elite projects in their own right, the new German and Italian states were also expressions of a popular, national, integrative principle.

Curiously, the implications of these ideas for secession were little discussed—curious because making a new state implies breaking another. Although states frequently changed their territory through war, which required justification, the kinds of territorial change that might be created *from within* by a politically engaged population received little attention. Philosophers, especially in the liberal tradition, spent much time considering the individual's moral right of revolution or emigration, but "the leading figures of political philosophy . . . [were] virtually mute on the issue of secession."[9] Even though some of these had the example of the American Revolution and the Spanish colonies' independence movements, their focus was on the formation of nations rather than the logical corollary of that process. And, after all, in a preview of decolonization in the twentieth century, vast salty oceans separated these new states from their imperial sovereigns; they didn't appear to raise the question of how to deal with secession from an integral state.

One place the question did arise was in the United States—unsurprising in a country formed by secession. The founders were divided on the question. Thomas Jefferson helped write the so-called Principles of '98, reserving the right of states to withdraw if confronted with unconstitutional actions by the federal government, while others, such as James Madison, vigorously opposed secession, describing it during the Nullification Crisis as "a violation without cause, of a faith solemnly pledged."[10] The view was finally laid in its grave, along with 750,000 men in their literal ones, after the Civil War, when the Supreme Court confirmed the rule against unilateral secession in *Texas v. White*. The case was about Treasury bonds, but the deeper question had already been decided at Appomattox Court House. Both doctrine and political power aligned in mid-century in favor of nationhood and unity.

The individual receded from political theory, public debate, and practice in the nineteenth century, which focused on collective, national interpretations, consistent with the apotheosis of the state as an ideal and an organizing principle. Self-determination found practical expression: From the 1860s, the plebiscites that revolutionary France had pioneered became an increasingly common—if abused—feature of European diplomacy.[11] By the end of the First World War, they were a ready tool, fit for the codependent rise of national states and popular participation. Self-determination's individual aspirations would only resurface, in altered form, from the 1960s on, in efforts to democratize states. In the intervening years, the principle became identified with collectives—given concrete form in what we recall today as Wilsonianism.

The Primitive, Preclassical Version: Wilsonian National Self-Determination

A Professor of Political Science, who was also President of the United States, President Wilson, enunciated a doctrine which was ridiculous, but which was widely accepted as a sensible proposition, the doctrine of self-determination. On the surface, it seemed reasonable: let the people decide. It was in fact ridiculous, because the people cannot decide until someone decides who are the people.

Ivor Jennings[12]

Until the beginning of the twentieth century, self-determination was largely an inchoate aspiration, a philosophical claim informing popular politics but not a coherent program of governance or law. The consolidation of the global imperial system, followed by the crisis of the First World War, impelled more explicit formulations.

The existential pressures of the Great War produced a rapid expansion of self-determination claims. Proposals to reorganize conquered enemy territory according to national principles were central to the diplomacy of the Allied Powers. The Central Powers had many nationalities living within their borders whom the Allies could entice with promises of independence. Thus, at various points, the Allied Powers committed, in the event of victory, to recognize a south Slavic and a Czechoslovak state on Austro-Hungarian territory, a Polish state on German territory, and Arab states and a Jewish homeland on Ottoman territory. Their commitment to self-determination was partial and positional; it was never a general principle, and only applied to enemy territory.

Late in the war, the new Soviet regime endorsed a more radical concept— radical both in content and because the Soviet state theoretically applied it to itself: The Decree on Peace, approved in late 1917, rejected

every incorporation of a small or weak nation into large or powerful state without the precisely, clearly, and voluntarily expressed consent and wish of that nation, irrespective of the time when such forcible incorporation took place, irrespective also of the degree of development or backwardness of the nation . . . , and irrespective, finally, of whether this nation is in Europe or in distant, overseas countries.[13]

Bolshevik views on liberating oppressed peoples had already found expression in an early Resolution on the National Question referring to the "right of all nations forming part of Russia to freely secede and form independent states[.]"[14] In contrast to the Allied Powers, the Bolsheviks advocated the liberation of colonial peoples, a view Soviet foreign policy continued to advance in the interwar period:

> The World War has resulted in the intensification of the liberation movement of all oppressed and colonial peoples. World states are coming undone at the seams. Our international program must bring all oppressed colonial peoples into the international scheme. The rights of all peoples to secession or to home rule must be recognized. . . . The novelty of our international scheme must be that the Negro and all other colonial peoples participate on an equal footing with European peoples in the conferences and commission and have the right to prevent interference in their internal affairs.[15]

But self-determination's most prominent and influential incarnation appeared in Woodrow Wilson's proposals for reorganizing the defeated Central Powers,[16] which found concrete expression in the new, national states that appeared in Europe after the collapse of the continental empires. At the risk of doing great intellectual violence, we shall call this the Wilsonian variant of self-determination— and also the 'primitive' or 'preclassical' model, for reasons that will become clear.

The clearest articulations appeared in Wilson's speeches, especially his "Fourteen Points" speech from early 1918, framed, improbably, as a program for global peace and justice. Wilson's proposals were an eclectic mix of restoration and self-determination. In part they reflected the Allied and Associated Powers' war aims, in part respected historical rights and sovereignties, and frequently equivocated as to what, exactly, was being promised. The choices are ad hoc, inconsistent: The Poles are to have a state, but very different language is used for communities in Austria-Hungary ("recognition of statehood or autonomous development") or the Ottoman Empire ("opportunity of autonomous development"). And, compared with the Bolsheviks' forceful demand for the liberation of non-European peoples, Wilson's model is circumspect: balancing interests, not absolute rights.

But alongside these qualified aims and nuances, there is a clear principle animating the proposals, a very different political calculus from the old norms of conquest. Communities—for Wilson, nations—are the fact around which

---

Wilsonian Self-Determination: From the "Fourteen Points"*

- A settlement allowing Russia to independently determine its development (Point VI);
- correction of the "wrong done to France by Prussia in 1871 in the matter of Alsace-Lorraine"—that is, its return to France (Point VIII);
- Adjustments to Italy's frontiers "along clearly recognizable lines of nationality" (Point IX);
- Recognition of the statehood or autonomous development of the peoples of the Austro-Hungarian Empire (Point X);
- Evacuation of Serbia, Montenegro, and Romania, with relations among the Balkan states "determined by friendly counsel along historically established lines of allegiance and nationality" (Point XI);
- Guarantees of sovereignty for the "Turkish portion of the present Ottoman Empire," but also "undoubted security of life and absolutely unmolested opportunity of autonomous development" for "the other nationalities which are now under Turkish rule" (Point XII);
- An independent Polish state "which should include territories inhabited by indisputably Polish populations" (Point XIII);
- "A free, open-minded, and absolutely impartial adjustment of all colonial claims, based upon a strict observance of the principle that in determining all such questions of sovereignty the interests of the populations concerned must have equal weight with the equitable claims of the government whose title is to be determined" (Point V).

*Wilson, "President Wilson's Fourteen Points" speech.

---

sovereignty is to be organized. Peoples—people, in the places where they live—animate the principle by which borders are to be drawn; they are the principle.

Parts of this principle and some of Wilson's proposals were validated in—at least not contradicted by—the postwar treaties with the defeated Central Powers: Versailles for Germany, Saint-Germain-en-Laye for Austria, Trianon for Hungary, Neuilly-sur-Seine for Bulgaria, and Sèvres for Turkey. New states appeared that more or less fit self-determination principles—certainly much more than had their imperial predecessors: Poland, and therefore a more ethnically German Germany; Czechoslovakia, Romania, and Yugoslavia,[17] and therefore a Hungary and an Austria each more monoethnic than they had been; the new Arab states and therefore a majority Turkish Turkey.

Most of these states were not literally creatures of Wilsonian self-determination or the peace process. New states were forming in any case, especially as Austria-Hungary imploded; self-determination and the conferences afforded conceptual and legal cover for what was already happening. But public advocacy of these principles reassured, reinforced, and emboldened nationalists. For example, in mid-1918—before the liquefaction of the Habsburg Empire—US Secretary of State Robert Lansing expressed support for Czechoslovak independence and declared "that all branches of the Slav race should be completely freed from German and Austrian rule."[18]

And although the postwar settlement was shaped by the victors' prerogatives, there were moments of constraint influenced by self-determination principles. French attempts to separate the abortive Rhenish Republic from Germany were opposed by elements of the American delegation, who viewed it as a violation of self-determination.[19] The establishment of a temporary administration and plebiscite for the Saar region represented a compromise between France's strategic interests and the wishes of the affected population, which was predominantly German.[20]

However imperfectly and preferentially applied, there was indeed a radical, even revolutionary principle at play in the wartime positions and postwar decisions of the powers who dictated the peace. So let's look at that principle and its application.

THE CORE PRINCIPLE The Wilsonian model recognized the right of national groups to form states on the territories they inhabited without relying on existing borders, and rejected the subordination of a people's interests to territory or the status quo. Concluding the fourteen points of his speech, Wilson noted:

> An evident principle runs through the whole program I have outlined. It is the principle of justice to all peoples and nationalities, and their right to live on equal terms of liberty and safety with one another, whether they be strong or weak.
>   Unless this principle be made its foundation no part of the structure of international justice can stand. . . . The moral climax of this the culminating and final war for human liberty has come. . . .[21]

The link between self-determination as the basis for states and popular participation in governance was clear:

> In this triumphal progress national self-determination and democracy went hand
> in hand. Self-determination might indeed be regarded as implicit in the idea of
> democracy; for if every man's right is recognized to be consulted about the affairs
> of the political unit to which he belongs, he may be assumed to have an equal right
> to be consulted about the form and extent of the unit.[22]

But Wilsonian self-determination was not principally popular and democratic: it was ethnic and national. Consistent with prevailing understandings—
and his own deeply racist views—Wilson took nationality as a given, a social
fact that had, and should have, political relevance. Not everyone automatically
assumed nations were natural or believed they should form the basis of the
state. But for advocates of this new form of politics, identifying certain groups
as self-determining nations—with different priority depending on their civi-
lizational level—was as much commonsense as justice. In the European context, Wilsonian self-determination represented the apotheosis of the national,
anti-imperial principle; although not necessarily democratic—in fact there
was very little democracy in it—the principle grounded legitimation on the
idea of popular sovereignty: The nation, the people, was the irreducible political unit.

The Wilsonian model gave identifiable ethnic groups the right to form states
(so long as someone with enough power identified them!), ensured minority
rights for groups not lucky enough to get their own states, and used plebiscites
to fine-tune borders. Creating new states that reflected demography solved certain problems, even as it created others. And although it was barely applied in
the colonial world, this new sensibility articulated a rationale that would later
be invoked to limit and eventually reverse colonial dominion. By then, though,
the concept would have undergone violent, disfiguring transformations and become, in effect, its opposite. But that came a few decades later. First, let's look
at the other features of the preclassical, Wilsonian model.

DETERMINING BORDERS: EXTERNAL IMPOSITION AND THE PLEBISCITE MODEL
Since Wilsonian self-determination had both a national and a popular basis, it
created a very practical problem for matching sovereignty with territory: any
change in borders to reflect national demography required some method of
determining where exactly those new borders should be. The solution had two
parts: a general assignment of sovereignty for self-evident cases, with borders

determined by negotiations or by fiat; and plebiscites to precisely delineate or fine-tune frontiers.

The first part, the assignment of sovereignty in obvious cases, began during the war: Both the United States and the Allied Powers made commitments to support new, national states, such as Poland and Czechoslovakia. In his "Fourteen Points" speech, Wilson simply assumed and announced that there ought to be a Poland, a matter anyone steeped in nationalist sensibilities could see as plausible. But where would Poland be? The precise borders of this and other units were not specified—in part because they depended on the fortunes of war, but also because, if Poland was an expression of popular sovereignty, the wishes of the people would have to be determined.

Beginning in 1918, the borders of the new states were established. Some were the product of continuation wars, such as the Polish-Soviet War, where military might determined the outcome. But others were determined, or at least recognized, in the peace processes: new states or changes to existing borders, largely along national lines. These adjustments could be enormous—the retrocession of Alsace-Lorraine to France—or tiny, like Belgium's annexation of the German-Belgian condominium of Neutral Moresnet (population three thousand, area one square mile).

In some cases the boundaries were delineated with great specificity in the treaties themselves, or by demarcation commissions. In other cases, however, in an application of the new principle, the final line was left to the people in a plebiscite. A number of plebiscites were held in the aftermath of the Great War.[23] In each case, there was a clear ethno-national choice. The plebiscites did not create nations, though the very fact of holding them increased the salience of national identity; rather, they were a mechanism for specifying the division between nations that, it was assumed, already existed.

MECHANICS: AN ELECTORAL MODEL Interestingly, although plebiscites were deployed in the service of ethno-national sovereignty, with campaigns mobilizing nationalist sentiment, the formal decision was a bare electoral choice. Elements of the plebiscite were informed by national demography: Voting rules for the zones of the Danish-German plebiscite varied depending on where Danes predominated; similarly, the cascading provisions in Klagenfurt and East Prussia gave areas in which different nationalities predominated the option to remain in their preferred state. So the plebiscites were not blind to ethnicity. But the

Designing Determination: The Schleswig Plebiscite

When Prussia conquered Schleswig from Denmark, it never held a promised plebiscite; the Treaty of Versailles required one. Versailles didn't mention ethnicity, instead declaring that the frontier "shall be fixed in conformity with the wishes of the population" in zones it describes in detail, including a map (Article 109). The northern zone voted as a single district; in the southern zone, decision was by *Gemeinden* (communes). The outcome contemplated adjustments "taking into account the particular geographical and economic conditions of the localities" (Article 110). Everyone twenty years old the day the treaty came into force, born in the zone or "domiciled there" since before 1900, or "expelled by the German authorities" was eligible; soldiers native to the zone could return to vote (Article 109, 2).

Zones favored Denmark. If Schleswig voted as one, Germany would win. But the north would go to Denmark, with German enclaves. In the south, Danes could win some areas. (In a third zone, no plebiscite was held.) In the north, Denmark won overwhelmingly. In the south, the pro-Denmark vote was lower than expected, and each commune voted to remain in Germany. Inside Denmark there was debate about annexing the entire area anyway, but having organized the plebiscite to its advantage, Denmark was effectively bound by the outcome.

Schleswig's demography presented a comparatively simple ethnocline: areas of almost pure Danish and German population and discernible dividing lines. (There was lots of intermarriage, and over time, areas had changed dominant ethnicity, which means individual families had switched across generations.) Yet even in Schleswig, many outcomes were possible, depending on how one designed the vote. It was an imperfect process—determined by outside powers—but it peacefully put many more people in states of their preference than most alternatives, or than doing nothing.

actual decision by individual voters did not require them to identify with a particular nation. Voters chose a sovereign for their territory, nothing more; their reasons were their own.

Everyone could vote, not just those of one nationality; and when they did, individuals chose between two sovereignties for whatever reasons they saw fit. Many did choose on the basis of national identity—the plebiscites mostly yielded outcomes one might have achieved by using external measures of demography—but not everywhere, and not everyone. In some places, the vote did not track preexisting ethnicity: Some 'Poles' voted to remain in Germany, as did some

'Danes,' and some 'Slovenes' to remain part of Austria. Wilsonianism assumed people wanted national states; but in the plebiscites, the outcome depended on what people actually said they wanted.

So the plebiscite system was only imperfectly consistent with the ideal of Wilsonian self-determination, but in practice it worked well. On its own terms, it was effective, creating frontiers that produced more homogeneous populations with fewer minorities, exactly as intended. The results were often refined to the level of villages; in the East Prussian plebiscite, for example, the great majority of the population and territory stayed with Germany, but a small number of villages were assigned to Poland, based on their inhabitants' preferences. Although the campaigns were often tense—owing to the difficult circumstances in which they were conducted and the uncertainty the process itself created[24]— the votes were overwhelmingly peaceful, as were the subsequent transfers of sovereignty they authorized.

This meant territorial revisions were accomplished with minimal violence— far more peaceably than the changes that arose out of the continuation wars in Poland and Anatolia, for example—and in general, issues of sovereignty and territory were resolved peacefully. "The plebiscites effectively defused six potential flashpoints—six sources of future inter-state discord—from the crowded agenda of European politics."[25] The areas that exhibited the greatest tension in the interwar period, and which contributed most to the outbreak of the next war, were not those whose sovereignty had been determined by plebiscite, but areas in which the principle of popular sovereignty had not been used to bring national identity and territory into alignment: Danzig, Sudetenland.

THE PROBLEM OF MINORITIES

The post-World War I settlements, though ostensibly based on the principle of national self-determination, in fact assigned tens of millions of people to nation-states other than "their own" at the same time that they focused unprecedented attention on the national or putatively national quality of both persons and territories.[26]

Of course, neither the plebiscites nor Wilsonian self-determination generally could be said to work well unless one accepted the system's premise that the sovereign people ought to be an ethno-national community. But even accepting that goal, on its own terms the system hardly worked perfectly. In many places, the principle was ignored or contradicted, but even where it was applied, the new system made many individuals and communities worse off. Indeed, in many respects, the solution of self-determination created its own problem: national minorities.

The mere fact that new national states came into being after the First World War reduced the average heterogeneity of Europe's states—a reduction by merely redrawing borders around populations, quite apart from the effect of forced transfers (to which we will come). However, this did not eliminate diversity, and in fact created new minorities, because members of old majorities suddenly found themselves in some other nation's state, like Germans in Poland. Moreover, by making the nation the legitimating spirit of the state, the interwar system gave heterogeneity a new and potentially dangerous salience.

Certainly before the war there had also been national sentiment, secessionist and irredentist movements, and ethnic, linguistic, or religious communities with subordinate status, like Jews in Czarist Russia or the Ottoman millet system. But with the creation of expressly national states, what had been coexisting, contending communities within imperial structures—and only one of many possible vectors for politics—became the touchstone of citizenship. As a consequence, those inside the new state who had a different national identity were often seen as disfavored, even treasonous aliens. The creation of new states on national lines practically created the problem of minorities as we know it.

This was obviously a danger—to the new states, to international stability (in many cases these minorities had kin across the new frontiers), and to the minorities themselves. This in turn suggested a regulatory response: the creation of a complex, internationalized system of minority rights treaties.

Most of the defeated powers and new states of Eastern and Central Europe were required to guarantee certain rights for minorities within their territory, usually through treaties. Each treaty was tailored to the circumstances of the country—the Polish rights system included specific provisions for Jews, for example—but in many respects the treaties were boilerplate, reflecting a common approach, since in each case, the creation of a national state had created national minorities needing protection.

The treaties were also embedded in the new international order. The League of Nations was given a supervisory role, and in short order procedures for petitions were developed—the nascent model for the human rights treaty system we have today, with its communications, complaints, and committees.[27] Minorities quickly found advantage in petitioning the League, seeking to internationalize disputes with their new states, but by the mid-1930s, the system was largely moribund.

Besides intruding on the sovereignty of the new states (not the victorious ones), the very idea of minority rights created real conceptual challenges. Should minorities be guaranteed literal equality or should they have special treatment, recognizing their uniquely vulnerable position in a national state not their own? Both approaches had their attractions and risks, and both were tried. In the *Minority Schools in Albania* case, for example, Albania's Greek minority complained about the closing of all private schools in the country—a facially neutral policy that in effect closed all Greek schools, since the public schools taught in Albanian. The Permanent Court of International Justice, which heard the case, had to choose between two interpretations: Did the treaty ensure the Greek minority perfect equality in law with the Albanian majority, or ensure differential conditions to compensate for its vulnerabilities and make it equal in fact? The court decided for substantive equality, but the question signaled the tension in a system of states premised on national identity—on one nation forming the state.

In the end, the minority rights treaties failed to do what they were supposed to; at least, they weren't able to stave off the interwar system's collapse, which was perhaps rather more than one might have reasonably expected of them. But fair or not, the approach—a collective, national understanding of rights—was largely discredited. After the Second World War, when the successor to the League was created, its approach was more individualistic—human rights. Minority rights received only slight mention and a vestigial presence in the institutions of the United Nations.

The interwar minority regime is sometimes conflated with the plebiscites—both were creatures of the self-determination principle, and both dealt with the problem of minorities created by Europe's decaying imperial systems. But they were quite different in their purposes and effects. The minority regimes, by design, took the new units as given. National states inevitably have minorities, and the purpose of the treaties was to create protections within them. The minority regimes were prophylactic, reactive, and ameliorative; they assumed—rightly—that majority and minority would clash, and sought to reduce the frequency and consequences of those clashes.

The plebiscites also assumed new states would be governed on ethno-national lines but didn't begin from the premise that existing states were a given. Quite the contrary: The point of the plebiscites was to determine the shape of states. Plebiscites tended to make the size of the underlying problem smaller. They did nothing to ameliorate problems between majority and minority as such—indeed, the very act of holding a plebiscite increased the salience of difference and exacerbated communal tensions. But in places where a plebiscite produced a clear line between two communities—impossible in some places, but quite successful in others—it could reduce the problem to a *de minimis* level.

Like many elements of the post–WWI settlement that came to be known as the 'interwar system'—and a better indicator of its failure we could hardly ask for—the minority treaties have been fairly criticized for their inadequacy and even destabilizing influence. But the plebiscites should not be confused with those: The minority regimes were ameliorative, designed to deal with minorities as a permanent problem; the plebiscites were designed to make that problem smaller and easier to handle—and they did this precisely by assuming borders were changeable.

THE OTHER METHOD: POPULATION TRANSFERS New states, revised borders, and minority rights were not the only models adopted in the aftermath of the First World War. There was another approach in the interwar period, often confused with secession, but which in fact operated on entirely different principles: the so-called population transfers, the most notorious of which occurred between Greece and Turkey.

After the 1918 armistice, one of the most significant continuation wars occurred in Asia Minor, where the major powers' efforts to carve out spheres of control from the Ottoman corpse were resisted by the nationalist movement led by a general later known as Atatürk. Greece tried to annex large areas with Greek populations, but its incursion ended in the panicked flight Hemingway described in "On the Quai at Smyrna":

> When they evacuated they had all their baggage animals they couldn't take off with them so they just broke their forelegs and dumped them into the shallow water. All those mules with their forelegs broken pushed over into the shallow water. It was all a pleasant business. My word yes a most pleasant business.[28]

Afterward, the powers acquiesced in a new treaty to replace the moribund Treaty of Sèvres. At Lausanne in 1923, Turkey and Greece recognized their mutual interest in consolidating their states, which, in the context of the time, meant homogenizing their populations. But rather than do this by exchanging territory, they exchanged people.

The exchanges were organized on religious grounds; those expelled shared their new countrymen's religion, but not necessarily their language. Orthodox Christians from western Asia Minor and the Black Sea coast were expelled to Greece—whether they spoke Greek or not—while Muslims from Crete and Macedonia were expelled to Turkey—whether or not they spoke Turkish.[29] Departure was mandatory; protections and compensation were included in the agreement, but most individuals were only compensated, if at all, with property seized from someone of the other religion who had also been forced to leave everything and move. The organized exchange forced hundreds of thousands over the frontier to new citizenship and new lives in a foreign land; larger numbers had already fled. The result was enormous suffering, and—in religious terms—two vastly more homogeneous states.

To this day, the transfers are recalled as an example of how not to conduct politics or treat human beings. But curiously, they are also invoked as an epithet cautioning against changes to frontiers.[30] Curious, because nothing of the kind occurred: The transfers were of human beings, not territory (though borders had changed recently, too, in the Balkan Wars of 1912–1913); they took place between two existing states, whose leaders perceived a grim mutual interest in purifying their lands by expelling people who didn't belong to the majority. Although they partook of the same tendency to think of states in ethno-national terms, the Greek-Turkish population transfers were not an inevitable aspect of self-determination—in fact, both in the context of the 1920s and logically, they represented a clear contradiction of its principles. The transfers were the very opposite of self-determination.

APPROACHING COLONIALISM: THE MANDATE SYSTEM Plebiscites and minority treaties were expressions of the new principle of self-determination partially and very imperfectly enacted in Europe after the Great War, and population transfers were a perverse departure from the principle. But one of self-determination's greatest imperfections was that it was only applied in Europe; the rest of the world was barely touched.

Wilson mentioned the colonies in his "Fourteen Points," but only weakly linked them to self-determination, in a way that just affected the defeated Central Powers. Yet the issue of imperial aggrandizement was unavoidable, since by the end of the war the Allies had taken control of Germany's colonial empire as well as the Arab parts of the Ottoman Empire; something would have to be done with those territories. Moreover, the war itself had made the question of colonial dominion salient: Although Europe's empires actually expanded after the Great War, their ideological and economic foundations were weakening. Britain's white dominions, which had sacrificed in the common war effort, were increasingly independent, and nonwhite subjects had participated in the war in great numbers for France and Britain, too. The very idea of colonial rule over nonwhite races was being questioned, even as those empires reached their faltering apogee.

The instrument by which the Central Powers' non-European territories were assimilated to the interwar order was the mandate system. At the end of the war, German colonies and the Ottoman Levant and Mesopotamia were converted into mandates, overseen by the League of Nations but administered by individual powers. Tanganyika was administered by the United Kingdom, while South Africa administered German South West Africa, and Belgium received Rwanda and Burundi. France held mandates for Syria and Lebanon; Britain for today's Jordan, Israel, and Palestine; Japan for many of Germany's South Pacific colonies; Australia for northern New Guinea; and so on. For the populations of German colonies, the effect was to swap colonial overlords; but Ottoman Arabs and Kurds, who had lived inside the empire, were for the first time reduced to colonial status.

The mandates marked the first conceptual constraint on imperial expansion, and the logic of self-determination provided the limit. The system created three classes of mandates: A, B, and C. Class A referred to Ottoman territories in the Levant; B and C to German possessions in Africa and Asia. Notionally there was an expectation that mandates (at least A and B classes) would move progressively toward independence—a process that implicitly brought colonial rule more broadly into question precisely because there was little practical difference between mandates and true colonies.

Progress toward independence was more than merely notional: by the end of the 1940s, all Class A mandates were independent. The others were converted into trust territories after the war, apart from South West Africa, over which South Africa asserted continued control, but even that was considered a matter of interest for the new UN. These territories in turn became the focus of the new, high classical definition of self-determination developed after the Second

World War, which defines our understanding of the term to this day, and to which we will turn in the next section.

PROBLEMS AND CRITICISMS

> *[I]t would be stupid to believe that there is much room in the world, as it really is, for such affairs as the League of Nations, or any sense in the principle of self-determination except as an ingenious formula for rearranging the balance of power in one's own interest.*
>
> John Maynard Keynes[31]

As the need for minority treaties and the temptation of population transfers demonstrated, the states that emerged after the Great War were far from pure examples of that rarest creature, a true nation-state. They contained large minorities (Czechoslovakia, Romania, Poland), or failed to include large parts of their own nation (Hungary, Albania), or divided a single nation between two sovereigns (Germany and Austria). Some nations had to share a state (Czechs and Slovaks; Slovenes, Croats and Serbs, along with yet unrecognized Macedonians and Bosnian Muslims). Some nations didn't get states at all (Ruthenians). Some territorial changes couldn't be explained as self-determination at all, and some of the territorial promises in the secret wartime treaties directly contradicted it. If the postwar settlement was supposed to demonstrate the principle, it didn't do it very well.

And that was in Europe. The principle barely figured at all in plans for non-European areas, such as the Arab and Kurdish provinces of the Ottoman Empire or the German colonies. And self-determination effectively didn't apply at all to the victors, except to limit their ability to expand by conquest; their own territories and populations were not subjected to the rigors of popular sovereignty. If self-determination was a principle, it was a highly selective one whose outcomes looked a great deal like a much older principle: *vae victis*—woe to the vanquished.

Many of the outcomes of the peace settlement notionally applied the principle of self-determination but were clearly the product of self-dealing, of not applying the principle—though one can ask if the principle could ever be applied neutrally by actual humans. And the problems went beyond defects in application: The Wilsonian system posed serious problems of arbitrariness, and though ostensibly based on a people's objective or affinitive qualities, the act of

One Town, Two States, Plus Time

The consequences of shifting frontiers can be observed over time in a single place. Subotica, in northernmost Serbia, has a mixed population, with a large Hungarian minority and a Slav majority, mostly Serbs, but also Croats, Bunjevci, and others. Prior to the First World War, the town, known as Szabadka, was in the Hungarian half of the Habsburg Empire, but even then had a mixed population. Then, the town's Serbs often knew Hungarian—the language of the state and dominant elites—and Hungarians often knew little Serbian. Today, most Serbs know little Hungarian, while almost all Hungarians speak Serbian.

The difference has been the border, and shifting policies and social practices that predictably followed changes in that border. Under Austria-Hungary, Magyarization was policy, but after Yugoslavia formed, priorities and patterns of migration changed, with more Serbs moving to the town from other parts of the new state. Lives in Szabadka had been oriented toward Budapest; lives in Subotica—which is the same place—face Belgrade. These shifting patterns reflect the circulation of people and ideas within a bordered territory that Benedict Anderson described in the formation of national identity in colonies;* it's applicable to states anywhere.

*Anderson, Imagined Communities.

drawing lines in effect created the very communities the lines were supposed to be drawn around:

> [T]he problem of identifying peoples under the Wilsonian principle is . . . a simple question of line-drawing. Depending on where the dividing line is drawn, an ethnic, religious or other community aspiring to nationhood can become either a "people," entitled to full self-government, or a minority, with only the minimal rights accorded to members of what was, in the Versailles scheme, a residual category.[32]

In many cases this was the same as saying lines can be well or badly drawn. The more important risk is that the status of the group ends up a function of the territory's status, rather than the other way round. As we shall see, this is precisely what postwar self-determination became.

The Wilsonian system did not solve the problem of distinguishing minorities (who must content themselves inside their current state) from peoples (who deserve their own state); arguably, it defined the problem into existence, since it is only once one acknowledges the idea of a self-determining nation that one must distinguish it from a mere minority.

Finally, Wilsonian self-determination radically threatened the status quo of borders. This disruptive danger was immediately apparent, and the response was to treat self-determination as a one-off, a new status quo to be defended against change and challenge. The postwar settlements expressly limited further territorial change in ways that disregarded or contradicted the principle. Germany and Austria were barred from unifying, for example, while the minority treaties confirmed the territorial integrity of the new, grudgingly multiethnic states. Capping the entire system, the League of Nations affirmed territorial integrity and included (ineffective) protections against aggression. Self-determination had shaken up the old imperial order, but the shaking was supposed to stop.

A new status quo made sense for the winners: Having used the principle of self-determination to achieve independence or expand their territories, the states in East Central Europe, supported by France, were particularly interested in preventing the defeated powers from pressing revisionist or revanchist claims.[33] Because self-determination had been applied to the detriment of the Central Powers, the victors—Britain and France—had a double interest in locking in the changes and inoculating themselves from any further self-determining disruptions. To whatever degree elements of the postwar settlement reflected principles of self-determination, the beneficiaries naturally now wished to keep and enjoy their gains, which continuing application of the principle might jeopardize.

There is one more thing: Whatever its attractions and flaws, as an early League of Nations report noted, Wilsonian self-determination in the wake of the Great War was "a principle of justice and of liberty, expressed by a vague and general formula which has given rise to most varied interpretations and differences of opinion."[34] Although it spawned important innovations and created new expectations, self-determination itself remained a principle, an aspiration. It was not a global law. That was to change in the wake of the next great cataclysm, which began twenty years later.

The High Classical Moment:
Creating a New Orthodoxy, 1945–1970

The collapse of the interwar Versailles system with its fragile national states and minority treaties discredited the notions of minority rights and ethnic self-determination. After the Second World War—at the beginning of our era, the era we still optimistically call 'postwar'—Wilsonian self-determination was eclipsed by a variant influenced by Leninism: decolonization. It was this that became, for the first time, a true legal norm, and more than that.

Effects of World War II and the Postwar Context

The rise of National Socialism conflated the defects of the interwar system with aggressive expansion, both in the Nazis' own policies and historical memory after it all came apart. Germany's absorption of Austria and Sudetenland—outcomes consistent with Wilsonian self-determination in principle, if not in method—were later little distinguished from the conquests on which Germany embarked with the absorption of the Czech lands and the invasion of Poland. The failure of the interwar system to prevent the rise of fascism was equated, in many minds, with the failure of preclassical self-determination as such. This is ironic, since the Versailles system was hardly a model application of self-determination, nor was self-determination the only thing Versailles tried to do, and did badly.

Early in the Second World War, the parties that would emerge victorious proclaimed self-determination as a general principle. In the Atlantic Charter, the United Kingdom and still-neutral United States declared that

> they desire to see no territorial changes that do not accord with the freely expressed wishes of the peoples concerned; . . . they respect the right of all peoples to choose the form of government under which they will live; and they wish to see sovereign rights and self-government restored to those who have been forcibly deprived of them.[35]

The United Kingdom wasn't referring to its own colonies—consistent with the previous war's model, self-determination applied to the defeated Axis—but in its own subsequent declaration, the United States pressed for a broader application. Still, although these principles were reaffirmed in the 1943 Moscow Declaration, with the Soviet Union's agreement, they did little to shape actual practice at war's end. Instead, the powers reassigned sovereignties and moved whole peoples like chess pieces.

The victorious powers oversaw the westward expulsion of twelve million to fourteen million Germans and the transfer of the emptied territory to Poland

and the Soviet Union, mirrored by the westward expulsion of over one million Poles and transfer of that emptied territory to the Soviet Union.[36] Germany and Germans shrank back hundreds of kilometers, Poles and Poland lurched westward by an equal amount. The political and philosophical difference between this and what Wilsonian self-determination imagined—or, as we will see later, what the rule proposed in this book would do—should be apparent to any moral observer. Borders were shifted, not to fit sovereignty to populations where they were, but as an exercise of geopolitics in which frontiers and peoples both were moved wholesale. It was a grotesque improvement on Lausanne's population transfers: Unrestricted by existing frontiers, in 1945 the victorious powers had evidently learned from those earlier expulsions only that such things could be done in an "orderly and humane" fashion, as the Potsdam Agreement called for, and on a vastly larger scale.

Still, the principle of self-determination had been mentioned, the war notionally fought to protect it, and this would have its effects in the new system of global governance. In its first article, the new United Nations Charter identifies self-determination as one of the organization's purposes. Yet in the very moment the principle acquired an authoritative legal form, its meaning was radically reversed: The Wilsonian model was superseded by one that defined self-determination in terms of preexisting territories.[37]

In short order, the new territorial definition acquired a specific addressee: colonies. The great colonial empires had been weakened by the costs of war and the rising expectations of their subject populations—many of whom had fought on their overlords' behalf, noticed the references to self-determination as one of the war's purposes, and drawn the logical conclusion. National liberation movements arose in Southeast Asia and Africa, and active Soviet and US encouragement for dismantling colonial empires rapidly undermined the position of the European powers.

Two of the earliest changes involved partitions decreed from above. The independence of India and Pakistan in 1947 became a byword for the dangers of partition. Preparing for withdrawal, a British commission delineated a border that left large populations of Hindus and Muslims on the wrong side of new frontiers, most prominently in Kashmir. The resulting dislocations and deaths of millions were among the largest mass movements of the postwar era, only exceeded during Pakistan's suppression of Bangladesh's independence twenty-five years later. In Israel and Palestine, the legacy of partition was ambiguous:

a mooted UN plan was never adopted—instead, a violent separation occurred; but to many observers, it was implausible to imagine continued coexistence without violence.

Decolonization as such was not mentioned in the UN Charter—indeed, the new system included an updated version of the League mandates—and there was resistance to the idea: "the United Nations, far from being the forum of a new and liberatory set of principles, appeared set at first on colluding in the attempted reimposition of colonial rule[.]"[38] Yet it was clearly on the agenda, and, in a "dramatic reversal on the international legality of colonialism[,]"[39] rapidly came to dominate interpretations of what self-determination meant. Within fifteen years, the broad outlines of a consensus were in place that decolonization was a necessary act of self-determination; within a quarter century, the edifice of a new orthodoxy was complete. The rise of this decolonizing variant was so thorough that it almost entirely displaced the Wilsonian concept in law and diplomacy; the preclassical model survived only in the persistent claims of outsider groups. But those claims could be ignored: In the bright, blinding, liberating glow of the early postwar period, self-determination became decolonization.

The Classical Model

In the new model, self-determination was declared a right of peoples who determined their own political status. This was what the preclassical model had said, too—but now peoples determined that status within preexisting units. Whatever self-determination meant, it had to mean it within the borders of the territory, without alteration.

This new doctrine was not created in one go, but step-by-step. Building on the UN Charter's ambiguous foundations, a series of General Assembly resolutions and human rights treaties articulated an increasingly dense network of legal and institutional commitments premised on this new, narrowed, colonial interpretation. Within a few decades, a new orthodoxy had arisen, with the same name as Wilson's model, but doing almost exactly the opposite—and later, increasingly, doing nothing at all.

LAYING THE FOUNDATIONS: TRUSTS AND NON-SELF-GOVERNING TERRITORIES IN THE CHARTER The UN Charter established a formal, legal regime with self-determination as a foundational pillar. In its very first article, the charter declares that one of the purposes of the UN system is "[t]o develop friendly relations among nations based on respect for the principle of equal rights and self-determination of peoples[.]"[40] And several chapters of the charter dealt expressly with colonies—or "non-self-governing territories," as the broader category was called.

Yet the text remained ambiguous, and to suppose this definition was inevitable would be a "retrospective rewriting of history."[41] The sections on non-self-governing territories do not expressly mention self-determination (though they refer to Article 1, which does), and the text is not clear about what was to happen with those colonies:

> Members of the United Nations which have or assume responsibility for the administration of territories whose peoples have not yet attained a full measure of self-government recognize the principle that the interest of the inhabitants of these territories are paramount, and accept as a sacred trust the obligation to promote to the utmost, within the system of international peace and security established by the present Charter, the well-being of the inhabitants of these territories[.][42]

Hardly an unambiguous affirmation: Those who remembered the League might have seen a reprise of the mandate system—a "sacred trust" to govern, not a promise of independence. As for when that might come, the words "not yet" carry all the weight. The mandates were continued as a system of trust territories: Ten of the trusteeships had been mandates (the eleventh was Italian Somaliland); these territories were to be assured "progressive development towards self-government or independence as may be appropriate to the particular circumstances of each territory and its peoples and the freely expressed wishes of the peoples concerned"[43]—a moving target.

But ambiguous though it may have been, the charter extended this "sacred trust" far more broadly than the League had done; non-self-governing territories included not only the former mandates, but soon extended to most of the colonized world.

Technically, the obligation states undertook for non-self-governing territories was not necessarily independence—but language even more qualified than the ambiguous promise made for the trust territories:

> to develop self-government, to take due account of the political aspirations of the peoples, and to assist them in the progressive development of their free political

institutions, according to the particular circumstances of each territory and its peoples and their varying stages of advancement[.][44]

There was an obligation to report:

to transmit regularly to the Secretary-General for information purposes, subject to such limitation as security and constitutional considerations may require, statistical and other information of a technical nature relating to economic, social, and educational conditions in the territories for which they are respectively responsible.[45]

Reporting is not the same as doing, but over time, reporting became the focal point for demands to decolonize.

In expanding beyond the mandates, the charter made some critical and very conservative revisions. It refers to "*territories* whose peoples have not yet attained a full measure of self-government"[46]—firmly linking the legal category, and the definition of people, to the territory itself. This completely reversed the Wilsonian imperative. And the charter's chapter on non-self-governing territories distinguishes between "territories to which this Chapter applies" and states' "metropolitan areas"[47]—making it clear that there is territory subject to decolonization and territory that is not.

Equating decolonization with self-determination was an act of interpretation; indeed, it's not clear that self-determination in the charter has *any* defined content. "[S]elf-determination, as envisaged by the drafters of the Charter, did not refer to the right of dependent peoples to be independent, or indeed, even to vote."[48] But the connection between self-determination and decolonization was quickly and generally accepted. Whatever self-determination meant as a founding principle, it was soon associated with the idea that colonies ought to be free. This sentiment had barely figured in Wilson's earlier formulation in the "Fourteen Points"—but then, all the other things Wilson *had* declared as the core of self-determination now found almost no place in the new global order.

ARTICULATING THE HIGH CLASSICAL MODEL: THE PROCESS OF DECOLONIZATION
The charter thus described a new model, retaining elements of the League that harkened back to Wilsonianism even as it overturned Wilsonianism's logic. Over the next twenty-five years, through declarations of the General Assembly, the rise of human rights, legal cases, and the politics of decolonization, the charter's sketch would be articulated into a fully developed system of self-

determination for and within predefined units—the classical model that still dominates our law and our thinking today.

The Colonial Declarations: The sketchy, underspecified commitments in the charter were given fuller expression through the practice of the UN's institutions, especially the General Assembly, which by the early 1960s had dozens of new members. The apotheosis of the new, classical orthodoxy was achieved in the so-called Colonial Declarations adopted by the General Assembly in 1960.

Resolution 1514, the Declaration on the Granting of Independence to Colonial Countries and Peoples, clarified the implications of self-determination, in what has become the classic, much repeated formula: "All peoples have the right to self-determination; by virtue of that right they freely determine their political status and freely pursue their economic, social and cultural development."[49] The resolution declared that "the subjection of peoples to alien subjugation, domination and exploitation constitutes a denial of fundamental human rights," called for an end to any "armed action or repressive measures" and the immediate "transfer [of] all powers to the peoples of those territories, without any conditions or reservations[,]" and rejected pretextual delays.[50] But in the very moment of declaring decolonization an imperative, the resolution also reaffirmed the new right's other implication: "Any attempt aimed at the partial or total disruption of the national unity and the territorial integrity of a country is incompatible with the purposes and principles of the Charter of the United Nations."[51] Self-determination was to be exercised by the whole people on the whole territory of a state.

Eighty-nine states voted in favor, none against; nine abstained, including the major colonial powers. The next day, by a narrower but still overwhelming margin (sixty-nine to two [Portugal and South Africa], with twenty-one abstentions) the General Assembly approved Resolution 1541. Although 1541 notionally concerned a technical matter—it bears the exciting title "Principles which should guide Members in determining whether or not an obligation exists to transmit the information called for under Article 73e of the Charter"—it defined the scope of decolonization. It identified possible end points: independence, free association with another state, or integration into the state. "Free association should be the result of a free and voluntary choice by the peoples of the territory concerned expressed through informed and democratic processes."[52] Integration "should be on the basis of complete equality. . . . The peoples of both territories should have equal status and rights of citizenship . . . without any distinction or discrimination; both should have equal rights and opportunities for representation and effective participation at all levels . . . of government."[53]

Technically, Resolution 1541 only talks about an obligation to transmit information about non-self-governing territories, but it has been understood as a command for independence.[54] Yet it also limited decolonization's scope. Resolution 1541 defined a non-self-governing territory: "*Prima facie* . . . a territory which is geographically separate and is distinct ethnically and/or culturally from the country administering it."[55] Geographic separation—the 'salt water' thesis—was the critical distinction: a territory would only be considered non-self-governing if separated from the ruling state by the sea. This inoculated states' contiguous territory from decolonization. (The alternative 'Belgian' thesis focused on ethnic difference and would have included, for example, Indian tribes within the United States. The major powers successfully opposed it.) States have no obligation to report on territories that don't meet the salt water test—which is the same as saying they don't have a right to independence.

A year later, in Resolution 1654, the General Assembly established a Special Committee on Decolonization (with 17 members, later 24, from which it became known as the Committee of 24 or C-24). Along with the Trusteeship Council, the C-24 formed the institutional architecture for decolonization, which, by then, was generally conceded as a principle, awaiting only its final realization.

The 1960 Colonial Declarations confirmed the main lines of the decolonization project, casting it firmly in terms of self-determination. Since that time, General Assembly resolutions on almost every conceivable issue have ritualistically invoked the self-determination of peoples *and* the inviolability of states' territory—proof that, whatever their theoretical contradictions, in the classical model, self-determination and territorial integrity are in almost total accord. Once its colony-breaking assignment was completed, self-determination served to justify the preservation of existing states:

> The result has been a series of lame and largely arbitrary attempts by various international bodies, including the United Nations, to endorse a "right of self-determination," on the one hand, in order to support Third World struggles against colonialism, while on the other hand restricting that right to only the colonial cases in order to avoid fueling numerous separatist movements within long-established nation-states such as Britain and Belgium.[56]

The Human Rights Covenants: After the confirmation of self-determination's nature as a decolonizing doctrine that preserved existing territories, the remaining moves, made over the next decade, simply refined the classical doctrine's contours.

The Universal Declaration of Human Rights, proclaimed in 1948, had not mentioned self-determination, but the two covenants that elaborated the UDHR proclaim self-determination prominently. By the time the two International Covenants on Civil and Political Rights and on Economic, Social and Cultural Rights (ICCPR and ICESCR) were finally drafted in the mid-1960s, opposition to self-determination as a legal principle had collapsed, or at least become muted.[57] The covenants' first articles repeat, in identical language, Resolution 1514's formula: "All peoples have the right of self-determination. By virtue of that right they freely determine their political status and freely pursue their economic, social and cultural development."[58]

That articles specifically mention the right of self-determination for non-self-governing territories, but debate over the covenants confirmed that self-determination was not confined to the colonial context—it had become "a free-standing human right" of all peoples and "a fundamental human right and a precondition to the enjoyment of all other enumerated individual rights and freedoms."[59] But as the colonial debates had so effectively established, that right, like those peoples, was to be defined within territorial units that already existed. Formally, self-determination was a right of the people: In practice, it was a right of the territory, which the territory's people enjoyed. Or not.

The ICJ: The classical orthodoxy was also enunciated in cases at the International Court of Justice. The court's most prominent decisions and opinions concerned African colonies—several involving South West Africa (Namibia)—but also, after the great wave of decolonization had been completed, cases that confronted self-determination's reach beyond the colonial context: East Timor, Palestine, and Kosovo. Surveying the charter and postwar course of events, the ICJ affirmed that "the ultimate objective of the 'sacred trust' was self-determination of the peoples concerned."[60] Whatever the precise content of self-determination, it is a right *erga omnes,* meaning that the right—and obligations arising from it—are a matter of interest for all states.[61] The court's pronouncements helped solidify an interpretation aligning self-determination with territorial integrity—with existing units.

The Last Piece: The Saving Clause of Resolution 2625: There was one final move—one that was to create what space there has been for ferment in succeeding decades. The postwar project had focused almost entirely on the liberation of colonies, with very little attention to the internal qualities of new states, apart from ensuring they were not run on overtly racist grounds by their former colonial overlords.

In 1970, the General Assembly passed Resolution 2625, known as the Declaration on Friendly Relations, to regulate relationships among the greatly expanded number of states. Resolution 2625 reaffirms states' territorial integrity in language that had already become commonplace, but adds a qualification, which appears to define self-determination as the exercise of inclusive, representative government:

> Nothing in the foregoing paragraphs shall be construed as authorizing or encouraging any action which would dismember or impair, totally or in part, the territorial integrity or political unity of sovereign and independent States *conducting themselves in compliance with the principle of . . . self-determination of peoples . . . and thus possessed of a government representing the whole people belonging to the territory without distinction as to race, creed or colour.*[62]

This appears to define self-determination as requiring governments to represent the whole people without discrimination—at least that such a government is a necessary indicator of compliance with self-determination. In turn, this formulation, read in the negative, suggests that the otherwise ironclad protection for territorial integrity leave one narrow window of vulnerability: a state *not* "possessed of a government representing the whole people" might not enjoy that protection.

Coming at the beginning of the end of the great wave of decolonization, Resolution 2625 signaled a repurposing of self-determination: the foundation for a great shift from its external focus on independence to an internal focus on democratization and human rights within the state. But its implicit promise—that the external and the internal would be linked, that there might be consequences for the unity of a state that did not treat its citizens well—did not prove very productive.

THE ACTUAL PROCESS OF DECOLONIZATION: FOSSILIZATION These legal positions were articulated against a backdrop of rapid political change, as colonies won independence or had it thrust upon them—shaping the process, being shaped by it, in short order turning self-determination into a doctrine almost wholly devoted to the liberation of colonies. Immediately after the Second World War, the major powers sought to reassert control of colonies that had been held by Japan, but by the late 1940s, the Dutch had given up, and the French did, too, after Dien Bien Phu in 1954. Although the colonial powers fought hard in certain conflicts in Africa, like Algeria and Kenya, and the General Assembly still complained about forcible repression of independence movements in 1961 when it established the C-24, in fact the argument was largely over.

By the time African decolonization began in earnest around 1960, the basic framework governing territory had been comprehensively altered by the new global settlement after the Second World War. Waging war to change territory had been rejected, and the only space in the system for violent change was for colonial peoples to liberate themselves from recalcitrant masters.[63] Territorial integrity had been enshrined as a core principle. So upon becoming independent, colonies entered into a system that guaranteed their borders.

But the process of decolonization impelled a further refinement of the new order. The doctrine of *uti possidetis*—developed during the Spanish American revolutions over a century earlier—was revived and reapplied in Africa. Compared to Spanish America, African colonial boundaries were relatively well established, mimicking in their clear delineation the model of European states. But those borders had been created in a very different way from European borders, which had gradually brought territory and demography into relatively homogeneous alignment; Africa's borders, in many cases only decades old, were notoriously unrelated to precolonial social, tribal, and political divisions, which had often been much less territorially fixed.[64]

Boundaries between colonies could change. The definitive incorporation of South Sudan into Sudan only dated from 1946, reversing a policy that promoted autonomy and even contemplated union with Uganda. Until 1936, the border between what became Mauritania and Mali was much farther west, and the predecessor of Burkina Faso did not yet exist, its territory distributed among the surrounding colonies. Had those borders survived to independence, they would have been sacrosanct, but under French rule, they remained fungible.

The new territorial orthodoxy limited that fungibility, demanding that colonial powers not change boundaries in the run-up to independence. But wherever they happened to be at the moment of liberation, colonial boundaries became

---

Mayotte: Preserving Borders or Disaggregating Peoples

Colonial borders often shifted, but in the classical era, there was an effort to lock in borders. In 1960, Resolution 1514 called on states not to change colonial borders before independence. It is on this basis that the Comoros (an archipelago in the Indian Ocean) claims the island of Mayotte, which France administers and which voted in 2008 to integrate into France as a *département*. Mayotte was part of the Comoros; in a 1974 referendum, the Comoros as a whole voted for independence, but Mayotte voted to remain with France. Comoros claims Mayotte was part of an integral colonial territory, and the General Assembly has supported the Comoros' claim, declaring, "the results of the referendum . . . were to be considered on a global basis and not island by island[.]"* France and Mayotte see the island as a more meaningful self-determining unit. Whatever the right answer, being an island helps: If there weren't salt water between Mayotte and the rest of the Comoros, France wouldn't have given its vote separate consideration.

*G.A. Res. 47/9 (1992).

---

the borders of independent states, and the foundation for an entrenched commitment to existing units as the vessels for self-determination:

> The political map of colonial Africa was virtually complete by 1914 and there has been little subsequent change. Within fifty years, that colonial boundary mesh would become the almost exact basis for territorial division of independent Africa then to be made fossilized by resolution of the Organization of African Unity (OAU) in July 1964.[65]

Before decolonization, some prominent African political actors had suggested repudiating the colonial frontiers.[66] But in the early 1960s, a conservative consensus developed that revising borders "might lead to conflict and to outside interference[.]"[67] One advocate noted that, though unjust, "it is also true that these boundaries have existed over a long period of time and it would be difficult to change them without raising more problems than would be solved. . . ."[68] The risk was real, though the true explanation was the opposite: It was precisely because the colonial borders were *not* ancient, *not* entrenched in locally legitimated politics, that they held such potential for dissension.

The new orthodoxy solidified in step with decolonization. The new interpretation found strong support among the decolonized themselves, in a virtuous circle. In 1955, at the Bandung Conference, newly independent African and Asian states, supported by the Communist bloc, adopted a Leninist interpretation that expressly linked self-determination to decolonization. By 1963, at the founding conference of the OAU at Addis Ababa, the consensus was nearly complete: The OAU Charter—adopted by states that mostly had not existed a decade earlier—was heavily armored with references to territorial integrity, defense of sovereignty, and noninterference.

Africa's new states quickly agreed among themselves that their withdrawal from imperial orbits would not be followed by further fragmentation. The OAU's 1964 Cairo Declaration called for member states "to respect the borders existing on their achievement of national independence."[69] Partly this was an effort to create a united front against the possibility that Europeans would use *divide et impera* strategies to maintain postcolonial influence, partly an effort to avoid ruinous competition, but also a recognition that the new states were indeed quite fragile and lacked the kind of shared identity—civic or national—that classic European states often possessed. So, at an OAU summit in 1963, President Philibert Tsiranana of the Malagasy Republic declared:

> It is no longer possible, nor desirable, to modify the boundaries of Nations, on the pretext of racial, religious or linguistic criteria. . . . Indeed, should we take race, religion or language criteria for setting our boundaries, a few States in Africa would be blotted out from the map. Leaving demagogy aside, it is not conceivable that one of our individual States would readily consent to be among the victims, for the sake of Unity.[70]

Here in one statement we find the new states' iron determination not to consider any changes to frontiers and their underlying concern: If they took the principle seriously, they might cease to exist—'they' meaning both the existing states in their present form and the elites governing them. "The leaders of these new states, though recent espousers of national self-determination, [we]re now perforce the defenders of multinationalism."[71]

Nearly all African states agreed on maintaining colonial boundaries (except Morocco, which had annexed the Spanish Sahara and wanted to keep it). The new states inherited well-defined frontiers—at least on paper. Some of the colonial overlords departed in such haste that new elites did not possess effective authority over their own territory of the kind normally expected for recognition of new states—one of the so-called Montevideo criteria[72]—but this doctrinal defect was overlooked, because the moral and political case for rapid decolonization was compelling. As we saw, the Colonial Declarations expressly prohibited any delay in independence because a population was supposedly unready to govern itself. In the aftermath of decolonization, the ICJ affirmed the new African consensus that borders should not be altered, and even declared it "a principle of a general kind which is logically connected with this form of decolonization wherever it occurs."[73] And so from a rule originally concerned with ratifying the actual holdings new states had achieved through military power, *uti possidetis* had been transformed into a doctrinal convenience affirming the sovereignty and shape of newly liberated colonies, whether or not they in fact controlled their own land and people.[74]

Still, it largely worked, at least on its own terms: New disputes were few, as were departures from the doctrine. Although there have been significant cross-border conflicts in Africa, most prominently in the Great Lakes region beginning in the 1990s, independent African states avoided the endemic contestation over frontiers that had marked Latin American independence:

> Whereas the African states became independent in an orderly and peaceful manner, each succeeding to a distinct colonial entity, the Spanish American republics were born in actual conflict and amidst the disintegration of the Spanish administrative divisions.[75]

Calling that process "orderly and peaceful" requires a serious qualification, as anyone familiar with the postindependence history of Africa will know. This more orderly transition made agreement on preserving frontiers easier, but it didn't reduce violence *inside* states or stabilize societies. Indeed, the postindependence decades were, in many African states, more violent than the colonial era, and that is saying something; most often, this violence was a contest for control, not *between* states, but *within*.

Still, decolonization had virtues quite apart from the mixed blessing of allowing misrule from Kinshasa or Bangui instead of Brussels or Paris. In principle, decolonization was simple and unambiguous—what Thomas Franck called an "idiot rule[,]"[76] not necessarily because the rule is idiotic, but because someone of limited capacity could understand it. The rule created an identifiable class of beneficiaries, and an equally identifiable limit to the benefit. A child supplied with the rule and a color map of the world from 1945 could accurately predict which bits of humanity would get statehood and which would not.

That child wouldn't get everything right. There were (and are) a few interesting line calls: Is Gibraltar a colony with the right to independence, or a territory that will revert to Spain if Britain ever abandons its rights under the 1713 Treaty of Utrecht? He might ask charmingly awkward questions about why India absorbed the Portuguese colonies of Goa, Daman, and Diu, and he would not have predicted the fate of the Soviet Union or Yugoslavia. But he would have gotten most of the map right, and until about 1990, his record would be nearly perfect. Some places already were states, and they would stay that way. Others were colonies; they would become states, and then stay that way, too. That was simple.

This new, simple rule also comported with a new sensibility that disfavored ethnicity or race as factors, while also helping the very ethnic groups and races previously disenfranchised. Treating a colony's whole population as its people emancipated and empowering the nonwhite populations—at least the parts that took power—without having to explicitly deploy the category of race. The whole population, not the racially subjugated part as such, would be liberated by self-determination.

But the point was to liberate the truly subjugated, and when it was essential to make this implicitly racial aspect clear, that was possible, too. States rejected white Rhodesians' claim that they were the beneficiaries of self-determination, since this denied the black majority any share in their own governance. But generally, as long as newly independent colonies didn't perpetuate a white-over-black hierarchy, self-determination provided few means for criticizing whatever happened inside.

The result, in many states, was domination by particular tribes, ethnic groups, or other subsets of the people. Violent, repressive ethno-kleptocracies comfortably found their place in the doctrinal framework of decolonization.[77] Still, the cases of antiracist self-determination laid down a marker—more accurately, picked up a marker the preclassical model had left lying about—which in time led to the most productive modification of the classical model: a first, halting attempt to identify internal aspects of self-determination.

By the end of the 1960s, the outlines of the system inaugurated in 1945 were largely defined. Most colonies had become independent states, or soon would;

Decolonization Plebiscites in the Classical Order

Plebiscites were held during decolonization, though inconsistently. They were mostly concerned with assigning populated territory to one or another state. This was similar to how plebiscites were used after the First World War, and therefore a departure from the new, rigid commitment to existing borders.

But there was another, novel purpose: not to choose between two states, but to ask if a new state should be created at all. As Resolution 1541 provided, colonies could choose their status: independence, integration, or a continuing non-self-governing relationship—as Puerto Rico, a US dependency, has done in four referenda between 1967 and 2012. In principle, the choice was the colonial population's to make.

However, the notion that colonial peoples were consulted was often just that: a notion. Plebiscites were held in some colonies—Comoros, Togoland, British Cameroons—but there was no standard practice for how to discern the wishes of the population. When Indonesia held a ballot in West Papua in 1969, it allowed about one thousand selected tribal leaders to vote, with soldiers guarding them.* In many colonies, there was no practice at all: The headlong abandonment of Belgian, Spanish, Portuguese, and some French colonies left little time for meaningful consultation, and the people's will—their preference for independence in existing borders—was often simply assumed.

Indeed, given the logic of classical self-determination, it made sense to *assume* a new state would come into existence. After all, a people was the population of a defined territory, and the territory was already defined; what was there to ask? Decolonization made plebiscites redundant: In the preclassical model, the purpose of holding a plebiscite had been to determine what the territory was; in the new model, a people might be interrogated about their preference, but the territory itself is not in question.

*Kingsbury, "West Papua," 491.

in most of those left after the 1970s—almost all small islands—the populations had indicated their willingness to keep their current status, beneficiaries of protection, economic transfers, and access to markets in the metropole. The last trusteeship, Palau, became a self-governing state in association with the United States in 1994, and the Trusteeship Council suspended operation.

There was still much uncertainty, but the main lines of the system were increasingly uncontested: Disputes over principles were increasingly replaced by

---

Self-Determination's Dead Hand: The Chagos Islands

The continuing influence of colonial borders after independence has recently been confirmed. Mauritius, together with various Indian Ocean islands, was a British colony. Shortly before independence in 1968, the United Kingdom separated the Chagos Islands and organized them into a separate British Indian Ocean Territory; it then removed the population and leased one island, Diego Garcia, to the United States for a military base. Independent Mauritius later objected, and in 2019, the International Court of Justice declared that the United Kingdom had violated Mauritius' right of self-determination by detaching Chagos and has continued to violate it by administering the islands.

There were important legal questions at stake: When did self-determination become a right? (Britain claimed it was after 1968; the court disagreed.) When is a country's consent freely given? (The court doubted colonial Mauritius' agreement had been a genuine expression of the people's will.) And there's little doubt the United Kingdom treated the population of the Chagos Islands abominably. But what does that have to do with Mauritius? Chagos is over 2,000 kilometers from Mauritius, its population's connection solely a function of their colonial status.

If the Chagossians are allowed to return, the case may prove a belated correction to colonial injustice. But little more: Running entirely on decolonization logic, it offers no principle that could ask meaningful questions about human beings and their politics elsewhere. It reaffirms the most rigid view of borders, confirming territorial integrity as a "corollary of the right of self-determination."* A better proof that self-determination has become a moribund, decadent category is hardly to be found.

* Chagos Islands Advisory Opinion, ¶ 160.

---

questions about how to implement what everyone now agreed upon. The remaining cases were holdouts, violations of a global norm admitting no exceptions. Or they were seen as quirky oddities and line-calls: the Falklands, Gibraltar, the Chagos Islands—the narrowing fascinations of an orthodoxy being worked out to scholastic finality.

This is not to say that there was no dissonance, or that the new doctrine's triumphant occupation of the field terminated all resistance. The colonial powers fought the full implications of the new interpretation for a long time and tried to carve out exceptions. Even as France granted independence to Tunisia, Morocco, and its Saharan colonies, it waged a protracted war to hold on to Algeria, which it considered an integral part of its territory. Major powers succeeded in heading off more expansive interpretations of self-determination, territorial integrity, or aggression that might have constrained their ability to dominate the economies of newly independent states.

And the ultimate heresy—the preclassical model itself, with its embarrassing focus on ethnicity and even more awkward potential to redraw borders—survived, if only as political claims by disaffected populations, or as memories that this doctrine once had meant something quite different. Self-determination remained the rallying cry of liberation movements, whether or not their demands fit within the new doctrine's increasingly rigid confines.

The developing orthodoxy implicitly conceded this persistent reality even as it tried to define it out of existence. In a joint declaration in 1964, Ethiopia's emperor and India's president affirmed that "the principle of self-determination should apply only to colonial territories which have not yet attained their independence and not parts of sovereign or independent states."[78] That the leaders of two such strikingly heterogeneous, almost jarringly diverse states should proclaim that, once the colonial yoke was lifted, there was nothing further to discuss is as instructive as it is ironic. Challenges have persisted, because populations continue to imagine, against all evidence and instruction, that the law offers them a path to statehood, or ought to.

But none of this nuance should distract us from recognizing how thoroughly the project of decolonization succeeded in displacing the previous model. For all the complexity, the new rule was triumphant; it had become what it remains even now: the classical system of self-determination. We are, ourselves, living in the classical era, if perhaps in its latter, decadent days. So let us now examine the operations of that system—our system—before turning to the assumptions that underlie it.

2

The Map of Our World:
The Limits of the Classical System

How do we make states today? What has self-determination achieved, and what is it capable of achieving?

BY THE 1970S, THE WORLD HAD SETTLED on the classical model of self-determination—a formal set of rules, elegant and stable in its principles and assumptions. Of course, in reality such models and moments are anything but stable, and ever since there has been almost continuous ferment and change. Indeed, one could say that as the classical model was announced, even while it was still forming, we entered into the postclassical era, in which the classical model persists, still dominant but increasingly indeterminate, insensible, decaying,[1] unable to explain its own premises or operate effectively: an age of self-determinative decadence.

But rather than succumb to a faddish postmodernism, let us keep our categories simple and just say we are still in the classical world. In the main, the model and even its critiques have remained within the confines of the classical structure. Indeed, those confines explain why self-determination has proven ineffectual and attempts to improve it so limited, which is why we may speak of its decadence.[2] The elements and operations of the classical model—including recent challenges—are the subject to which we now turn. These questions will guide us:

- Who has the right of self-determination?
- What does the right consist of?[3]

Such is the convoluted, tautological, and self-referential nature of self-determination—rightly described as *"lex obscura"*[4]—that it is impossible to discuss any part of it without considering all the others: in order to know what a people is, we must know what rights different peoples have, but to know what rights self-determination includes, we must know the nature of the territory, which means we must know . . . and so on. In fact, if what we want is clarity of definition, 'the people' might be the very worst thing to start with, but we must begin somewhere, and so we'll start with the human beings with whom we should be concerned, before getting lost in gyres of doctrine and definition. Besides, the reasons it is so troubling to begin with the people—the problems that arise when one tries—are quite revealing about what is defective in this, the decadence of our classical doctrine.

The People Who Self-Determine: The Holders of the Right (Whatever It Is)

At the heart of every self-determination claim is the idea of a people—or, as we shall soon be compelled to qualify them, a self-determining people or a people possessed of the right to self-determination, formulations that immediately suggest there must be other peoples without the right.

Two Models: The Dominance of the Territorial Principle

When we speak of a people, we mean something other than just plain folk: We are dealing with a definition in law, where the plain and commonsensical are not held in highest regard. A people refers to a coherent group, joined together by circumstance or history into a political community with identity, meaning, perhaps purpose. And in law, a people has particular qualities, or at least particular rights.

There are two main ways to define a people. Objective tests describe observable, often fixed qualities, while subjective tests ask if the individuals feel they constitute a people. Definitions can combine these test, and usually do.[5] The primitive, preclassical model was just such a mix, insisting on some observable markers, such as shared ethnicity or common history, as well as subjective recognition by the community itself that it constitutes such a group—the distinction between a politically aware nation and a 'mere' ethnicity.[6] The heart of the classical definition, by contrast, is almost wholly objective, adopting a very particular criterion for a people: citizenship of a preexisting territory.

Peoples are mentioned in the classical order's foundational documents. The UN Charter declares that peoples possess "equal rights and self-determination[.]"[7] Both human rights covenants declare self-determination a right of "all peoples."[8] These documents don't actually explain who these peoples are, but the classical rule's definitional core is straightforward and impressively objective: A people is the entire citizenry of an existing territory—a state or non-self-governing territory that could be a state—without reference to ethnic or national qualities, or anything other than citizenship. (Citizenry, not population: There may be humans in the territory illegally, or with guest status, such as *Gastarbeiter* in Germany or green-card holders in the United States, or refugees; these aren't part of the people.) A legal people and a state are not the same thing, but they overlap; the legal theorist Hans Kelsen assumed the reference to peoples in the charter effectively meant states as such[9]—not the view that has prevailed, but telling for its assumption that although we talk about humans, we are really dealing with the units.

The simplicity of this definition is supposedly one of its chief virtues, in contrast to the line-drawing judgment calls of Wilsonianism. In fact, the operation of the classical rule has created complexity, propagating peoples in bewildering number and variety. This complexity—redolent of medieval scholasticism or the Islamic schools' closing of the gate of *ijtihād*—is a hallmark of the decadent style.

HOW MANY PEOPLES ARE THERE? COUNTING UNITS First, how many peoples are there? It should be a fairly straightforward calculation if peoples are based on existing territories. But the definitional periphery around 'existing political territories'—the thing we need to know in order to know who's part of which people—turns out to be quite ragged: the more one considers the problem of identifying the units in international law's flat, anarchic system, the harder it is to say how many units there are.

Recognition of states by other states is the heart of the conceptual problem with counting units in a horizontal system. Is South Ossetia a state? It is recognized by 5 widely recognized states, as well as a few units themselves recognized by almost no one else. Israel is clearly a state, though not recognized by about 30 other states that are universally recognized. Palestine is recognized by 136 states, though not a functioning state in important ways—less than So-maliland, which is recognized by no one. One could analyze secession entirely through the lens of recognition.[10]

Even so, this is hardly the most difficult part, because it's possible to get close to consensus: the roster of generally recognized states and non-self-governing territories, plus a short list of plausible claimants that have secured some recognition or control enough territory to be taken seriously in politics.

The populations of all generally recognized states are peoples who have already exercised their right to self-determination by forming a state. If we use membership in the UN as a proxy, that makes 193 units, plus Palestine and Vatican City.[11] In addition, the populations of the remaining non-self-governing territories are self-determining peoples; currently there are 17 on the official list.

So the first cut is territorial: Peoples are the populations of states, non-self-governing territories, and a few other territories that claim to be states. But although its basic criterion is territorial, the classical definition has echoes of earlier, ethnic Wilsonianism. A colony was supposed to have two characteristics distinguishing it from the metropolitan state: It should be "geographically separate and . . . distinct ethnically and/or culturally from the country administering [them]."[12]

The more important of these has been the geographic qualification—the 'salt water' clause from Resolution 1541—that limits external self-determination to overseas colonies, not states' contiguous territory or nearby islands: part of why Corsica isn't a French colony but New Caledonia is. (New Caledonia held an independence referendum in 1987, and under the 1998 Nouméa Accord it held another in 2018 and may hold two more in 2020 and 2022.) The requirement of ethnic or cultural difference receives less attention, though it actually carries the weight of classical self-determination's project of liberating non-European peoples. Together, the combined rule of salt water and brown skin has had a double effect: justifying independence for communities living under racially defined colonial regimes, while keeping the territories of states, however diverse, off the table.

And there is a third, essential criterion: that the population (really, the territory) be non-self-governing. After all, the core of the project was to ensure that peoples govern themselves, so it made sense to apply it to populations that didn't. Of course, being non-self-governing is a relative judgment, and in making that judgment, it greatly helps to discover a physical separation. France claimed Algeria as an integral part of its metropolitan territory; that claim, difficult to justify given the differential treatment of its ethnic Arabs and Berbers, was made even more implausible by the awkward interposition of the Mediterranean Sea. That may seem obvious, but modern internal self-determination favors certain forms of territorial differentiation—autonomies, federalism—that can actually be hard to distinguish from non-self-governing status in nondemocratic and repressive regimes.[13]

In practice, the territorial aspects of the classical definition came to be the most essential: overseas colonies could claim independence, but the contiguous territory of a state, no matter how it was governed, belonged to a people already exercising self-determination. This insulated existing states from challenge: Even if not democratic—even if the people didn't rule themselves at all—existing states were safe from territorial challenges so long as an equal despotism was applied to everyone.

Whatever the demerits of this definition, it at least simplified the list of peoples. It ensured multiethnic states would not be carved up from the inside, as had happened to the European land empires after the First World War. It also allowed liberated colonies to head off threats to their territorial integrity: Once a colony achieved independence, no further exercise of the right was needed, or possible. Territorial change could still happen, but only consensually: The *whole* people would have to agree (at least, the government or legislature would), not just any territorially discrete part.

As we have seen, the ancient doctrine of *uti possidetis* and the new principle of territorial integrity were invoked to convert colonial boundaries into international frontiers and to forestall any further secession from the new states. This was done, not in contradiction of self-determination, but fully consistent with it—consistent with what the doctrine had become. Self-determination had become a legal principle, but—stripped of its Wilsonian focus on the substantive qualities of a people—it had become a right for colonies to gain independence and nothing more.

Although there is a racial component to self-determination's decolonizing logic, it is not clear that it often made a difference in deciding if an overseas territory was non-self-governing. In theory, the requirement that the community be ethnically or culturally different could justify continued rule of territories populated by the same community as the majority state—places like the Falkland Islands or Gibraltar. (The United Kingdom has acknowledged Falklanders' and Gibraltarians' right of self-determination.) But distance and separate governance seem to matter more. By contrast, it is difficult to think of any cases in which ethnic or cultural distinction has been the basis *without* geographic distance. Diverse populations in western China or Russia's periphery or Africa's states have never been covered by the classical definition, because they lack the blessing of an ocean between them and the majority.

Instead, the requirement of ethnic or cultural distinction looks like a vestige from the preclassical era: a substantive criterion that doesn't derive from the unit, but instead provides meaning to it. It is the only part of the definition capable of doing generative work—of producing a new shape—yet so powerful has been the decolonizing principle's focus on existing units that this clear reference to ethnicity and culture in the core documents is largely invisible. It has only surfaced in a set of cases involving alien rule or occupation—the next complications in the definition we have to consider.

PEOPLES UNDER RACIST RULE AND OCCUPATION In parts of southern Africa, local whites sought to appropriate the colonial unit for themselves, excluding the black majority—South Africa during apartheid until 1994, and Rhodesia from 1965 to 1980. This was rejected as a form of alien or racist rule that violated self-determination principles.

Alien occupation was always a problematic category to describe these cases.[14] There is little doubt that the aliens ruling South Africa and Rhodesia were an integral part of the self-determining people; their sin was not being alien, but denying a portion of their own people the right to take part in the shared project of self-determination. Moreover, South Africa was already independent before the UN era, and not a case of decolonization. So all the work was done by the idea of a 'racist regime.' The common trope that speaks of South Africa's *liberation* in 1994 shows how strong the antiracial norms underpinning decolonization are; in legal terms, the idea is a nonsense—an already independent South Africa merely changed its internal governance—but the idea of liberating *the whole people* is compelling.

Not so compelling as to be generalizable: The ethical sense attaching to the South African case has not yielded much support for the idea that colonial domination's *equivalent* can occur outside the colonial context. This lack of definitional slippage should indicate to us the intensity, if not the clarity, of classical order's conviction that self-determination was about ridding the world of a particular set of imperial legacies, not a more general principle of liberation.

Military occupation presents a clearer case, at least in theory: It really is about outsiders imposing their rule on a separate people by force. It doesn't rely on racial or ethnic difference: So long as the occupier is from a different self-determining unit—if Canada were to invade Minnesota—the conditions for a denial of self-determination are fulfilled. Occupation is not necessarily illegal—it is a status under international humanitarian law—but it *can be,* as the most common view considers Israel's occupation of Palestine;[15] and legal or not, occupation suspends a people's right to self-determination.

In practice, occupation has had a very narrow application: Although well-developed in the laws of war, in self-determination it is mostly invoked to condemn Israel's occupation of Palestine. Occupation nicely demonstrates and reinforces the state-centered logic of self-determination. If a portion of a state is occupied, that portion's population only has the right to rejoin the state from which it has been separated. (For example, Crimea would not have the right to become an independent state, only to rejoin Ukraine.) When we speak about occupation and self-determination, we invariably speak about preexisting territories that are wholly or partly occupied.

Thus, through the doctrines of alien rule and occupation, the territorial definition of a people was expanded to include populations facing burdens similar to those of colonized peoples—more accurately, *territories* whose populations bear those burdens. These two categories have potentially broad application—occupation or alien rule might happen to anyone—but have been developed for very particular cases: South Africa, Rhodesia, Palestine. Expanding the list to include alien rule and occupation is conceptually a small step, and in practice it hasn't increased the number of recognized peoples. Its more important contribution has been to claims about internal self-determination—about the quality of governance inside an independent unit—to which we will turn shortly.

ARRIVING AT A NUMBER Beyond recognized states and non-self-governing territories, and the tiny number of cases of occupation or alien rule, there are a few line calls—territories whose populations might be considered self-determining peoples, at least by part of the international community. The population of Kosovo is clearly a people to states that have recognized Kosovo, clearly not to those that haven't, and the same could be said for Taiwan, South Ossetia, Abkhazia,

Northern Cyprus, and Nagorno-Karabakh. Counting these peoples is fraught, since they and their territories are considered parts of other self-determining units: Serbia considers Kosovo part of its territory, China considers Taiwan part of its, Georgia claims South Ossetia and Abkhazia, Cyprus claims Northern Cyprus, and Azerbaijan claims Nagorno-Karabkah. Counting them builds in disagreement and dispute.

But even with all these qualifications and line calls, we readily arrive at a figure in the low two hundreds for territories whose populations are peoples for purposes of self-determination.[16] The ragged edges create confusion about what the units actually are, or what territory they exactly encompass, but we can all, 'idiots' or not, produce just about the same list, and that is significant. The confusions truly are on the literal and metaphorical periphery: Self-determination is one of those things about which one can learn more by attending to the main lines than to the marginalia.

Although there have been fascinating speculations about the self-determining status of peoples without territory—a practical concern for some Pacific states—the doctrine remains solidly married to the union of a population with a defined plot of land, which is really the only way we know a population is a people in the first place. Indeed, speculations about disappearing islands simply prove the hold territory has on our law and politics: These pathetic cases only seem *legally* interesting because they so obviously run contrary to the normal state of things—and we only recognize them as cases because, for now, those peoples still have a territory, just barely above the waves.

The List Expands—and Loses Coherence

But we are not finished. Along those ragged edges we have seen, the classical model has gradually incorporated other qualities—and new territorial qualifications—into its definition, so now there are many more recognized peoples: a growing, even metastasizing list. But their inclusion has destabilized the magisterial clarity of the classical rule.

In 2007, after long debates, indigenous communities were recognized as peoples for purposes of self-determination. In certain respects, an indigenous people recalls the preclassical model's ethnic definition; Wilson himself wouldn't have imagined that most of today's indigenous groups could have qualified as self-determining peoples, but the logic is similar. And indigeneity is closely linked to territory: As the name implies, indigeneity presumes a preexisting relationship to a piece of land. This is an echo of the decolonizing impulse, since indigeneity is constructed in relation to some subsequent, *arriviste* population that was, in its own origins, colonial or imperial.

There is no precise definition of indigeneity, but estimates suggest there are 370 million indigenous people—5 percent of the world's population—belonging to five thousand separate groups.[17] This dramatically multiplies the number of peoples with the right of self-determination—and layers them, since every indigenous person is also a member of some state's people. But this layering has been achieved—and neutralized—by articulating a new, disaggregated or deconstructed form of self-determination to which profoundly different rights attach, as we'll see in the next section. Indigenous communities are peoples possessed of the right of self-determination, but not the same right.

There are, and logically must be, still other peoples. Some constitutions identify self-determining peoples within the population, even (rarely) with a right to secession. The United Kingdom recognizes within its borders four separate historical countries that arguably have a right to self-determination. Many socialist constitutions, following the tradition developed by Lenin and Stalin, recognized the right of national communities to self-determination, although this was generally a paper right. Yugoslavia's republics were recognized as successors to its dissolved sovereignty. Similarly, in the Soviet Union, the existence of republics with a notional right of secession smoothed the path to the state's dismemberment.

At the least, the chances that a group recognized in a domestic constitution will be internationally recognized as a people if the state dissolves are higher than for some random fraction of a state's population. And this affects our estimate of how many peoples there might be: Anyone trying to make a list of self-determining peoples in 1990 might not have included the populations of the fifteen Soviet republics or the seven successors to Yugoslavia, but later he would have wished he had.

Moreover, peoples may exist in latent form, coming into being—or being acknowledged—only when certain, very unpleasant conditions arise. The doctrine of remedial secession (to which we will later turn) suggests that groups may secede for exigent self-protection. By the very act of becoming a new state they become a self-determining people. So remedial secession implies the existence of potential peoples, who only emerge through acts of oppression and assertion of independence.

The number of such peoples might be limited by a requirement that they exhibit some ethnic or cultural difference from their oppressors. The Canadian Supreme Court, in its famous advisory opinion on Quebec, said the Quebecois are, or might be, a people; the court declined to define the term but suggested it has something to do with traditional marks of ethnicity, a view that looks decidedly like the preclassical Wilsonian model.[18] Still, the court's reasoning could apply to any persecuted ethnic group, not just those already identified as nations; in that case, there could be as many peoples as they are ways to persecute our fellow human beings, and that is a great many ways indeed.

To add to the complexity, it is clearly possible for one person to belong to more than one people, by having multiple citizenships or indigenous status. A group claiming remedial secession has membership in both a persecuted people and in the persecuting state (until it secedes).

Finally, beyond all these categories, outside even the growing complexity the existing law itself creates, there are many human communities whose members, apparently still reading tattered glosses on the "Fourteen Points," *imagine* themselves to be self-determining peoples, even though the classical rule gives them almost no reason to believe such an implausibility. They annoyingly continue to act as if they are peoples with the right to form a state.

So, beginning with a simple, magisterial rule, articulated in seemingly pure form between the 1940s and 1960s, we have arrived in a few short decades at something quite different: beneath the sheen of the classical rule's absolute equivalence between a people and a territory's population, an enormous, unstable, indeterminate complexity. How many peoples are there? No one can say.

Beyond mere counting, the qualities peoples have are less clear than originally imagined, and certainly less coherent. Attempting a typology of various peoples with various rights to self-determination simply confronts us with the question: What distinguishes them? One might imagine peoples would have different rights based on some independent quality, but as we'll now see, the only basis *is nothing other* than the rights each people gets. The distinctions have no independent rationale: Peoples are only differentiated based on the different rights they are accorded. Wilsonian self-determination at least tried to give people different rights based on different qualities; the classical rule divides the world into territories and then classifies human beings depending on their place in that scheme.

Problems with the Two Definitions of People

Some people or nationalities were thus destined never to become full na-
tions. Others had attained, or would attain, full nationhood. But which had
a future and which did not?
Eric Hobsbawm[19]

The two models of self-determination—the present classical mode and primitive, preclassical Wilsonianism—represent two different understandings of
people: the population of a predefined territory, or a community based on shared
identity. Each have their qualities and their problems.

The classical doctrine lacks almost all substance, and arguably that is the
point: Populations that could not possibly meet any substantive definition of
community other than shared confinement within existing frontiers are treated
as self-determining peoples. There are as many examples as there are countries,
but two will do. The Congo has barely existed as a coherent state since its independence; its population does not share much of anything except a legacy of
colonial brutality and violent, chaotic postindependence statehood. But it is not
only failed states that fail the test. A political and cultural unit we call China has
a historical coherence that Congo utterly lacks, but China *in its current borders*
includes populations that have little connection to the unit, lack objective markers or subjective perception of shared identity with the Han, and whose inclusion
in a self-determining Chinese people is a function of little other than being in
the same bordered unit.

By contrast, the preclassical model focused on finding a substantive basis for
shared statehood. As we have just seen, this logic persists as a minor key in the
classical model, a counterpoint from the past, underpinning the marginal expansions and alterations in classical doctrine to include persecuted peoples, indigenous peoples, people under alien rule. But while this has admitted more groups
to the category, it has not expanded the number of peoples *with a right to form*
a state, and in the process the classical rule's definition has been rendered less
and less coherent.

The objections to each approach are readily apparent. The present model
crowds human communities together on the basis of often arbitrary, contingent,
even cruel demarcations, without regard to whether or not those groupings reflect anything else at all, let alone if the people subjected to them wish it. Some-

times this works out all right—after all, history's demarcations are also people's history, marking them and perhaps, over time, shaping them into a true, if imagined community. This is arguably what has happened in the United States, where state patriotism has melded highly diverse populations into a community whose patriotic identity is difficult to distinguish from nationalism. Still, in many places, this simply has not happened.

So although the classical rule's definition of people appears simple, it is in fact quite complicated, with layers derived from the operation of the rule itself. This suggests there is in fact another kind of idiocy at work in the classical rule: a constellation of distinctions far more arbitrary than primitive Wilsonianism ever was. For whether a group of humans is a people with certain rights or a people without them, or not a people at all, turns out to be a function not of anything intrinsic to them, but of the political status of the territory on which they live. The principle that under the present model is supposed to determine humans' political status is in fact determined by the status they already have.

WHY MINORITIES AREN'T PEOPLES To understand this, it will prove instructive to consider a kind of community that is not a people: a minority. There is no agreed definition of minority,[20] but in fact minorities differ from a nation or people in just one way: It is a group within a state whose majority belongs to a different group. Whether any given person is a member of a majority or of a minority depends only on where the border is: With one border, you are a member of a minority; with a different border, your group is the majority. Kosovar Albanians were a minority within Serbia; in an independent Kosovo, they are the majority—and this would have been true even if independence had come without all the bodies in wells and the roads swelled with refugees. By the same token, Serbs in Kosovo—part of the majority nation, obviously—became (obviously) part of a minority when Kosovo became independent. For fun, we could run the experiment in a different direction: Neighboring Romania has a much bigger population than Serbia, so if we annexed the whole territory of Serbia to Romania, the *entire* population of Serbia—including its Serb majority and Kosovar minority—would become minorities at a stroke. (Almost everyone, that is: The small Romanian minority would instantly become part of the new state's majority. Such thought experiments suggest why rules against violent acquisition of territory are a really good idea.)

Of course, a person belonging to a minority *is* a member of a self-determining people, because he is part of the state's population.[21] It is just that he is *also* a minority because of his affiliation to some other group that, to his misfortune, either resides outside the state's territory or otherwise doesn't constitute a majority inside the state. The very idea that a minority could have the right to self-determine is tautologically excluded. A minority, by definition, is a group that doesn't have that right:

> The restrictive view of the non-applicability of self-determination to minority groups is strengthened by a consideration of General Assembly Resolution 1514—the Colonial declaration. . . . The holder of the right of self-determination is, once more, declared to be the people. . . . Minorities, therefore, may not secede from States—at least, international law gives them no *right* to do so. The logic of the resolution is relatively simple: peoples hold the right of self-determination; a people is the whole people of a territory; a people exercises its right through the achievement of independence.[22]

This purely territorial view has been widely criticized since it "fails to take account of the enormous impact of linguistic, cultural, and religious factors on the way in which populations identity themselves. Populations do not in general consider themselves as one 'people' by virtue of the fact that they happen to reside within certain territorial limits."[23] Although definitionally excluded, minorities are precisely the groups that the earlier model had in mind as the beneficiaries of self-determination: Wilsonianism turned minorities into majorities by moving borders. But that purpose has been abandoned in the classical model, which defines political identity by—and subordinates it to—the borders we already have.

Yet the preclassical model is equally troubling. The Wilsonian definition was rigid and ascriptive, assuming peoples *should* be defined by ethnicity. Making political affiliation depend on ethnicity assumes individuals share identities that may not be salient: In some places religious ties truly bind people together and separate them from others, but in others, religious difference is trivial or private. Markers for ethnic difference can be studied and described, but their subjective value, their meaning for those marked by them, is always complex. It is rare that political identity can be reduced solely to such markers, and is usually unpleasant and violent when it can.

Even when they work as advertised, ascriptive identities create exclusion. Giving the status of self-determining people to one group—implying its authority to sovereignty over territory—can reduce the status of other groups living there. As we saw, by creating national states, Wilsonian self-determination practically created the problem of national minorities. Since governing territory is one of the essentials of human politics, these other groups are disadvantaged, both in the places where they live and in relation to the larger society.

As we'll see, the new rule in this book suggests a third definition, closely tied to the act for which a people's political identity is most relevant—claiming sovereignty over territory—but based neither on ascriptive qualities, like Wilson's nations, nor on accidents of history, like the present rule. Before we get to that, however, we must consider the rights a self-determining people actually has. As we'll now see, one of the central problems with our present model is not only that it has multiplied the kinds of people, but it has deconstructed self-determination and, in the process, gutted its original purpose—to help communities create states that serve their interests and desires—letting it fade to a near nullity.

What Self-Determination Actually Consists Of: External and Internal Variants

The classical model is immediately unsatisfying, as it arbitrarily divides human communities into different categories. There have been two responses to this dissatisfaction: one, to revisit the categories of people to whom the original meaning of self-determination applies; the other, to devise new meanings for self-determination. The world has largely chosen the latter.

As we have just seen, the definition of people has been expanding—but in ways that have reshaped the right self-determining peoples enjoy. The doctrine's original focus on independence has been disaggregated; as a result, self-determination applies to an increasing number of peoples, but also increasingly means a variety of things—and only rarely what it originally meant.

In the process, politics and law have become suspicious of the very thing self-determination was originally supposed to do: create new states. With the end of decolonization, this thinking goes, that kind of self-determination has been completed, and should not be exercised anymore. With few exceptions, no more peoples need states;[24] now the task is to make the states we have better for the peoples they contain. If self-determination is to have a future, it is only by promoting change within states; that is precisely the turn we find in recent decades.

So, having cataloged the various kinds of people who have some right to self-determination, we must now look at the increasingly variable content of that right. In particular, we will find self-determination complexly divided into two distinct forms: external and internal.

External self-determination is the part most clearly associated with Wilsonianism and Leninism: the right to form an independent state. Internal self-determination refers to a people's right freely to choose the form of governance within a territory that has already exercised external self-determination—"the choice of a system of governance and the administration of the functions of governance according to the will of the governed[.]"[25] The right to govern oneself has increasingly been expressed as a right to democracy for the whole population, but also as autonomy or special rights for minorities.

This division is dogmatic: The two halves of the doctrine are separate, so that a people might possess some right of internal self-determination, but not external self-determination. The division is so entrenched that it is common even to think of the two forms of self-determination as separate rights.[26] As we shall see, however, this division rests upon arbitrary distinctions derived from assuming the very thing that self-determination ought to decide, and arises out of an almost desperate desire to keep using this magnetically compelling doctrine without actually confronting what it logically means.

The Limited Varieties of External Self-Determination

External self-determination—the formation of new states—is possible under very limited circumstances, and far more limited than they used to be. New states continue to form, but it is not clear what self-determination has to do with the process—or rather, self-determination is clearly supposed to have as little as possible to do with it.

THE BASIC METHOD: NEW STATES THROUGH DECOLONIZATION Decolonization is the core of the classical right's external aspect. The people of a non-self-governing territory have a right to govern themselves. This may be expressed through independence, integration into the metropolitan state, as some of France's overseas departments (like French Guiana) have done, or "emergence into any other political status freely determined by a people."[27] A colonized people can remain in association with the metropolitan state—as Puerto Rico and some island colonies have—but this is supposed to be the free decision of the group.[28]

Who Should Vote in Western Sahara?

Spain relinquished its colony on the African coast in 1975. Morocco occupied it, claiming historical title, but its claim is widely contested. An indigenous movement, the Polisario Front, declared an independent republic and is recognized by many states. The territory is the largest still on the UN's list of non-self-governing territories. Under a UN-sponsored plan, there was supposed to be a referendum in 1992.

The Moroccan government and Polisario Front have different views about which populations should be included in the much delayed vote. Polisario wants to rely on the 1974 census. The government wants to include descendants of Sahrawis who moved to Morocco during Spanish rule; if they and the tens of thousands of Moroccan settlers took part, they could tip the balance. Both the departure of indigenous inhabitants, under complex circumstances, and the importation of new populations affect the likely outcome, and an effective response would have to account for both.

Almost all colonies of any size have become independent. Only occasionally was this choice actually put to a popular vote—when the great wave of decolonization was underway, self-determination didn't require democracy—though there's little reason to doubt that independence was most people's preference. This lack of actual choice shows the degree to which self-determination had become about the territory rather than the people living in it: External self-determination gives a people the right to claim independence, but only in and because of a territory to which they already belong.

CONTINUING EXTERNAL SELF-DETERMINATION: INDEPENDENCE AND TERRITORIAL INTEGRITY After independence, the right of self-determination is not extinguished: It continues, providing the legal basis for protecting the state against external or internal threats. Once formed, the state—the shaping vessel for its self-determining people—is proof against almost all challenges. Although a state can divide itself, it cannot be forced to, by outsiders or groups within, even if those groups themselves otherwise have a claim to self-determination. Some states have provided a constitutional pathway to secession, but "[t]hese clauses are rare indeed"—eight, in fact.[29]

Thus, the whole people of each state possesses the right of external self-determination, which they have already exercised and continue to exercise by remaining independent. Only the populations of colonies, occupied territories, or territories under alien rule are presently deprived of their right. And once they exercise it, they become states, too, and continue to exercise their right by remaining a state. This is a closed system, a tautology.

NEW STATES THROUGH DISSOLUTION The basic framework ensures independence for colonies and continuing independence for states. The rules protecting existing borders are extraordinarily rigid, but that does not mean borders never change. Things fall apart surprisingly often, and law has to respond. One way is through dissolution: When a state simply ceases to exist owing to internal turmoil or dysfunction, new states can form out of it; by definition, the new states' populations become self-determining peoples.

The Yugoslav collapse is typically described this way. Yugoslavia's republics didn't have an *international* right of self-determination before the country's collapse. Following standard Communist theory, the last Yugoslav constitution confirmed that each nation (*narod*) had the right of self-determination, but that right had supposedly been perfected when the titular republics—Slovenia, Macedonia, and so forth—joined Yugoslavia; the constitution also provided that Yugoslavia's frontiers could not be altered without the approval of all the republics and autonomous provinces.[30] And whatever the constitution said, in international law the matter looked sublimely simple: The entire population was a single self-determining people. Certainly other states weren't proclaiming the right of Slovenes or Macedonians to form their own states *before* Yugoslavia's collapse.

Yet now that single people is at least six, and seven for those that recognize Kosovo—a lot more than one people, which is what every state counted until 1990. After Yugoslavia's collapse, those constitutional provisions—and the strong inclination of international law and diplomacy to work with existing units—led to the quick identification of Yugoslavia's republics as holders of a latent right of self-determination. *Uti possidetis,* which we saw in Latin America and Africa, was repurposed in Yugoslavia to explain why its republics should be recognized. Faced with the factual problem of the state's disappearance—at least, this is one way to describe what happened—international law found other vessels to contain the missing state's populations, which were declared self-determining peoples.

A similar story is told about the collapse of the Soviet Union. Its 1977 constitution declared that the Union of Soviet Socialist Republics had formed "as a result of the free self-determination of nations and the voluntary association of equal . . . republics[,]" and confirmed that each republic "retain[ed] the right freely to secede[.]"[31] It is not clear, however, if these republics were actually self-determining in the international legal sense—certainly they weren't in practice. But when the Soviet Union dissolved, the republics became states, and their populations, self-determining peoples. Russia was considered the legal continuator of the Soviet Union, while the others were new states (or, in the case of the Baltic states, continuators of states occupied during the Second World War). Each new or continuing or resurrected state's population was now a legally self-determining people: from one, fifteen.

But while dissolution happens, it is not common. The two main instances in which it has been invoked were quite fecund, converting two states into twenty-two, but otherwise the category has not been used much. So when do we recognize dissolution, and when not?

Law does not automatically make new states just because an existing one collapses. States may suffer civil war and anarchy without jeopardizing their statehood—or their people's right to self-determination. For decades Somalia, the *locus classicus* of state failure, was treated as a state, maintaining its seat at the United Nations; no state has recognized Somaliland, the only functioning state on its territory.[32] Even the principal example, Yugoslavia, is questionable, since the proof that it had dissolved was that its units declared independence— but that is supposed to be a *consequence* of dissolution, not its cause.[33] Indeed, the Yugoslav dissolution is notable for having happened at all—for being treated the way it was. We can look far and wide for other cases in which states have recognized division simply because a state's institutions are in disarray; Somalia may be an extreme example, but it's still the mainstream, and Yugoslavia the outlier. Dissolution is both rare and selective; it is difficult to find any principle governing it, other than the vagaries of attention and interest.

Moreover, the few cases we have actually reconfirm the strongly territorial orientation of the classical system. When Yugoslavia and the Soviet Union dissolved, the clear practice in each was to default to existing substate units. There, the territorial logic of the classical model played out in miniature: a unit was identified, whose population now took over the right of self-determination, which is the only way to know it was now a people. Groups that contested the new dispensation by forming a unit that didn't match favored internal boundaries—

in the Republic of Serbian Krajina, Transnistria, Nagorno-Karabakh, South Ossetia, Abkhazia—found almost no support for their legal claims. (Some of these had defined territories, but were not republics, the preferred units.) Even Russia, the backer of many of these breakaways, did not recognize them; instead it took part in peace processes that assumed the territorial continuity of states within their old republican boundaries. (Russia only recognized South Ossetia and Abkhazia in 2008, after its war with Georgia.) Even when confronted with dissolution, the default response is to hold on to the units and the borders that are already there; the conceptual distance between this and what was imperfectly attempted after the First World War is enormous.

NEW STATES THROUGH VOLUNTARY DIVISION Dissolution encourages us to imagine the collapse of a state as an event subject to the laws of physics—like the impact of a meteor—but in fact it is the consequence of human choices: a social construction. The Soviet Union's dissolution was not an act of nature—it happened through a series of political decisions and formal acts. In Singapore and Malaysia in 1965, separation was a conscious policy choice to resolve an increasingly dangerous political stalemate. But there needn't even be a crisis, because nothing in international law prevents a state from dividing voluntarily: This is what happened between Slovakia and the Czech Republic. Legally, this process is not terribly interesting, although later we will have much to say about what it means for a single people to divide itself when there *isn't* agreement.

But whether through voluntary division or dissolution, the result is not only a new state, but a new people with the right of self-determination. (If we were to return to the previous section and ask how many peoples there are, our answer would depend on how many states decide to continue as they are or divide.) So powerful is the inverted, territorially defined logic of classical self-determination that even if some group has never thought of itself as a people, the moment its territory achieves independence, it becomes a self-determining people. And the proof is that it has its own state.

NEW STATES THROUGH SECESSION—IN GENERAL Another way new states form is through secession: the creation of a new state out of part of an existing one. This can be done with the agreement of the existing state—in which case it looks very much like voluntary division—or without its agreement in a unilateral secession. Unilateral secession forms the central concern of this book, because while not strictly illegal, it is heavily disfavored in ways that effectively guarantee the territory of existing states against internal challenges.[34]

In practice, the distinction between secession and other ways of forming new states is often blurry. Some unilateral secessions have been cosmetically papered over as voluntary divisions. Eritrea withdrew from Ethiopia by consent, but only after Eritrean rebels and their allies conquered the state and created a legal pathway for consensual departure. Similarly, South Sudan fought for decades before Sudan agreed to a referendum. To pretend that these were not effectively unilateral secessions seems unhelpfully formalistic: Voluntary division is not always so voluntary.

And as we saw, dissolution may be driven by secessions—even defined by them. How would we have known Yugoslavia dissolved except that Slovenia and Croatia withdrew? As a matter of plain language and sense, it's clear they seceded, though most international lawyers resist the characterization, as would many Slovenes and Croats, because secession is such a suspect category.[35] Even decolonization is a special form of secession: An asymmetrically governed territory withdraws from a globalized state, with or without its consent. Yet so complete has the current system's eclipse of the preclassical logic been that while we think of decolonization as self-determination, we rarely think of it as secession.

Thus, in recent decades, especially since the end of the Cold War, various groups have attempted to expand 'peoples endowed with self-determination' to groups within states—to return to a more Wilsonian vision of self-determination.[36] These claims run directly up against the restrictive definition of classical self-determination, which does not imagine giving the whole right to groups other than the whole population. These claims also face a radically unfavorable context: Whereas colonial self-determination forced distant overlords to withdraw from overseas empires, today, claims would require states to accept the division of their own territory. Whether seen as a problem of how to define a people or as a problem of what content to give the right, efforts to form new states have been singularly unsuccessful: There are very few examples of recognized secessions.

REMEDIAL SECESSION For groups other than a state's population, the classical consensus gives no "primary right" to external self-determination.[37] There may be a narrow exception, however, which depends not on the group's identity, but

Trains of Abuses: The American Remedial Revolution

The American War of Independence was an early instance of remedial secession. Although the Declaration of Independence invokes the consent of the governed, it also counsels caution: "Prudence, indeed, will dictate that Governments
long established should not be changed for light and transient causes; . . . man-
kind are more disposed to suffer, while evils are sufferable, than to right themselves by abolishing the forms to which they are accustomed." The impetus is
therefore framed as exigent necessity: the right is invoked to abolish a government "destructive" of life, liberty, and the pursuit of happiness, and only after "a
long train of abuses and usurpations . . . evince[d] a design to reduce them under
absolute Despotism" do they assert a right (even a duty) to rebel.

Given this heritage, the relationship between oppression and a right to withdraw was recognized even by opponents of secession in the antebellum United
States: "[T]he right of seceding from intolerable oppression . . . is another name
only for revolution, about which there is no theoretic controversy."* Some eighty
years later, the seceding southern states directly modeled their declarations on the
original Declaration.

*"James Madison to Daniel Webster, March 15, 1833."

its treatment. Through remedial secession or "remedial self-determination[,]"[38]
groups subjected to extreme persecution might claim the right to form a state as
an act of self-protection.

Under the theory, a group that otherwise has no right to secede might do so
if the state fails to observe even the minimum duty of tolerance and noninterference necessary for the group's continued existence.[39] Remedial secession shares
many features with a much older principle: the right of revolution. It differs in
the oppressed community's strategic choice to withdraw from the state rather
than replace the government.

One basis for remedial secession is the Saving Clause of the Friendly Relations Declaration. As we saw, Resolution 2625 appears to qualify the guarantee
of territorial integrity by restricting it to states "possessed of a government representing the whole people belonging to the territory without distinction as to
race, creed or colour."[40] This suggests that populations that *are* excluded might
be able challenge the state's territorial integrity, since whatever the state is doing
somehow doesn't comply with self-determination. (In turn, it might authorize

other states to intervene on the excluded population's behalf, in the same way states might support colonial liberation movements.)

Thus, the Saving Clause arguably allows remedial secession when the state fails to provide equal rights and political participation to racial, ethnic, and religious minorities. Such discrimination could defeat the normal presumption of territorial integrity, since "[t]he guarantee of integrity is contingent upon the existence of representative government."[41]

This view has been reinforced in subsequent analyses, such as the Canadian Supreme Court's opinion in *Reference re Secession of Quebec,* which elaborated the conditions under which a community might make a claim. As the court explained, remedial secession is not limited to denials of democratic participation, as the Saving Clause might suggest; it has been invoked as a response to various harms, and the list typically includes genocide, ethnic cleansing, and extreme persecution. The court suggested that a people might have resort to secession as a last, remedial option to protect themselves against oppression. Quite sensibly, it rejected this possibility for the Quebecois, who are not the least bit oppressed, but under the court's reasoning, a great many groups around the world would qualify.

This view has recently been advanced by states supporting Kosovo's independence, who argued that Kosovo's Albanians had a right to withdraw from Serbia because of extreme violence and human rights violations.[42] Finland, for example, argued for accepting remedial secession in a range of circumstances, including "abnormality, or rupture, or revolution, war, alien subjugation or the absence of a meaningful prospect for a functioning internal self-determination regime[.]"[43]

The oppressed group's identity might matter: Most remedial secession theories expect persecution will be directed at some group with identifiable characteristics—an echo of the Wilsonian assumption that groups ought to have some objective identity. The Saving Clause refers to "race, creed or colour," so perhaps remedial secession is only available to communities that exhibit some difference from the main population (presumably the basis for their persecution). But this could create an anomalous situation in which identically gruesome levels of persecution would give one group the right to secede, but not another, based solely on their ethnic qualities. It seems perverse to insist that people suffering grave human rights violations also share ethnic characteristics to deserve relief.

For its advocates, remedial secession represents either a continuity with long-standing norms[44] or a repurposing of self-determination after decolonization to regulate the internal qualities of the state; either way, it continues the emancipatory spirit underlying both Wilsonian self-determination and decolonization. In his separate opinion in the *Kosovo* case, Judge Cançado Trindade noted:

> The principle of self-determination has survived decolonization, only to face nowadays new and violent manifestations of systematic oppression of peoples. . . . [P]eople cannot be targeted for atrocities, cannot live under systematic oppression. The principle of self-determination applies in new situations of systematic oppression, subjugation and tyranny.[45]

Many states strongly resisted this claim, however, including China, Spain, Slovakia, Cyprus, and Iran.[46] Romania disputed that such a right, even if it existed, would apply to Kosovo,[47] suggesting a very high threshold for its application, given the level of violence and repression that occurred there. Even the foundations of the right in the Savings Clause have been questioned.[48]

The ICJ itself took no view, but noted:

> Whether . . . self-determination confers upon part of the population of an existing State a right to separate from that State is, however, a subject on which radically different views were expressed. . . . Similar differences existed regarding whether international law provides for a right of "remedial secession" and, if so, in what circumstances. There was also a sharp difference of views as to whether the circumstances which some participants maintained would give rise to a right of "remedial secession" were actually present in Kosovo.[49]

Such a sharp divergence argues against easily assuming the existence of such a right.

Remedial secession's status is far from clear. On the one hand, "[t]his idea is today supported by a vast number of writers."[50] But states are far less sanguine about it; after all, they are the ones who will do the remedying, or not. As for practice, there is only one widely recognized case of secession grounded on a remedial claim. That is Kosovo, and it remains highly contested, its implications even more so. Even states arguing on behalf of Kosovo's independence claimed that the province's circumstances were sui generis—a logically untenable position, but a telling one.[51] The idea of remedial secession is also supported by the opinion in *Quebec Reference,* but that is an abstract, hypothetical exercise by a single country's court and can hardly be expected to bear the weight of such a doctrinal shift.

The most one might say for the doctrine is that it is in flux, and there is weak evidence for such a radical expansion of the law. And, as we will see, remedial secession is not so radical after all: Even those in favor effectively accept the default of territorial integrity with the narrowest exception for situations of great suffering and abuse. Remedial secession, though of practical potential for mitigating particular harms, does little more: It merely gives the semblance of restoring a robust external right to self-determination's moribund doctrine. It is a remedy that proves the rule—that territories define peoples—and yet another symptom of self-determination's doctrinal decadence.

LIMITED SCOPE FOR CREATING NEW STATES All of these categories, taken together, describe a very narrow field. The possibilities for creating new states— by unilateral secession, remedial secession, dissolution, voluntary division, or otherwise—are quite limited. With the possible exception of the remedial category, secession is considered a political matter, neither required nor forbidden, subject to minimal regulation; yet the strong priority given to territorial integrity in the international system means that unilateral secession—the *involuntary* division of a state—is effectively barred and almost never recognized by other states.

On the rare occasions when it has been—Bangladesh, Kosovo—that new state's population becomes a self-determining people. But it is difficult to say that Bangladeshis or Kosovars enjoyed the right to self-determination *before* they seceded; they were not exercising a previously recognized right, as a colonial people might in fighting for independence, but created it through effective action, by seceding and being recognized. So if we are concerned with the content of self-determination, we are forced back in a circle, to ask what kind of people this is; and to answer that, we have to know what kind of territory they live in. Before independence, Bangladesh was part of Pakistan, and Kosovo part of Serbia, the humans living there each part of a single, larger self-determining people. After independence, each became a new state, so the humans living there formed a new people. But classical self-determination provides no insight into this change, and no justification for it until after it happens.

Outside these limited pathways, self-determination offers the overwhelming majority of the earth's people only the right to live in the state they already do. Outside the colonial context, the moments in which new states are formed are rare indeed. And this really does appear to be a kind of ideological commitment, not cynical self-interest: In a world governed by political interests, one might expect that things occasionally would align in favor of breaking existing states, but this almost never happens. That rarity should signal something curious: In the sphere of international relations—in a world of hard-nosed realism—we find an actual ethical, ideal principle in operation, and a very restrictive one.

Internal Self-Determination

If external self-determination has been moribund, its counterpart—internal self-determination—has been a source of ferment and innovation. But this internal turn has radically deconstructed and undermined the capacity of self-determination to do the very thing it used to do: generate peaceful change in the shape and number of units. The multiplication of peoples has been accompanied by—has occurred precisely through—a balloonlike expansion of self-determination, a thinning out of its core definition; the turn to internal governance has been the principle path by which self-determination has lost its vitality as a generative principle. The florescence of internal self-determination, though welcome in its own right, reveals the empty space at its heart: an almost palpably desperate effort to avoid the very thing it originally and logically promised, which was the right for people not just to govern themselves a certain way, but to do so in places of their own.

A DEMOCRATIC RIGHT The most significant development in the classical model has been the reconceptualization of self-determination as democratization. The link to internal governance was always present, even in the Wilsonian era, however little it shaped actual practice. Later opposition to racist regimes implied an internal component: After all, South Africa was already independent, so only its internal governance could violate self-determination. After 1970, the Saving Clause appeared to condition territorial integrity on respect for the right of the whole population to take part in governance. So the idea that self-determination should not only create external independence but also shape the internal qualities of the state was always available; it was a short leap from this to discovering a right to democracy.

Still, although the democratic aspects of self-determination may seem intuitive, so powerful was the territorial imperative of the classical model that democracy was hardly needed: Independence made colonies self-governing—a clear improvement, whatever was happening inside. The politics of the Cold War suppressed the doctrine's democratic logic as well: The contesting blocs did not agree on democratic principles beyond the most vacuous abstractions.

It was only with the end of the Cold War that this intuition about self-determination resurfaced. In 1992, Thomas Franck published an influential article entitled "The Emerging Right to Democratic Governance"—a title suggesting even its author was unprepared to say the right already existed. That came soon enough, however, and now it is commonplace to suppose that people everywhere have a right to participate in their government, and that this entitlement is historically rooted in self-determination.

Democratic self-governance implies the participation of each member of society as citizens, not merely subjects. It is not clear this newly asserted right actually specifies that much—if it does, then many countries are in violation of it—but one element seems clear: Whatever form governance takes in a state, the population must share equally in it.

Consistent with classical self-determination, democratic governance applies to the *entire* population. Subgroups as such only have a right to be meaningfully included in the state's governance like other members of the population. As we saw, remedial secession presupposes minorities enjoy the right of self-determination as part of the entire people 'without distinction,' and it is only when this is denied that they might make a new state as a desperate last resort. The default is integration.

Here we see the vitiating effects of self-determination's deconstruction across a half century: Today, the most ambitious avenue for external self-determination is subordinated to a highly integrative, internal vision, which assumes the preferred, progressive path is for communities to find their way within the confines of existing states. The idea that a group might better flourish in its own state, or simply desire the benefits of statehood—the original idea of self-determination—is nowhere to be found.

AUTONOMY AND MINORITY RIGHTS Participating in society on the basis of perfect equality without distinctions is only part of the matter. The postwar system was premised on universal rights but also included a limited continuation of the minority rights framework. The history of minority rights is marked by the endemic tension between equality and differential treatment, responding to distinctions of "race, creed or colour" by offering minorities both inclusion and internal self-governance or special rights.[52] Thus, the ICCPR provides that "persons belonging to [ethnic, religious, or linguistic] minorities shall not be denied the right, in community with other members of their group, to enjoy their own culture, to profess and practice their own religion, or to use their own language."[53]

As this cautious formulation suggests, the forms minority rights take are as diverse as the states and societies that create them. Protection may be given to the group, to its members, or to individuals through facially neutral laws that protect practices. Groups may have territorial autonomy (as in Iraqi Kurdistan, Alto Adige, or Aceh) or cultural autonomy (as in Israel or India, where religious groups govern members' personal status in matters like marriage). States can devolve decision-making to federal units in which a group's members can dominate politics. Ethiopia's federalization was explicitly designed to accommodate its diverse ethnic groups. By contrast, the American constitution doesn't allow ethnic states (except for Indian nations), but its federal structure allows Mormons to dominate politics in Utah. Some groups may be expressly identified, or there may be a process by which a group can seek status; in Hungary, thirteen groups are specifically named in minority rights legislation, and there is a formula by which others can claim eligibility. Finland uses a population formula to decide if Finnish, Swedish, or both will be used in a given district, but ensures bilingualism in the capital. Some autonomies are governed by international treaties, like the interwar minorities treaties; for Muslims in Thrace, personal status law is still governed under regimes deriving from the Treaty of Lausanne. Many autonomies are largely fictive: Autonomies within China proper do not translate into real local self-governance, though in this respect Tibetans and Uighurs are not necessarily worse off than their fellow citizens, apart from living in a country organized around someone else's language and habits.

Indeed, for all the diversity, in international law no group has an absolute right to autonomy or any particular form of it. As with remedial secession, claims to special treatment can be defeated by constructing a state with formal equality. As a result, in some states minorities have special rights, autonomy, or asymmetrical power in a federal system; in others, minorities with similar qualities have no special rights, only the right to be included in governance of the state they happen to be part of.

THE MAP OF OUR WORLD

Internal Colonization and the Clock

Uighurs constituted "the vast majority" of the Xinjiang region's population in 1949, when the Chinese government established control; they are now 46 percent, and Han Chinese are 40 percent.* Similar shifts have occurred in the Tibet Autonomous Region. Some migration is a matter of individual choice, but much is facilitated by the government; policies of military settlement date from the imperial era. Nor is migration only a process of importing members of the dominant group: China has relocated two million Tibetans since 2006.† Eventually, Han Chinese will constitute a majority in those regions. If Uighurs and Tibetans ever hope to have their own state—unlikely as that is—they'll have to hurry.

*Buckley, "27 Die in Rioting in Western China."
†"They Say We Should Be Grateful," Human Rights Watch.

The deepening of self-determination has actually been quite shallow. It has largely been limited to restricting wholesale exclusion—and that is something, considering the alternatives that have been tried. But while internal self-determination *allows* more generous approaches, it does not *require* them; that would be inconsistent with the integrative logic of the classical model. Minorities can use self-determination to argue—politically—for special arrangements that acknowledge their different identity. But not more, and certainly not to claim the rights a people has. Because a minority by definition isn't a people, since it doesn't already have a state of its own:

> The right of self-determination in the Covenants is universal. . . . [but] [s]ections of the people—minorities—enjoy more limited rights than the people itself. . . . The essence [of self-determination] is political control. . . . The rights of minorities are enumerated and finite, and do not include political control.[54]

INDIGENEITY A final major development is the growth of indigenous rights. Indigenous communities have been recognized as peoples with a right of self-determination—one of the definitional expansions of the term "people." But the rights this kind of people gets are quite different.

Indigenous people have rights to control their traditional lands and resources and protect their traditional culture. But expansive as the list is, it is expressly qualified: The same declaration confirming the self-determining status of indigenous peoples also notes:

> Nothing in this Declaration may be interpreted as implying for any State, people, group, or person any right to engage in any activity or to perform any act contrary to the Charter of the United Nations or construed as authorizing or encouraging any action which would dismember or impair, totally or in part, the territorial integrity or political unity of sovereign and independent States.[55]

That language may look familiar, since it tracks closely with the Saving Clause—except the critical part about the state's territorial integrity being conditional on good behavior is awkwardly missing. All indigenous rights must be exercised within the confines of the existing state and cannot in any way affect its territorial integrity. Indigenous self-determination is a purely internal exercise. (If indigenous people happen to form the majority in a state, as they do in Bolivia, they could in effect act like a full self-determining people. But no indigenous community has a right to external self-determination *as such.*) Being indigenous does give one certain rights, but not the one right that, in the colonial context or the preclassical era, was essential to the very idea of self-determination: the right to form a state.

The way indigenous rights have developed—identifying a new category of people but defining that people's rights restrictively—illustrates better than any other change the deconstructive tendencies to which the classical doctrine has been subjected. More groups are now peoples with the right of self-determination, but that right no longer means the same thing for every people. Self-determination comes in more and more forms, less and less for the purpose it originally promised.

The Varieties of Self-Determination

We have now seen the kinds of peoples who have some right of self-determination and the varied forms that right takes. If we combine them, we can see the shape of the classical model in its current articulation.

Two things are apparent: Rights are a function of the territory people live in—not any quality those people possess; and self-determination no longer does much useful work.

First, the classical rule has no independent rationale for its categories. Much

Who Gets What Rights to Self-Determination?

	Independent state (external)	Remedial secession* (external)	Democratic participation (internal)	Autonomy (internal)
Whole population of an existing territory				
State	Yes	—	Yes	—
Non-self-governing (colony)	Yes	Yes	Yes	—†
Under alien rule or occupation	Yes‡	Yes	Yes	—
Subsets of an existing territory's population				
Indigenous people	No	No**	Yes	Yes
National/ethnic minority	No	No**	Yes	No
Population not limited to an existing territory				
Cross-border ethnic group	No	No	No††	No

*Assuming this right exists at all, which is controversial.

†A colony cannot be integrated against its will into the metropolitan state, so in this sense it has a right to autonomy, but the metropole could simply force independence on a colony.

‡But if only a part is occupied, its right of self-determination is realized by rejoining the rest of its state.

**If the group were seriously oppressed—but it would not have the right as an indigenous people or minority as such.

††Members of these groups have this right as part of the whole population of their current states.

of the rule's seeming diversity collapses into two categories: groups that are the whole population of a territory, and groups that are a subset of a territory's population. These get very different rights, but the differences between these two types are a *function* of territory. Under the classical system's logic, whether the two million people in Kosovo are a minority or a people is entirely a function of whether or not there is an international frontier between Kosovo and Serbia. Yet since the very question self-determination supposedly answers has to do with forming units, using existing units to decide who self-determines simply reverses the equation, emptying the inquiry of all meaning. Classical self-determination is supposedly a right of peoples, but really, it is a right of territory.

Second, as a consequence, the doctrine lacks generative capacity. The only people with an *absolute* right to their own state are those who already have states (or are still living in colonies). The right to form a new state—the heart of the preclassical project—is largely a spent force. Internal self-determination must be doing all the work, for otherwise precious little is being done.

The circularity and tautology of the classical rule's distinctions is evident. It does not matter if we start with the definition of a people or with the content of the right—either way, we arrive back where we began, with a right given to a rightholder whose identity is based on the rights he is given, and who has the rights he has because he has them. But circular or not, these distinctions constitute the accepted lines of self-determination today, which reflexively considers certain human beings the holders of the right to form states, others not, based entirely on the incident of the very borders that, in theory, should be determined by the humans they contain.

Self-determination is a universal right with far from universal content; the very effort to expand the definition to peoples beyond the colonial context has destroyed its universality, and with it, self-determination's original purpose and promise. In the past, the right had a narrow (if numerous) class of addressees to whom it promised very clear benefits. Indeed, as critics like Lansing understood, the disruptive potential of self-determination was precisely that it gave a single type of people a very expansive right. Now there are many self-determinations, almost none of which do what the original idea promised. It has been deconstructed into congeries of different and quite limited rights, held by communities distinguished only by their territorial distribution, not any independent quality.

Any effort to understand internal and external self-determination separately from classification by territory is a hopeless and hopelessly confused endeavor. There is no governing principle: In the classical model—in our world—peoples are what their territories make them. The current model does—can do—no generative or transformative work with borders. Assuming one never wishes to change borders, this might be a virtue. But if, in a changing and fluid world, one ever wanted, even needed, to change borders, the current model looks less useful. And very different from the original, preclassical one, which imagined human communities constituting themselves and seeking meaning for their shared existence based on something other than where borders already happen to be.

The Broader Framework of the Classical System:
Reinforcing Territorial Integrity

So far we have considered states' continuity and change as a matter of self-determination, but that doctrine is embedded in a broader framework that shapes how we make and maintain states. These other elements of the postwar order protect states against threats to their territorial integrity; after all, the right to a state would mean little if it could be conquered by outsiders. The entrenchment of classical self-determination occurred in parallel with a series of shifts in the structures regulating the territory of states, their sovereignty, and use of force, which have limited the scope for states to predate on each other. Classical self-determination is also part of the modern human rights movement, which itself, in surprising ways, reinforces the territorial orientation of the system.

Formally, these other norms are distinct from self-determination—and territorial integrity in particular is often thought, mistakenly, to be in contradiction with self-determination. In practice, they are closely bound together, complementing and reinforcing self-determination's strong territorial conservatism. Together, they complete the contours of the classical system.

Territorial Integrity and Sovereignty

Sovereignty is notoriously difficult to define, and it is not clear the word is actually useful.[56] But whatever it is, "[t]erritorial sovereignty is best understood as a set of *jurisdictional* powers over territory, conferred upon the state."[57] The legitimate power to control borders, the territory within those borders and what humans do within them, captures most of what we mean by sovereignty.

Countless pronouncements reaffirm nearly absolute guarantees for states' territorial integrity and sovereignty. They appear in almost all the major enactments of the postwar world—the UN Charter, the Helsinki Final Act, the human rights covenants—and in documents on every conceivable issue. Reference to these two principles is a rhetorical reflex in international law and diplomacy.

These guarantees are valid whether or not a state behaves well. Even if a state violates its international obligations, including human rights, its territorial integrity is generally protected. If a state is placed under some form of international supervision that limits its sovereignty, the state's territory may be violated temporarily, but almost never is its territory permanently altered. Indeed, while territorial integrity is often violated—by military operations, as when the

Security Council authorized intervention in Libya—it is extremely rare to find a state's territorial integrity *permanently* disabled.

Although the Savings Clause arguably creates a narrow exception by justifying remedial secession in case of serious rights violations, there are no clear cases in which a state's territory has been divided on these grounds—only Kosovo, but that is controversial and creates a data set of one. If remedial secession exists, it operates at an extremely high threshold, when communities are subject to massive persecution and ethnic cleansing; it doesn't cover political marginalization, let alone the bare undesirability of being a minority in someone else's country.

International law also reinforces territorial stability through its rules on treaties. New states are not necessarily bound by all treaties ratified by their parent states.[58] However, a more conservative principle prevails for boundary treaties.[59] When colonies become independent, they inherit their international frontiers as well as the internal boundaries between different colonies belonging to the same metropolitan state (following the principle of *uti possidetis*). For example, Senegal maintained its borders with The Gambia and Portuguese Guinea, which had been international frontiers, but also the colonial demarcations with Mauretania, Mali, and Guinea, which had also been French colonies. Likewise, when a new state forms out of the territory of an existing state (and therefore necessarily creates at least one new international frontier), its other external frontiers remain. When Slovenia withdrew from Yugoslavia, it formed a new frontier along the old, internal boundary with Croatia, but inherited Yugoslavia's borders with Italy, Austria, and Hungary without change.

It is commonly supposed that territorial integrity and self-determination are in tension with each other; but given how conservative classical self-determination is, in fact they are almost entirely complementary and mutually reinforcing.[60] Self-determination legitimated independence for colonies, but by identifying the *continuing* right of self-determination with the whole population of existing states, it protects states almost exactly as territorial integrity does. In theory, self-determination can disrupt states—and the preclassical model really did— but in practice, classical self-determination only disrupts colonial empires; it reinforces the legitimacy, borders, and territorial integrity of existing states.

Even internal self-determination reinforces this complementarity. Internal self-determination takes the state as a given, a necessary unit, and focuses on the quality of its internal governance, not its shape. The most expansive form of internal self-determination, indigenous rights, explicitly reaffirms states' territorial integrity. The supposed tension between self-determination and territorial integrity is a tension of ideal types, and for self-determination, that ideal is inaccurately characterized, as if it were still doing things it has not done since Versailles.

Prohibitions of Aggression, Use of Force, and Conquest

Closely related to the guarantee of territorial integrity—and the very idea that a state's existence might be guaranteed at all[61]—is the prohibition of aggressive war. States used to be free to go to war and conquer territory, but now the use of force against another state is prohibited in all but the narrowest circumstances, and territorial gains resulting from illegal use of force are not supposed to be recognized. Russia's annexation of Crimea has been widely repudiated, and Russia subjected to sanctions; this has not prevented Russia from consolidating its hold, but the legal norm is clear.

So we have prohibited war for all but a few purposes. Anyone reading the news may notice the prohibition is leaky, and a great deal of blood seeps through the breach. Still, these restrictions have probably reduced resort to interstate war and helped ensure that states don't lose territory to the neighbors; we find few examples of annexation in the postwar world compared to preceding centuries. But these same postwar regulations say far less about *internal* conflicts, which have not declined in the same way. As we shall see in the next chapter, internal conflicts are of the greatest relevance to the problem of changing political communities and borders.

Human Rights

Finally, the classical model of self-determination has been articulated in the era of human rights. Self-determination is ritualistically declared to be the very core of human rights, but it is a very unusual right: one of the few that is collective in nature. The orientation of human rights is strongly individual in focus, with many theorists expressing skepticism about the utility or even coherence of group rights. Some human rights have collective aspects, such as the right to exercise one's religion or to vote, or require a plurality of beneficiaries to be meaningful, such as freedom of association; others, such as minority rights, can be conceptualized as group or individual rights. But there is general agreement that self-determination really is different: It is applied by the collectivity as such.

This singular quality—perhaps we should say plural quality—is clear in the texts: Other rights typically refer to 'everyone,' as in 'everyone has the right to x.' But self-determination is a right of 'all peoples.'

This makes self-determination, despite its notional centrality to human rights, an outlier. But while the fit may be uncomfortable in theory, in practice the distance is narrower. Self-determination's internal focus on democratic participation is fully compatible with civil and political rights. Its reaffirmation that peoples freely dispose of their own resources is consistent with socioeconomic rights (although this frustrates advocates of more egalitarian distribution *among* states). Finally, as we will shortly see, the classical model relies on human and minority rights to ameliorate its own harshness and rigidity.

These broader features of the global system—nonaggression, human rights— have likely contributed to a safer and more stable world. (Likely, because the effects are hard to measure—a point we are about to see for territorial integrity.) Along with their positive qualities, though, the main features of the classical system exhibit a mutually reinforcing conservatism about borders. They not only stabilize global politics but also ensure the continuity of existing units and discourage new ones. Perhaps that is a worthy goal, or at least an acceptable price to pay for peace and stability. But what if it weren't necessary? If one could capture the benefit of these features, but leave open the possibility for human beings to choose the states in which they wish to live—well, that might be an inquiry worth making.

It is to that inquiry we now turn. Before doing so, we should sum up the classical model. It may be stated like this—a description even those who disagree with my thesis might plausibly agree with:

The Rule We Live Under: The Classical Commitment to Fixed Borders

- The international order is organized around territorial integrity. We live in states with fixed borders, and the legal and political system reinforces that.
  - This is expressed directly in formal, legal rules about self-determination, nonaggression, and territorial integrity, and indirectly in human rights norms.
  - This principle also closely reflects political practice.
  - Bordered, territorial states remain relevant.
  - The units in existence in 1945 are the default. States and colonies in

existence at that time are presumptively self-determining units. Other units can come into existence but require special justification.

- States have a nearly ironclad guarantee of their territorial integrity. Their borders are protected against unwanted alteration, from without or within, in almost all circumstances.
  - States may change their own borders voluntarily, through cession of territory, merger with another state, or consensual secession.
- Self-determination gives peoples the right to govern themselves. Peoples are defined as the populations of existing territories. This means that:
  - the populations of non-self-governing territories (colonies) can form independent states;
  - the populations of existing states continue to enjoy the right to self-determination, through their state's continued independence;
  - other groups as such—minorities, national or ethnic groups, regional populations—do not have any right to form a state.
- The only grounds for creating a new state *against* the will of the existing state are:
  - remedial secession (which is controversial) because of:
    - gross violations of minority's human rights; such as genocide, or
    - systematic exclusion on invidious grounds from participation in the whole state's self-governance;
  - total dissolution of the state—that is, the state ceases to exist—in which case the successor states will, if possible, be drawn from existing sub-units, rather than by drawing new borders.
- When a new state does form, law and politics strongly tend to analyze this as a voluntary act or the product of dissolution, rather than unilateral secession or self-determination.
- Increasingly, self-determination focuses on the internal governance of states. This includes a right to democratic participation for the population as a whole.
  - States must include their entire population in their governance, without distinctions of race, religion, or ethnicity.
  - Subgroups enjoy self-determination as part of the whole population.
  - Internal self-determination may also be expressed through autonomy or minority rights.

- But states are not *required* to give minorities or other subgroups any particular rights as part of internal self-determination.
- Indigenous populations are peoples with a right to self-determination, including extensive autonomy, but not independence.
- Practice varies widely.

This is the general shape of the present rule in context—the classical system in full. Its main lesson is clear: Making new states is difficult. A successful claim to secede is highly implausible; and where that claim does not involve an existing territorial subunit, like a province, it is nearly impossible. There is simply too much weight of opinion and practice against the proposition that anything other than the whole population of a territory is a people with the right to form a state. In effect, those peoples who have states are the ones who are supposed to have states. Classical self-determination—the system we live with today—offers almost no hope to people who don't already have a state.

In fact, when it comes to forming states, the classical doctrine does almost no work at all. The UN Committee on Decolonization uses an interpretation of self-determination that follows the classical definition's limitations: External self-determination will be completed when these cases—Western Sahara, Gibraltar, and fifteen islands—become independent or integrate. After that, external self-determination will have only a latent function, applicable only in response to extreme repression, after the occasional state collapse, or when states voluntarily divide. Decolonization is nearly complete, and—despite the notorious tendency of bureaucracies to perpetuate themselves—there is no evidence of a new push to discover new states-in-waiting. It doesn't make for a very exciting annual meeting.

This moribund quality is part of why scholars and practitioners have refashioned self-determination to improve *internal* governance, with some success. But as we will see in the next chapter, that success has been limited, because the internal doctrine is self-limiting: not without value, but unable to effect the kind of change many of its supposed beneficiaries desire, especially in the hardest cases. The reason is simple: In focusing entirely on internal structures, self-determination has abandoned the purpose for which it was conceived. It is now oriented entirely toward humanizing existing states, and therefore never asks—even when the question is obvious and urgent—if the existing state is the problem.

For all the ferment in self-determination, the broad lines have been remarkably stable: Independence is available only to non-self-governing territories separated from the parent state, and all other expressions of self-determination are internal. Those who do not govern themselves must be freed from the dominion of others—and once that has been done, no further 'others' are to be discerned within that new whole, even if their new rulers are even more brutal, exclusionary, and cruel than their former masters. Innovation in the external right—through remedial secession—has been extremely limited. The principle *appears* to have expanded but has only been diluted and deconstructed.

Whatever the relationship of self-determination as doctrine to the real world, there have been few instances of new states being formed by secession, and almost none by groups not already living in an identified territorial unit, like Kosovo or Bangladesh. Our global system offers little hope for groups who wish to form new states. It is a separate question whether that is a good or bad thing, and that is what we must now turn to. What effects does this rule actually have? What assumptions underlie the rule: What do we believe it does? How would we even find out?

3

The Measure of Nations: Testing the Assumptions behind the Classical Rule

What do we think the prevailing model actually does? How do we know?

He had hit upon the paradox of excessive order, the perfection of which inevitably brought inaction in its train. . . . For some indefinable reason, order seems to bring on bloodshed!

Robert Musil[1]

THE CURRENT, CLASSICAL RULE of self-determination is historically bounded: Its borders are history's borders; it favors the outcomes of historical processes over current realities. The classical rule effectively draws a line under claims from before 1945: If you were a colony then, you could become a state; if you were already a state, you could remain one; but if you were neither—perhaps you just had a region in someone else's state, like the Ibo or Tibetans had—you were out of luck in the self-determining lottery. In 1945, that rule *felt* revolutionary, because it justified independence for colonized peoples. But it was a revolution whose course was predetermined, and since the end of decolonization it has operated to bar new claims, reinforcing historically received borders. Under the classical rule, whenever a conflict arises within a state, we are compelled to look for solutions that work within the fixed borders we already have. Unsurprisingly, those are the only solutions we find.

This constraint is thought to be a virtue. The explicit purpose of the system put in place at the end of the Second World War—territorial integrity, self-determination, human rights, and prohibition of aggression—was to stabilize global politics and reduce the resort to war.[2] Rigid borders were an intentional part of that project.

But *has* that been the result? Have fixed borders produced a more peaceful world? What if territorial integrity has not reduced violence but increased it— if, as Musil suggests, the quest for order actually causes bloodshed? And what if that order's positive effects are being purchased at a high price in other things we value: human rights, autonomy, self-governance, justice? To answer this question, we have to measure the effects of the classical rule, and as we will now see, that is very hard to do. How are territorial inviolability's effects to be measured? Even if we accept that borders have been unusually stable and violence has declined—which is far from clear—to what should we ascribe these effects? What is the proper way to test this central tenet of the global order?

Although it's hard to test the rule we have, there are indications of what it's doing, and we can think logically about the assumptions behind our rule. This chapter does that, and suggests borders are not doing what we think they are. But before we can get to that, we must consider an epistemological problem: How would we even know if the current rule is working or not?

Something We Can't Know: The Problem of Testing a Global Norm

Claims about the effects of our territorial rule are empirical claims, though they don't get far before tripping over their normative underpinnings. But even if we stick to the claim that territorial integrity stabilizes global politics and limits violence, problems arise. How can this be measured? Territorial integrity is a global rule, and global rules, by their nature, aren't readily amenable to empirical testing.

It's always challenging to design rigorous social science experiments— problems with incomplete data, selecting variables, and the like. But empirical analysis confronts special problems in international law and relations simply because the data is so thin.[3] What counts as a large-n study in international relations would be disturbingly small in the harder sciences, because the n of all states is very small: 193 UN members plus a few territories. Considerable random variation would be expected.[4]

And although some social sciences get by with small data sets, they use subjects that are similar so that discrete qualities can be held constant. By contrast, the subjects called states—Russia and San Marino, Indonesia and Paraguay, Norway and Somalia—are shockingly dissimilar, nothing like human subjects,[5] let alone white mice. Cross-state comparisons can be particularly fraught, because controlling for variation between cases can consume the entire enterprise, or should.

Empirical techniques are useful for understanding many aspects of the international system. But here we deal with something different: Territorial integrity is not the type of rule we can easily subject to a scientific experiment in which we control the environment and replicate results, because the rule encompasses the operations of the entire system. The rule is not a rare event about which we have little data; it is an all-pervasive factor, whose omnipresence makes it difficult to construct conditions in which it varies. It is an *in*variable: a global condition for which we lack an adequate control.

Certain *types* of global rule may be measurable. A discrete change in the global system at a specific time, leaving other elements in place, might allow a longitudinal analysis. But while territorial integrity fulfills part of this criterion—its origins can be traced to a discrete date—it doesn't allow meaningful comparison. That date—1945—was quite a year: the end of an unprecedentedly large conflict; the realignment of global politics in the crystallizing Cold War; the introduction of nuclear weapons into global security; the creation of the UN and the advent of the human rights era; the beginning of the colonial system's collapse; the start of a thirty-year period of economic growth. These many moving parts—some closely linked to new territorial norms, others not—make it difficult to design some longitudinal study with pre-1945 levels of violence as a baseline, territorial integrity as the treatment or independent variable, and post-1945 levels of violence as the dependent variable.

Similarly, we might imagine testable claims about a global norm gradually applied—the relationship between the spread of democracy and the likelihood of states going to war, or the behavior of states that sign human rights treaties.[6] But this too is different: However universal the norms of democracy or human rights may now be, precisely because their application has been gradual and partial, we can test their effects over time and in different places. By contrast, territorial integrity and self-determination have been norms at all times and places since their introduction; they have operated in peace and war, even in places where borders have changed, either shaping behavior or not.

All of this makes it difficult to say what the rule has done. We have experi-

enced the border changes we have, suffered the wars we've suffered, either despite this rule or because of it. Or something else: Despite seven decades of
rigorous and innovative social science research, the current rule turns out to be
entirely untested—unsurprisingly, since we have no second earth on which try
an alternative. If there is some way to measure a global rule of this kind, it
would be good to know what it is. And if not, what approximation might we use?
If we cannot test the rule itself, what aspects or incidents of the present rule,
what proxy for it, might we test?

The Little We Do Know: The Assumptions
We Make about the Current Rule

> *Fixity of national boundaries and of national allegiance, and political sta-
> bility would disappear if this principle was uniformly applied.... What
> effect will it have on the Irish, the Indians, the Egyptians, and the national-
> ists among the Boers? Will it not breed discontent, disorder and rebellion?
> Will not the Mohammedans of Syria and Palestine and possibly of Morocco
> and Tripoli rely on it?*
>   Robert Lansing[7]

Untestable does not mean inscrutable, and there are aspects of the current rule
we can describe, letting us indirectly evaluate what it actually does. If we consider why we have this rule—what we *think* it does—we find three assumptions:

- Territorial integrity promotes stability and limits violence.
- Territorial integrity encourages cooperation among diverse communities.
- Territorial integrity best reflects the liberal values of international society.

We can further specify these assumptions, with accompanying predictions:

- First, fixed borders are stabilizing, and therefore flexible borders would
  - lead to endless fracturing into small, unviable states; and
  - increase violence within and among states.
- Second, the present rule improves political discourse within states, and
  therefore
  - flexible borders would lower minorities' incentives for cooperation.

- Third, the present rule provides more support for liberal or cosmopolitan forms, and therefore
  - flexible borders would lead to the creation of illiberal and nationalist states.

We should add a fourth assumption, which has to do with the mechanics of the system:

- Whatever the shortcomings of the current rule, the turn to internal self-determination provides enough protection and flexibility to mitigate its harshness, and therefore
  - the present rule is not in need of significant reform.

This adequately summarizes the main assumptions about why we have a system of rigid borders—why we *should*. Each assumption is both empirical and normative: Each makes some objective claim about the world, but also suggests some value or preference. So let's examine each—not to provide definitive answers, since an empirical test is all but impossible and values are never testable—but to identify areas in which more rigorous examination might be profitable, or not.

Assumptions about Stability and Violence

FRACTURE

> [T]here is a very large number of potential nations on earth. Our planet also contains room for a certain number of independent or autonomous political units. On any reasonable calculation, the former number (of potential nations) is probably much, much larger than that of the possible viable states. If this argument or calculation is correct, not all nationalisms can be satisfied, at any rate not at the same time. The satisfaction of some spells the frustration of others. . . . [V]ery many of the potential nations of this world live, or until recently have lived, not in compact territorial units but intermixed with each other in complex patterns. It follows that a territorial political unit can only become ethnically homogeneous, in such cases, if it either kills, or expels, or assimilates all non-nationals.
>
> Ernest Gellner[8]

EMPEROR JOSEPH II: *". . . there are simply too many notes, that's all. Just cut a few and it will be perfect."*
MOZART: *"Which few did you have in mind, Majesty?"*
Amadeus[9]

It is commonly supposed that relaxing territorial integrity would lead to endless proliferation of ever-smaller states. A destabilizing competition would cause continuing divisions as each community carved out its own territory, only to be carved up by smaller groups seeking the same advantage, as populations are displaced in campaigns of ethnic cleansing.[10] This is the fear that animated Lansing's concern about Wilsonian self-determination.

Implicit in this assumption is a belief that without some rigid rule, this process might have no end, leading to literally thousands of states. One common basis for nation formation is language, and there are over seven thousand languages.[11] Half are spoken by tiny numbers of people, but that still leaves over three thousand sizable nations. Each might seek its own state, unleashing "a Frankenstein of unrestrained proliferation and fragmentation."[12] The current rule guards against this by giving each state a veto on territorial changes and enforcing a default regime of rigid frontiers. Occasionally a state might voluntarily divide, as Czechoslovakia did, or totally break down, as happened to Yugoslavia, but these are occasional, manageable events. Fixed borders reduce the risk of uncontrolled fracture.

But how great is that risk? There are many incentives for communities to voluntarily surrender their autonomy and integrate. These incentives—seen in things like currency and customs unions, or the European Union with its goal of "ever closer union"—don't disappear just because secession is an option. (The United Kingdom chose to exit the EU, but others want to join.) There are many dangers in this world—reasons to be afraid and to seek the protection of the group—which is why states join military alliances. Those dangers wouldn't disappear just because territorial change is an option.[13]

It is not clear how many communities would abandon the benefits of mutual protection and economies of scale for the brass ring of sovereignty. Many wouldn't, and on this we actually have empirical evidence. There are still non-self-governing territories—almost all small, almost all islands—that have chosen to remain in that status rather than become fully independent, because their populations (or elites) perceive the benefits of not being states: subsidies, access to markets, security. What has proved true for colonial populations with an unimpeachable right to independence would also affect the thinking of other groups.

In some cases a flexible norm would lead to secession. The option of exit in the peace deal between Sudan and the Sudan People's Liberation Army yielded an almost unanimous vote for South Sudan's independence,[14] and Kosovars overwhelmingly favored separation from Serbia. But as Scotland shows, populations don't necessarily exit even when they can. When states acknowledge the possibility, they can actually mitigate secessionist sentiment: Separatist sentiment in Quebec declined considerably after Canada's Supreme Court issued the *Quebec Reference*. The causal relationship is difficult to discern, but Canada's cooperative attitude probably helped deflate support for secession.[15]

A more flexible rule would probably lead to more fracturing. But this begs the question: What's wrong with that? Assuming it were peaceful, why is fracturing a problem? What is the right number of states? There is, in other words, a *normative* belief embedded within our supposedly empirical assumption about fracture's risks: Even if the likelihood of fracture were great, it is a separate question how we should feel about it. Perhaps more states *are* a problem—they certainly create a more complex network, which increase challenges of coordination. But that sits uncomfortably with the four-fold increase in states since the war. We typically think decolonization was a great thing, so which ones should have remained colonies? It's an awkward question, and the only answer that avoids awkwardness requires a Panglossian belief that we have just the right number of states today—that, by the most amazing chance, we created the right number of colonies, and then freed them.

There's another value judgment implicit here—though it runs opposite of the way one might expect. Fracturing is not some natural process governed by a law of physics; when it happens, it is the result of individual decisions by actors trying to preserve one state or make another. In each case, it only happens if some population (or elite) wants its own, smaller state. The risk of fracture simply means that given a chance, human beings would make more states, not fewer. In deciding this is a bad, even dangerous idea, we are constraining their preferences and choices. We are tying our fellow human beings to the mast on the 194 ships we have already built for sailing past the sirens and clashing rocks of this world. And God help the passengers for whom the ship itself is the danger.

NONVIABILITY

> *[W]hat can words like "independence" or "sovereignty" mean for a state of only six millions? . . . To-day it is only under quite peculiar presuppositions that such small state formations can have a possibility of life. . . . [H]ow should a state which was but the size of a single province succeed?*
> Adolf Hitler[16]

Some of those ships of state are less than seaworthy. If fracturing is less likely than we assume, that's partly because the world is a dangerous place, and more dangerous for the weak. Tiny islands choose to remain tied to their imperial mothers because they perceive the costs of going it alone—costs that can make independence not merely risky, not just not worth it, but practically impossible.

Here we confront one of the most common, if also ideologically fraught objections to secession: a bias toward assuming new states may not be viable, which if true would contribute to instability.[17] States must support a functioning economy and ensure their security, and smaller units may find this more difficult. Thus, fracturing is not only a problem for coordination among units, but for the new units themselves. Dysfunction may only increase in conditions of interdependence and globalization, with small units floundering in the brutal contest of coordination-competition among globally connected actors. In turn, this increases the pressures on the international system—and, as Herr Hitler reminds us, the opportunities for external powers to exploit vulnerable units: The Habsburg Empire could at least hold its own in the world; little Austria, about which Hitler was speaking, hardly could.

But it's not clear the risk is real, and here again we actually have evidence. Many small states exist today. Thanks to India and China, states' average population is about 36 million, but the median is about 7.6 million; there are thirty-eight states—one in five—with populations under 500,000; twelve below 100,000; and the very smallest under 1,000.[18] Likewise, states range in physical size from giants like Russia, Canada, the United States, and China, to tiny Andorra, San Marino, and Vatican City. These states actually exist, so it's hard to argue that any population or size is too small—certainly, current doctrine wouldn't dream of questioning the sovereignty or territorial integrity of *those* countries.

Many small states do quite well. Eight of the ten wealthiest countries (by GDP per capita) have populations below average, six under 1 million; "[c]learly size and prosperity do not go hand in hand."[19] Luxembourg, with fewer than 550,000 people and an area just over 2,500 square kilometers, has the highest GDP per capita in the Euro zone. Singapore has 5.5 million people, a territory of 719 square kilometers, and is one of the wealthiest states in the world.

They're hardly typical: Luxembourg is embedded in a prosperous economic and political union with many shared values, while Singapore is a trade entrepôt and banking center. But this simply shows that such cases are possible and indicates some conditions that make them so: economic specialization and embeddedness in broader economic, political, and security structures. And while there are small countries that are poor and unstable, there is no reason to think small countries are more likely to be so—no evidence that small countries are necessarily poorer or more unstable than large ones.[20]

The value of being embedded in larger structures suggests that another part of this assumption is wrong, too: In an interconnected, globalized world, it is *more* possible for small states to prosper.[21] With antiaggression norms protecting against external threats, small states should be safer than they were when Hitler was eyeing his neighbors. Cross-border incursions still occur, but rarely lead to annexation: One reason Russia's taking of Crimea was so striking is that such things are so rare. Globalization might make a mockery of pretensions to total independence but also provides a framework of interdependence in which small units can maintain the kind of qualified sovereignty that has always, in fact, constituted statehood. If anything, the conditions of the contemporary world make small states more, not less viable—the average state is much smaller today than it was one hundred years ago.

For secessionist territories, the argument is no different. Some territories that have broken away, like the Baltics, Slovenia, and Singapore, have done quite well. Some were already relatively wealthy, but this hardly makes the nonviability assumption more persuasive.[22] In fact, often the larger states from which these areas secede are already dysfunctional, which is part of why the region wishes to exit: not Slovenia but Yugoslavia, not Katanga but the Congo, not Somaliland but Somalia.

Incentives to integrate, which limit the likelihood of fracture, also mitigate its supposed harms. Smaller units are often embedded in larger economic and security blocs: The EU has seen a resurgence of secessionism in part because European integration makes secession less costly.[23] There is also a self-regulating effect: Populations are unlikely to attempt secession unless it is plausibly in their interest to do so. In Scotland, fear about the effects of independence on prosperity and security were a significant factor for many voters preferring to remain in the United Kingdom. If voters in a prosperous, well-governed community exhibit such concerns—Scotland risked only relative decline, not actual unviability—it is reasonable to expect voters in truly marginal places would be at least as cautious.

Finally, as with fracture, there is a normative belief hidden in claims about viability. Even if it could be shown that, all things being equal, small states tend to be less stable and prosperous, this would still not tell us what to do. It is possible, for example, that Kosovo's population is economically worse off than it would be in a union with Serbia—and secession certainly made them worse off in the short term—but I have never met a Kosovar Albanian who would prefer that deal.

In the real world, all things are never equal, and measurable increases in prosperity must be balanced against claims of justice and moral preferences. As an observer of the tumultuous interwar period—which produced both new states out of Mitteleuropa's empires and economic misery—noted:

> It was easy enough to condemn the peace settlement as the "balkanization of Europe" from arm chairs in London. It was all very well for the economists to demonstrate by industrial and banking statistics that the new grouping of the states was unworkable, and to a large extent they were right. But national sentiment takes little account of statistics. To the traveler who witnessed the ecstasy with which all the liberated peoples were reveling in their newly won freedom, it was obvious that the peace settlement was in its broad lines not only right but inevitable.[24]

There is no reason to believe larger units are inherently preferable—certainly no reason to pretend their own populations necessarily think so. By definition, in societies with secessionist movements, someone thinks the state is too big, not too small. In some cases small states actually turn out to be more stable and prosperous; that doesn't tell us what we should do, either, but it's worth noting.

Concern with viability is mutable and has sometimes mattered less. In self-determination's high classical moment, viability was expressly rejected as a reason for delaying independence for colonies: The General Assembly declared "the inadequacy of political, economic, social or educational preparedness should never serve as a pretext[.]"[25] Colonies were admitted to UN membership

Is Slovenia Viable?

Size looks different depending on who is measuring it. Prior to Yugoslavia's collapse, the European Community, as it was then called, sent an envoy to try to dampen the crisis. In Ljubljana, he cautioned Slovenia's authorities against independence, warning that their republic was too small to be viable. Today, Slovenia is a member of the European Union. But the ironic part concerns whom the European Community sent to deliver that message about smallness: Jacques Poos, foreign minister of Luxembourg.

whether or not they met the traditional standards for recognition, which required real control of population, territory, and a functioning government.

Concerns about viability are exaggerated. They are mostly a fiction predicated upon the all-too-human tendency to overvalue the way things happen to be, treating them as necessary or just.[26] Emphasizing viability is a pseudo-objective way of preserving existing states for their own sake and discounting the wishes of actual human communities. If we judge viability empirically, we should judge on the actual circumstances, not some prophylactic notion masking ideological preference for the status quo.

VIOLENCE

> *Unjust laws exist. . . . Men generally . . . think that they ought to wait until they have persuaded the majority to alter them. They think that, if they should resist, the remedy would be worse than the evil. But it is the fault of the government itself that the remedy is worse than the evil. It makes it worse.*
>
> Henry David Thoreau[27]

It is not merely the number of states or their viability that raises concerns; it is change. Change is destabilizing. The creation of new states is often accompanied by violence, as elites are replaced, scores settled, a new order imposed. The strongest argument against a flexible rule may be negative—avoiding greater harm: It may be we support territorial integrity because we assume the status quo is less violent than any possible alternative. We assume—we fear—that a more flexible rule would lead to great violence, although in truth we mean *greater* violence, because the present rule is very violent, too.

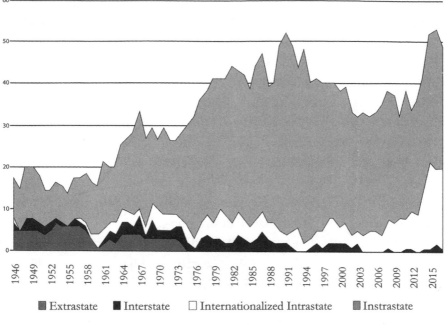

State-based armed conflict by type, 1946–2017
(drawn with data from Pettersson and Eck, "Organized Violence")

So has the present rule reduced instability and violence—not just from what came before, but more than any alternative might? Measuring the relationship of violence to territorial integrity is difficult, the evidence complex: While the number of *international* (interstate) conflicts has declined since 1945, the number of *internal* (intrastate, including internationalized intrastate) conflicts has increased—and at almost all points in the postwar era, there have been many more internal than international conflicts.[28]

Those internal conflicts are the very ones of greatest relevance to changing political communities. It might be that the classical rule has not reduced violence so much as redirected it from cross-border conflicts to internal ones. It is even possible—though just as hard to prove as the prevailing assumption—that the current rule has *increased* violence, by creating conditions for groups locked inside to engage in all-or-nothing struggles to control states from which there is no exit.

Still, if secession correlates with increased violence, why is this not an irrefutable objection? The answer lies in that correlation, and its likely, logical

causes: Violence is not caused by secession as such, but by *resistance* to secession. New states can form without violence: for example, the many peaceful
decolonizations, or the division of Czechoslovakia. States routinely negotiate
peaceful border corrections, just as the territorial plebiscites after the First World
War were peaceful, even though they were a consequence of the war. And in
those rare cases in which a state has allowed its people to consider seceding—
Scotland, Quebec—there has been no significant violence.

It is easy to misinterpret the violence that accompanies the breakup of states.
Observers point to the decade of war and one hundred thousand deaths that
accompanied the collapse of Yugoslavia, and conclude that secession is too
dangerous. But we can read those same facts differently: Resorting to war to
preserve Yugoslavia was what killed those people. Few would blame Bosnia's
Muslims and Croats for the slaughter that followed their withdrawal, rather than
Serb leaders in Belgrade and Bosnia who resisted. Likewise, one could conclude that the decades-long war in South Sudan, which led to millions of deaths,
proves the danger of secession; but it was Sudan's refusal to allow secession or
reform—and its capacity to resist, which the international order facilitated—that
caused those deaths. Similarly, Myanmar has been subjected to nearly continuous separatist conflict: Much of it can be traceable to the government's refusal to
honor the secession provisions of its own 1947 constitution and its campaigns of
centralization and suppression. *Violent resistance* to secession is the problem.

In many cases, the state has chosen to resist a movement that was, or could
have remained, peaceful. Sometimes secessionists are the first to use violence,
but that choice is also shaped by the normative framework. States have no obligation to tolerate secession, and they have considerable leeway to use coercion and violence.[29] Some states constitutionally prohibit or criminalize even
peaceful advocacy of secession, as China does. There are groups that resort to
violence without first trying other means; a group that loses an election and
then stages a coup cannot legitimately claim all other pathways were blocked.
But that is analytically and morally different from a group abandoning peaceful
means in frustration, or rationally recognizing that it would be pointless, even
dangerous, to try.

Kosovo is a powerful example: A Gandhian movement for autonomy and
independence was ignored and repressed by Serbia and eventually replaced
by a radicalized, violent (and successful) movement, after a decade of fruitless
attempts to effect peaceful change using nonviolent means. When the Kosovo

Liberation Army (KLA) began its attacks, Serbia reacted with ethnic cleansing. So in which ledger should we count that violence: with the dangers of secession, or the dangers of a system that permits states to use almost any means to defend their territory against the people living on it?

Yet the assumption that somehow secession itself is responsible for violence—that the correlation between territorial change and violence is the only analytically relevant fact—seems deeply entrenched in political and scholarly thinking.[30] Here is how one prominent human rights scholar poses the problem, in terms that practically assume the problem is not the state, but the people in it:

> States in the age of human rights have to reconcile human rights observance with containing a dissident or oppressed opposition or an ethnic minority seeking self-determination. These secessionist challenges, often backed up by terrorism, sometimes jeopardize the unity of the state.[31]

Missing from such arguments is the possibility that the state might be the terrorist, or that commitment to the state's unity—and very idea of a state's 'containing' its own people—might be the problem.

We think of secession as requiring justification, whereas the state does not. But territorial integrity is not self-enforcing: The continuity of state territory is often accompanied by and accomplished through great violence, even in the absence of separatism. Acknowledging a more plausible causal account might alter our normative evaluation about the violence that accompanies secession. For here too a normative question is embedded in our assumptions. In weighing up the relative costs of the current rule and of alternatives, we must weigh *all* the sources of violence to arrive at a moral accounting. In that equation—unless we give overwhelming weight to mere peace—we must also consider when it is justified to oppose a regime that purchases peace through repression. Force is sometimes justified to resist occupation or oppression—this is the logic of humanitarian intervention—and there is no reason why such logic shouldn't apply to a secessionist group, if its claim were *otherwise* justified but denied by the state. After all, the current system does not place an absolute priority on peace: Instead, it tells us that it is moral to use violence to preserve the state. That is not an empirical law, but a normative preference—a design choice with real consequences. Even if we don't prefer a particular secession, it does not follow that the state is justified to resist it with force.

No less a realist than E. H. Carr made clear, in his seminal work on international relations written just before the Second World War, that any society failing to provide avenues for peaceful change can expect the other kind:

> Every solution of the problem of political change, whether national or international, must be based on a compromise between morality and power. . . . But the defence of the *status quo* is not a policy which can be lastingly successful. It will end in war as surely as rigid conservatism will end in revolution.[32]

This truth—which for Carr was as much about morality as power, since politics consists of both—operates just as much in a world that has supposedly prohibited war across borders, if not within them, as in that more openly violent age.

If the present rule actually ensured stability and reduced violence, there might be little point in proposing an alternative. Yet the examples we have just seen and the broader evidence of the postwar period suggest that despite the near-total ban on nonconsensual change to territory, existing states do not feel sufficiently confident to relax about the minorities in their midst. The history of postcolonial nation-state building is one of tremendous human costs, and around the world regimes suppress minorities, fearing the claims they might make. So the present rule, despite handing so many cards to states, has not handed them enough to quiet their fears and ensure peace.

But this is not because there are other cards to give; it is because human beings persist in making claims even in the face of a stacked deck. States suppress groups that pursue secessionist or autonomist claims despite those groups' low chances of success. To blame those groups for the violence that ensues seems morally perverse and analytically unhelpful. Instead we ought to focus on the structures and incentives we have created and the effects they have: The current rule of territorial integrity has not in fact created a peaceful world—and whether it has produced a *more* peaceful world than any alternative could is precisely the question we need to answer.

Effects on Internal Politics: Lowered Incentives to Cooperate

The very existence of a right to secede, moreover, is likely to dampen efforts at coexistence in the undivided state . . . which might alleviate some of the grievances of putatively secessionist minorities. . . . Efforts to improve the condition of minorities ought to be directed at devising institutions to in-

crease their satisfaction in existing states, rather than encouraging them to think in terms of exit options.
Donald Horowitz[33]

Evils which are patiently endured when they seem inevitable, become intolerable when once the idea of escape from them is suggested.
Alexis de Tocqueville[34]

There are also assumptions about what might happen *inside* existing states if we relaxed the rules on territorial integrity. The current rule assumes that relaxing the locked-in quality of the modern state would lower the incentives of nonmajority communities to cooperate; this would lead to less effective negotiations over governance in diverse societies—"blackmail, strategic behavior, and exploitation"—and "reduce the prospects for compromise and deliberation in government."[35] Thus, minorities

> entitled to self-determination will lean towards rigidity and intransigence; convinced that the right to self-determination entitles them to absolute independence, they will be reticent to negotiate if sovereignty does not immediately appear in the offing. All too often, invoking a legal right renders the right holder less flexible and receptive to compromise.[36]

This is true—the tendency for "rights talk" to descend into rigidity is a general problem,[37] and there is no reason to think minorities wouldn't seek advantage—but it is equally true for majorities. To the same degree the current rule incentivizes minorities to cooperate, it *lowers* incentives for *majorities* to cooperate.[38] Under the current rule, majorities have an effectively absolute right to preserve the existing state; they don't need to give minorities almost anything. Locked borders and no exit mean that, even in a democratic society, the majority knows it need give only some minimum to avoid either the extremely high and controversial thresholds for remedial secession or the risk of radicalizing the minority. Basic game theory suggests that when one side controls the distribution of a good and the other side has no option to exit the game, outcomes will favor the dominant side.[39] So majorities will *also* "lean towards rigidity and intransigence . . . be reticent to negotiate . . . [and] less flexible and receptive to compromise." And, of course, they control the army, the courts, and the police.

The limited empirical evidence does not bear out this assumption about mi-

Madrid's Incentives: The Predictable Parameters of a Crisis

In Catalonia in 2015, a coalition won parliamentary elections on a promise to promote independence. When the new government set a date for a referendum, a collision was assured. Catalonia passed legislation nullifying Spanish law; Spanish courts and government invalidated those acts. In October 2017, Spanish police intervened to stop voting. Hundreds were injured; by European standards, the violence was shocking. The outcome was an overwhelming vote for independence on low turnout—an ambiguous result. When parliament voted for independence, Spain suspended Catalonia's autonomy. Catalan leaders were jailed; others fled the country. New elections returned the separatists to power.

Catalonia's crisis may seem volatile, but the real lesson is its *predictability*. Things needn't have come to this, but that they *could* should never have been in doubt. It is the logical consequence of the state's Weberian power. From Spain's perspective, Catalonia's moves were intolerable and illegal, though that just begs the question of why they were. Because those moves would be tolerable, and legal, if Spain allowed them. But Spain has no incentives to be tolerant. Catalonia's steps contravened the constitutional order and gave Spain opportunities to assert its authority. The international order, viewing secession as an internal matter, supports the exercise of police powers that favors the state.

Catalan separatists pushed a radical agenda. But the Spanish state is radical in its own way. There are consequences: If Spain had allowed a vote a decade ago, it would have won handily and perhaps put the issue to rest. Instead, Spain has firmly resisted any internal path, thereby increasing sentiment for independence. Which is a lesson about cause and effect: Rather than a right of exit radicalizing separatists, insisting that no exit is possible did that. Yet such intransigence is what the current rule enables.

nority intransigence, or at least suggests the dynamic is far more complex. In Quebec, an effective right to negotiate withdrawal indeed produced a dynamic in which Quebec sought, and Canada conceded, greater autonomy. Yet that and the availability of the right itself arguably helped moderate Quebecois separatist sentiment.[40]

And this is evidence from a state with a liberal, rights-respecting political system and a willingness to grant considerable autonomy to diverse communities. In many states, the central authorities and majority are dismissive of minorities' interests, and there is almost nothing in the structure of the global system that incentivizes them to act differently. Indeed, what the assumption about incentives hides from our gaze is that the current rule naturalizes a system of rigidity, in which a wide range of possible solutions to existing social tensions are taken off the table. There is no reason to believe that the relationship between majority and minority is made more moderate by locking the borders of the state. It is simply skewed to the advantage of the majority.

Insisting that borders cannot be changed by the minority, the majority, or anyone unless everyone agrees, reveals an atavistic commitment to the state. Locking in works—except where it doesn't. Unfortunately, "doesn't" covers a great many places for which our present doctrine has no answer; worse, though it springs from humane impulses, it proves harmful to other liberal values.

The Kinds of States Produced: Illiberalism

> . . . a covenant with death and an agreement with hell.
> William Lloyd Garrison[41]

That is ironic, because a third assumption concerns what sort of state would arise under a more flexible rule: Secession, it is thought, tends to produce illiberal polities, because only retrograde nationalists want to secede. Even sympathetic treatments tend to assume this.[42] Thus, rigid territorial rules act as a brake against illiberal tendencies by locking unreliable communities into larger, more liberal states.

Obviously this is a normative preference, but there is an empirical question here, too: *Are* secessions in fact illiberal? There is actually no evidence that secessionists are necessarily more or less liberal than the majorities or states they leave behind. Sometimes breakaway groups are more illiberal, like many Sudeten Germans in 1938, but recent noncolonial cases have often been seen as efforts by a more liberal community to escape a repressive state, as with the Baltic states from the Soviet Union, or Slovenia from Serbian-dominated Yugoslavia. And of course it is difficult to assign an empirical score to the 'before' and 'after' conditions of liberated colonies: Even though in many of them matters got far worse after independence, being a colony seems an example of illiberalism nonpareil.

The only valence secession necessarily has is toward smaller units—and a worldview in which integration and ever greater union are not automatic values—

but there is nothing necessarily liberal about larger (or preexisting) units. Of course, neither are secessions necessarily *more* liberal. But that is the point: Secession either produces more-liberal states or less-liberal ones, depending on circumstances; it has no tendency. So while we may prefer liberal states, relying on this preference to oppose secession is problematic: It rests on an unfounded assumption that many residents of the former Soviet Union, or Russia today, or China would find hard to swallow.

But another objection is that whether or not secessionist states are *worse* than the state they are leaving, they are nationalist-oriented and illiberal by definition. Here too we find the empirical and normative problematically mixed: One prominent legal scholar criticized Catalan separatism as a "frenzy for secession and independence[,]" associating it with the "mindset" of the "poisonous logic of national purity and ethnic cleansing[,]" and calling secession "irredentist Euro-tribalism which contradicts the deep values and needs of the [European] Union."[43]

It is true secessions tend to produce more ethnically homogeneous units, but this isn't the same thing as a nationalist orientation: It is simply a description of the demographic qualities shared by a population within a given territory. Often, a seceding group is seeking to escape *another group's* nationalism—the rationale for remedial secession is to escape persecution directed against some identifiable group—so it is hardly surprising that separatists often have an ethnonational character.

To call such bounded demography undesirable is pure preference. And one would have to account for the many *existing* states with high levels of homogeneity. States in northern Europe remain highly homogeneous compared with most African states,[44] and when they first developed liberal policies they were even more homogeneous—a reminder that there is no necessary relationship between a territory's demography and the liberality of its policies. Or, indeed, if there is a relationship, it probably runs in the other direction: Homogeneity may be more likely to correlate with decency and lack of conflict.[45]

And what about the states we already have? Are they in fact the best units? All states are diverse, and are so in their own particular ways. We may celebrate diversity, but those differences also create challenges of internal coordination: Diversity is partly a description, partly a value, but not a formula for ease of governance. A state's demography affect its prospects for effective internal governance and civil discourse—some combinations will find Habermasian deliberation or Rawlsian fairness easier to apply than others (we'll look at these thinkers later)—and even the likelihood of violent conflict.[46] Since human identity is fluid and demographics changeable, why would we assume that rigid units are best? Yet that is precisely the assumption—the bet—that the current model makes.

A Fourth Assumption, That This Is the Best Possible Rule

Finally, we should add a fourth assumption implicit in the ones just looked at: that the rule we have is satisfactory because we already have the right means to tame existing states. Since the end of the Cold War, many new states have been created, and recent developments—human and minority rights, democratization—ameliorate the harsher effects of rigid borders by humanizing governance within existing states. So perhaps the system is already responsive enough?

Surely not. Each of these protective structures suffers from specific shortcomings that make them inadequate counterweights for the defects of the current rule, because each is limited by a logic that takes existing states as givens: Human rights are reactive and statist; minority rights are irreducibly complex and context-specific, practically guaranteeing a suboptimal distribution of resources; democratization, by its very nature, assumes the existing state as the default unit; and remedial secession addresses only the most urgent, violent cases and creates perverse incentives.

These tools are tremendously valuable in their own right—they can humanize politics and offer protection from grave danger—but they are not adequate to the challenges posed by secession and the state's often violent reaction to it. Instead, they suggest the limits of the classical model's attempt to turn self-determination inward, to make perfect that which happens to exist—to work only with and within the units we have, rather than make something anew. Let's look first at the most directly relevant device, remedial secession, to see why it does not redeem the current rule, and cannot.

THE PERVERSE INADEQUACY OF REMEDIAL SECESSION As we've seen, remedial secession is designed to protect groups suffering persecution by the state, allowing them to escape and form a new state. So this looks like a useful mechanism for maintaining rigid units while also protecting against abuse. But remedial secession is an extremely unwieldly instrument, rarely used and troubling in its implications when it has been.

The few involuntary secessions that have occurred have come after great violence and long delays: years in Kosovo, decades in South Sudan and East Timor, unprecedented violence in East Pakistan. Not all of these are examples of remedial secession: South Sudan became independent with Sudan's consent, while East Timor was delayed decolonization. But the doctrine remains a rare resort—Bangladesh and Kosovo are the only significant examples in half a century[47]—available in only the most extraordinary circumstances; the death toll in Bangladesh was at least three hundred thousand (and perhaps as high as three million).[48] And we must consider the many noncases in which, despite suffering marginalization, persecution, and terror, populations don't succeed in exiting—violence that the current system simply allows or abets without providing any remedy.

But worse, remedial secession can exacerbate the very problem it seeks to resolve. Remedial secession is a remedy, and remedy implies a harm. It relies on a harm-threshold logic, requiring some quantum of injury to trigger a response. So even in applying the doctrine, we only create new states *after* first allowing great suffering to occur; indeed, we effectively *require* great suffering as a proof and a prod before we will act. Cases falling below that threshold receive no benefit, so secessionist groups have perverse incentives to demonstrate they have suffered enough to deserve exit.

This is precisely what happened in Kosovo, where the KLA adopted a deliberate strategy of provocation killings to prod Belgrade into reacting and widening the war. It was successful, luring the world's mightiest military alliance into action that secured the province's liberation, but also a costly one: more than eight thousand Kosovars killed and nearly a million expelled. Yet given the logic of remedial secession and humanitarian intervention, this violence was a necessary part of the strategy: Had the Serbian state not subjected its own Albanian population to an adequate measure of terror and ethnic cleansing, NATO would not have moved to aid them.

Even then, NATO undertook only a protective intervention, not a war of liberation. It took nearly a full decade to move from intervention and international administration to a unilateral declaration of independence and widespread recognition. Even then, states supporting Kosovo's independence strongly resisted the idea that this was a precedent for any other case. The Kosovo conflict pre-

---

Enough Death

Remedial secession does not allow partition until *after* genocide or ethnic cleansing; consider the incentives that creates. I was working at the Yugoslav war-crimes tribunal during the Kosovo War, and I recall a painful conversation in which a group of British officials expressed their hope that the prosecution might discover the civilian death toll had exceeded ten thousand—a magic number they seemed to think would help justify NATO's intervention. We were sorry to disappoint them.

---

cipitated renewed discussion of humanitarian intervention and the Responsibility to Protect (R2P, cautiously endorsed at the 2005 UN World Summit), and it suggests the limits of remedial secession as a protective measure: The global default is still for reintegration of contested territory into the existing state. Remedial secession doesn't offer much hope to many peoples, and none to those not prepared to suffer terribly first.

The focus on extreme violence suggests how few cases remedial secession actually applies to. Remedial secession cannot provide a remedy for the many cases in which a population is seriously disadvantaged but not subjected to extreme violence (or unwilling to provoke it). The threshold is very high. There are no examples of remedial secession based on a violation of the Friendly Relations Declaration's Saving Clause—for denying a population its right to participate in society. The problem with the doctrine is not only that it incentivizes violence, but that even then it helps so few communities.

We might gradually lower the threshold for remedial secession, so that it encompassed a broader range of harms, perhaps covering the entire human rights corpus. But there are reasons to suppose this will not happen—reasons we will see when we look at human rights in a moment. States' resistance to the doctrine is considerable, so it is hard to imagine they would readily accept an even more intrusive remedy. And even if the threshold could be lowered, remedial secession would still be insufficient to ameliorate the system's rigidities. There is an entire class of cases it could not address no matter how low the threshold: By its nature, remedial secession cannot provide a remedy when a population simply has a strong conviction that its incorporation into the present state is an injustice or is undesirable. Remedial secession is a repackaged right to revolution, only triggered in response to crisis. In treating secession as a remedy, the doctrine excludes the more radical idea that secession might be a right.

Indeed, the logic of remedial secession shows the dead-end quality of classical self-determination. Remedial secession focuses not on the desire to rule oneself, which was the animating genius of preclassical self-determination, but on analogies to genocide and colonial oppression as "an *ultima ratio*"[49] to excuse violent self-help and intervention in extreme cases. It accepts territorial integrity as the norm, anticipating only the rarest and most pressing exceptions for great suffering.

This limited vision sits uncomfortably with intuitions about why humans form political communities. If one thinks Kosovars deserved independence not because of ethnic cleansing, nor even because of their marginalization in Serbian society, but because they believe themselves to be a people deserving a state—and recognizes the perversity of insisting they go through a kind of earthly hell to claim independence—then the limitations of remedial secession should be clear. Surely, the better view is that if Kosovo's Albanians deserved independence, they deserved it before all the killing. The same logic suggests that as few non-Albanians should be forced into the new state as possible. But the harm logic of remedial secession, combined with a default preference for existing units even when they make bad international frontiers,[50] makes it impossible for us to ask substantive questions about which people and places actually needed protection. The whole doctrine is fatally self-limiting—guided by a harm threshold that contemplates secession only in extreme situations, and therefore actually discourages us from considering the larger group of claims based on human desire.

THE LIMITED UTILITY OF HUMAN AND MINORITY RIGHTS The other favored tools for humanizing the system's rigidity are also problematically self-limiting—even less capable of producing solutions outside the existing framework of the state. The most practical reason to doubt that human rights can mitigate the harsher aspects of the current system is the notoriously poor record of rights enforcement. Much of the human rights project is focused on norm transformation rather than remedying specific violations. Scholars speak of compliance rather than enforcement—a nuance that hints at how little enforcement there is. Rights may change attitudes over time—but in the meantime, humans dissatisfied with their state have little practical recourse.

Even when remedies are available, they rarely ameliorate the harmful effects of rigid borders. Human rights are creatures of states: Their purpose is to protect human beings by policing and reforming *existing* states. Their response to violation is shaming, compensation, reform, the end of abuses—not the creation of new states. There is simply no support for the idea that significant rights violations, below the thresholds required for remedial secession, are to be remedied through territorial revision.

This sounds like a challenge of enforcement, but the problem is deeper: Rights don't cover a range of social and political realities of precisely the kind that lead communities to secede. Even a liberal, rights-respecting state has considerable latitude to shape its policies in ways that dramatically affect human identity. Liberalism "allows for a state committed to the survival and flourishing of a particular nation, culture, or religion . . . so long as the basic rights of the citizens who have different commitments . . . are protected."[51] And basic rights don't necessarily imply equal treatment:

> Each state/society has considerable latitude in how it treats, for example, particular minority religions. It would be completely consistent with international human rights standards to (merely) tolerate minority religion A while actively supporting the majority religion and minority religion B. . . . States may choose to treat all religions identically . . . but that is not required by the Universal Declaration Model.[52]

A state can favor particular ways of being, disfavor others, yet fully comply with human rights. Even if all rights are respected, it makes a difference if one's religion or language is the dominant one, takes social precedence, has to accept a marginal position, or is merely tolerated. So it is decisive, even in a liberal state, which group constitutes the majority—but since majority or minority is a function of borders, it matters where those borders are.

This does not mean we should give up on human rights: They have inherent value and can improve people's lives in real ways—and as we'll see in chapter 7, they provide a model for how to implement a right of secession. But they don't do enough to help groups wishing to alter or escape from the states that rules them. They are no substitute for a state of one's own.

As a subcategory of human rights, minority rights might appear more promising, since they focus on the communities historically most likely to challenge states' territorial integrity. A well-designed set of minority provisions—including federalism, autonomy, and group rights—can mitigate the harms that lead communities to secede. But not only do minority rights confront the same limitations as human rights, they have two additional features that makes them less useful in mitigating the harshness of borders: They are enormously variable, and their variation is almost entirely determined by the state.

There is no universal model of minority rights. What a given minority can claim—even its recognition as a minority—is subject to political discretion. Some states grant extensive rights, including autonomy, while others restrict rights to the personal realm. Article 27 of the ICCPR provides for rights "[i]n those States in which ethnic, religious or linguistic minorities exist"—so some states deny the existence of minorities.

What these diverse outcomes have in common is that they are negotiated within each state. Although there are international principles governing minority rights (and sometimes a treaty creates rights, as in the interwar minority treaties or the Dayton Peace Accords), their development is a function of each state's politics. Minorities get the deal they can negotiate, under conditions in which there is no exit, which means minorities predictably get deals that are less good than if exit were possible.

The state doesn't only rely on superior numbers; it has tools that limit the usefulness of minority rights. Given the principles of equality and nondiscrimination animating the contemporary global system, states often have an attractive alternative: integration. Rather than descend into a thicket of particularisms, a state can commit to common citizenship and full equality. From the perspective of a minority, the right to join the majority is a mixed blessing: Integration can look like subordination and the denial of difference. But the global system has a hard time explaining why this might be a problem.

The diversity of minority rights is a virtue, since it allows a variety of tailored solutions that can improve the situation in ways that satisfy minorities' concerns. The problem, as always, is those cases in which they don't. When the problem is not circumstances, but the fact of being in a state—being a minority in someone else's country—minority rights offer no meaningful remedy. Minority rights can lessen the hardship of being a minority, but not remove it. And whatever is won can be lost: In 2017, Russia refused to renew an autonomy agreement with Tatarstan, and reduced once-mandatory Tatar language classes to two voluntary hours a week. As Tibetans, Eritreans, Kosovars, and others have learned, and Hong Kongers are beginning to, guarantees of autonomy don't always last.

Even more than human rights, minority rights as such cannot justify a new state, because by definition a minority is that part of a population *not* entitled to its own state.[53] The very idea of a minority reinforces the conceptual priority of existing states. It is a powerful example of the classical model working itself out to its logical conclusion, its unending termination: devising ever-greater expressions of complexity within the paralytic confines of a paradigm so dominant it is hardly perceived.

THE DELAYED BENEFITS AND PRESENT DANGERS OF DEMOCRATIZATION A right to democratic participation should be the most promising development, because it is expressly an exercise in internal self-determination, humanizing the very doctrine that created rigid borders. But democratization is unlikely to respond to the kinds of social and political tensions that call states' integrity into question. Like human rights, it is conceptually ill-fit to the challenge: Democratization assumes existing states are the default in which the work of democracy must be carried out.

As with human rights, democratization's normative impulse is integrative. Although it is possible to differentiate populations to achieve deeper, substantive equality, the most common approaches favor formal equality: one person one vote, a state for all its citizens, and the like. Democratization can give minorities a more prominent voice in governance—especially in consociational systems that share power—but its main focus is integrative, concerned with giving voice to the *demos*.

Shocking, egregious denials of participation might justify independence as a protective measure. Yet even in a well-functioning democracy, discrete communities can be permanent, structural losers. Though not excluded, they may be permanently unable to realize their preferences—and this inability registers not as failure, but as the system functioning correctly. Nothing in democracy actually ensures that the state will serve the interests of a minority as such, rather than as part of the broader community. Democracy promises inclusion, which is hardly an unadulterated good for communities that might prefer not to be included in someone else's state.

And democracy presents a special problem—a unique danger that limits its protective value. *Democratization*—the transition to democracy—can prove deeply destabilizing, especially in divided societies.[54] A democratic culture is harder to develop than elections, and that lag can be dangerous, inducing an all-or-nothing contest in which elections are little more than a demographic census.

In Yugoslavia, the introduction of multiparty democracy, in a context in which ethnic and republican rivalries had reasserted themselves in the vacuum of central authority, exacerbated tensions and made it more difficult to hold the state together. Yugoslavia's collapse was not inevitable, but sizable parts of its populace were insufficiently committed to it and found other state projects appealing. In such a context, asking people about governance may make it harder to ignore what, in some societies, is obvious: Many people do not want their current state to rule them.

This danger is unlikely to abate. In consolidated democracies, it is relatively minor: It's principally an effect of transition. But that's a large category, and as the post–Cold War experience with the end of the 'End of History' has shown, we can expect to be in a democratizing rather than democratic world for a long time. That uncertain progress will make the problem of a democratic citizenry's identity—and states' demography—even more salient in coming decades.

THE INSUFFICIENCY OF INTERNAL SELF-DETERMINATION   Rights and democracy are core elements of the postwar global order. They are also expressions of internal self-determination, which has become the only avenue for change within the classical model. New states are not the thing, so we must improve the states we have: thus, democracy, human and minority rights, constitutionalism. Each can improve the internal governance of states, humanizing the harshness of the territorial norm upon which the global order is premised.

But the good work they do is self-limiting. Each assumes an existing state and operates within it, literally and metaphorically. The pathways of rights and democracy are inside the state; they are conceptually ill-fit to claims whose resolution challenges that state itself. (Even remedial secession—in addition to being rare, ineffective, and perverse—assumes a default of integration.) It is precisely the hardest cases in which these devices do the least good. Like rigid borders themselves, they work except where they don't—and when they don't, we have no answer: Tellingly, opponents of secession who rely on internal processes fall back on the unwritten right of revolution if things don't work out.[55] If we must depend on rights and democracy to mitigate the classical rule's rigidity, that is further reason to doubt our easy assumptions about the rule and what it does.

So we should note one last feature of our current rule—a fact available to us despite the system's untestable nature: It leaves many people living under the domination of some state other than they might wish. We know this because they frequently try to form new states and often are killed in the process. Surely this is not the best of all possible rules.

PART TWO

THE NEW RULE

4

A New Right to Secession

What might a right to secession look like?

WE HAVE JUST LOOKED AT the assumptions underpinning our collective faith in territorial integrity—our belief that it does certain things—and seen reasons to doubt those assumptions. But these are merely indications, not tests in their own right, and as we have seen, it may be impossible actually to evaluate the current rule's effects. If the current rule and its assumptions are intuitively unsatisfying but also annoyingly untestable, we should consider how we might nonetheless take their measure.

A Hypothetical Alternative to an Impossible Test

One way would be to do what was not done in 1945: make a discrete change in territorial integrity without altering other parts of the system, and examine the effects over time. Is the future more or less violent, more or less stable? Are more or fewer people living in societies they prefer? While social scientists might be happy to have such amazing data, it would be impractical—and could take a frustratingly long time—as would subjecting, say, only one hemisphere to a different rule.

Instead, we can try to do the same thing through a kind of thought experiment: devise a different rule, and think about its likely outcomes. That's the point of this chapter and the rest of this book: to propose an alternative—both to test the current rule and because it might actually be better. Here I outline *one* basic model for an international right to secession, to test the idea that an idea *like this one* might be a good thing and better than what we have now. So here it is:

The New Rule: A Right of Secession

A. The existing system of territorial integrity is maintained, with *one* change: A state's territorial integrity can be challenged from inside by a self-defined community constituting a local territorial majority.

B. Such communities vindicate their claims exclusively through a plebiscite, leading to negotiations with the state.
   1. The community determines the plebiscitary territory, subject to these limits:
      a. some minimum population;
      b. some minimum contiguity of territory; and
      c. no plebiscites across international frontiers.
   2. Other communities within that territory can form and make a counterclaim not to secede, in a cascading process.

C. A community wishing to secede must win a (super)majority of votes among all those living in, or having long-standing ties to, the plebiscitary territory.
   1. No proofs of harm are required.
   2. Historical claims have no special weight.
   3. However, plebiscites resulting from recent occupation, ethnic cleansing, or serious violations of human rights can be rejected.

D. In addition to winning its plebiscite, a secessionist community must:
   1. accept all residents of the territory or others with legitimate ties as citizens;
   2. negotiate in good faith with the parent state;
   3. undertake to respect all relevant human rights provisions; and
   4. accept ongoing international supervision.

E. The parent state must:
   1. allow and facilitate the plebiscite;
   2. negotiate secession in good faith if the plebiscite succeeds; and
   3. accept all residents with valid links to its residual territory.

F. The right is iterative for any territory or population.

G. All other commitments within the international state system (human rights, nonaggression, succession rules, and so on) are unaffected.

We have already examined the problematic assumptions underlying the current rule. Now we'll see how this new rule responds to those assumptions. Let's briefly look at its elements, taking them on their own terms. We will return to them in the remaining chapters to consider in detail their effects and rationales and the objections to them. Here, we simply wish to see what the rule would look like if it worked as imagined—which, of course, nothing ever does.

The Basic Features of the New Rule

Truly Self-Determining Peoples

In the empty space at the heart of self-determination is the question of who, exactly, is a people. That was the objection to Wilsonian self-determination: its indeterminacy. The classical version refuses even to ask the question, but that doesn't make it go away. Answering that challenge is the heart of *this* proposal: Only the people can decide what they want, so first they must decide who they are.

The classical rule defines self-determination using territories rather than peoples. The new rule reverses that formula: The holders of the right are communities who define the territory on which they determine their own governance. A people is not the population of an existing state, nor the state itself: It is a self-defined, self-constituted community forming a majority in some part of an existing state—a part the community's members themselves define. In so doing they define themselves.

But if the new rule reverses the classical one, it also abandons the troubled logic of the preclassical model: No shared national identity is required. The self-determining community does not exist in any objective sense; it is socially constructed, not primordial. Its sole identity, for legal and political purposes, is as the democratic expression of a population's preference, which in turn serves as the basis for recognizing 'its' territory as a state.

The new rule allows communities to identify themselves without reference to preexisting units. It takes the democratic aspects of self-determination seriously, prioritizing them over the diktat of borders. But the rule is also territorial, since it requires the group to constitute a local majority. It expects political communities to be territorial in nature, just as the current system does.

The rule does not rely on theories of ethnic naturalness or any claim about identity other than that human beings are by nature capable of sharing political preferences. Any group could make a claim: In practice, the new rule is likely to be employed by ethnic groups, but it is theoretically available to other coherent communities who constitute a local territorial majority—industrial or rural regions, island populations, 'blue' or 'red' states. If enough people gather in one place, they can make a claim.

The new rule solves the key flaw of Wilsonianism, which assumed an objectively determined ethnicity was necessary for peoplehood. The dream of identifying "peaceful, impartial mechanisms for legitimate self-determination"[1] is quixotic, which is why the new rule adopts an overtly subjective method: It asks people to determine themselves, rather than relying on outsiders' notionally neutral estimates. The only basis for claims under the proposed rule is an electoral outcome.

This removes the problem of proving some group is real enough to merit its own state—that it is a historical nation, has a high culture, or otherwise meets some standard. Critically, it removes the problem of proving this to outsiders: Although recognition is an important part of vindicating this new right, the rule does not require outsiders to validate the group's identity as such. It only requires outsiders to observe and validate the results of an election, which is something that, for all the challenges it presents, we actually know how to do.

The Plebiscite

A community's right to define itself and its territory is the legal and moral heart of this new rule; the plebiscite is the engine. The plebiscite is the procedural and political expression of the right—the way the community announces its claim and constitutes itself as a recognizable, legally relevant unit.

The plebiscite is the mechanism by which a local majority's democratic preference is expressed and recognized. The plebiscite both legitimates the community's claim and allows the community to constitute itself—in a way the classical rule's reliance on existing territories simply cannot do, but also without the pre-classical model's reliance on externally imposed proofs. What is being decided in the plebiscite is only sovereignty over some territory; the identity and motives of participants will matter tremendously to them, but are formally irrelevant—they are decisive, but not decisional.

This is very close to the model we adopt in elections, which aggregate preferences without interrogating them. Voters have their reasons for choosing a given candidate or party—we hope!—but on election day, it is their choice that matters, nothing else. Voters can choose Candidate X because he has promised to do something, or because they think he has, for good reasons, bad reasons, even no reason at all. Some people voted against Barack Obama in 2008 because he was black, and while this was racist, it did not invalidate their votes—any more than those of people who voted *for* him because he was black. The only limits are vote selling, fraud, or intimidation, but those limits aim to ensure the integrity of the individual voter's autonomous choice; once that is ensured, we do not inquire into the reasons for his choice, which is simply valid and, if part of the majority, authoritative.

The new rule's electionlike agnosticism is its key feature: Unlike the current rule, which is hostile to ethnicity as an organizing principle, the new rule need not exclude or disfavor solutions that have an ethnic valence, or indeed any valence. The rule *requires* groups to mobilize through a democratic process, but doesn't *rely on* any particular identity. It allows communities to decide that they wish to form a separate political community for reasons they alone know, insisting only that they then construct a society whose norms are reasonably rights-respecting.

We will consider these mechanisms briefly in the following subsections and return to them in a separate chapter. But one thing here: The plebiscite is the mechanism, but independence is not necessarily the goal: The very fact of a right to secession with a robust mechanism alters the negotiating dynamic between states and their own populations; that should lead to more favorable outcomes even for communities that choose to stay. The right is independence, the mechanism is the plebiscite, but the outcome, often, will be better negotiations about the reasons to stay.

Limits on the Plebiscitary Territory

The borders of the plebiscitary zone are determined by the claimants. This does two related things: It requires a community to define itself in relation to a specific territory, and it creates self-regulating incentives. Separatists need to define a territory on which they can win, and this should lead them to limit their claim so as not to include too many unsympathetic people: "A modest boundary including only areas densely inhabited by one's own people is the surest route to success."[2]

In addition, the plebiscite territory would be subject to certain limits.

MINIMUM POPULATION SIZE AND LIMITS ON SHAPE There are prudential grounds to require a minimum group size. A minimum population helps legitimate secession by demonstrating its democratic qualities—and politically, a larger population suggests greater importance. A population requirement threshes out less weighty or less salient claims and helps address concerns about fracturing. One could analogize minimum populations to thresholds for winning seats in a legislature, which limits the influence of small or fringe groups.

Just as there are pragmatic reasons for a minimum population, there might be reasons to regulate the territory's *shape,* though there probably doesn't need to be a minimum *size.* The new rule expresses itself in territory, but its rationale is human beings who have a relationship to territory, not territory itself. There is no principled reason for a minimum territory—under the current system, states come in all sizes, from Russia to Vatican City—and a minimum population already offers protection. But as we'll see, it might be necessary to place limits on extreme gerrymandering or require some contiguity.

NO PLEBISCITES ACROSS A FRONTIER Finally, no plebiscite could be held across an international frontier. This runs directly counter to the intuition that it is the fracturing potential of secession we should fear—this provision keeps seceding units smaller!—but it has a purpose: to discourage revanchism and foreign intervention by limiting pretexts for involving neighboring states.

Cascading Plebiscites

Plebiscites would be cascading. Those opposed to secession not only could vote against it, they could organize their own countervailing plebiscite, allowing their smaller area to remain in the existing state. So if a group overreached in defining its territory, it would run two risks: losing outright, and triggering a cascade that would reduce its area. The effect would be final borders more closely aligned with the preferences of those on either side—a better fit between borders and people.

In principle, there might be unlimited rounds, until no more were demanded or no more majorities could be produced.[3] In practice, however, cascades could

---

Repeating a Successful Experiment

Cascades are modeled on the plebiscites used after the First World War: In East Prussia and Carinthia, plebiscites included secondary zones activated if the larger zone voted to secede. Both had large communities expected to be uncomfortable with the likely outcome: Germans and Poles, Austrian Germans and Slovenes. Because of how the voting went, the cascades weren't actually deployed, but their inclusion in the model helped make those plebiscites successful, producing borders much more closely aligned with populations' preferences and doing it peaceably.

Back then the secondary zones were identified by outsiders—a preclassical exercise in imperial other-determination—and introduced the very sort of problems Wilsonianism suffered from: Zones were premised on highly rigid (and often incorrect) beliefs about individuals' likely voting behavior—that ethnic Poles would vote for a Polish state, and ethnic Germans for a German state. But in this new model advocates of a cascade would self-identify, just like supporters of the initial plebiscite. Both groups would be subject to the same game-theoretic logic about which population and territory to include to ensure an outcome (and avoid including large, disruptive minorities).

Although they were externally imposed, the postwar plebiscites worked quite well, and this is not surprising: People's identities and preferences are complex, but ascriptive markers can be remarkably good predictors of voting behavior. One *could* use such data to fine-tune a line, but leaving the decision to the communities—a true act of self-determination—yields a high level of specificity without assuming anything about individuals' identity or giving ethnicity an explicit role.

---

be limited to two or three rounds, after which further changes could be negotiated as border adjustments—a model already used in the current system. This would minimize the negative effects of border changes, producing a better fit between populations' preferences and the new frontier. But, in turn, cascades introduce or reinforce other complications: They can increase the complexity of the final territory, because finding the best fit may be in tension with maintaining contiguity.

Conduct of the Plebiscite

In addition to provisions governing the shape of the territory, the rule includes basic requirements for how the vote is conducted—including a (super)majority and international supervision—as well as excluding certain elements typically associated with secession that are extraneous to an electoral decision, such as requirements of harm or historical claims.

(SUPER)MAJORITY A successful plebiscite has to achieve a majority, possibly a supermajority. A bare majority could be enough, and has been used in many cases, such as the Scottish referendum and Brexit; a supermajority clearly biases toward the status quo, "a mechanism to prevent a side from winning."[4] But the pull of settled expectations, the risks of uncertainty and transition—the start-up costs of nationalism—might argue for more than bare majoritarianism. This is consistent with principles of constitutionalism, which make it harder for casual, transient majorities to overturn core values, since we desire a more decisive expression of popular will to make fundamental changes than we do for normal legislation.[5]

The bar could be quite high: say, 70 percent. That is a level rarely reached in statewide elections—in many systems, it would constitute a crushing electoral victory, enough to amend the constitution—and thus indicates a high level of consensus and seriousness. If a pro-secession group can identify a territory in which it could achieve 70 percent, that suggests a very high level of dissatisfaction with the current state. Many separatist movements would not make the grade (I once presented my ideas to an audience in Barcelona, which was very enthusiastic until I suggested a supermajority), but a high threshold would ensure that successful claims would have high support.

But whether 70 percent, a bare majority, or something in between, the principle is general: A higher level creates greater legitimacy and precision. It ensures the directly affected population is, to a greater degree, actually in favor of the change, and reduces the number of people subjected to the sovereignty of a new state against their will. At the same time, the higher the threshold, the fewer communities benefit, either through independence or the ability to negotiate more effectively with the state. There is no inherently superior number; it is a sliding scale, a balance.

NO NEED FOR HARM: THE NEW RULE TREATS DEMOCRATIC SECESSION AS A RIGHT, NOT A REMEDY The new rule is a claim of right, not a response to human rights violations or systematic exclusion. Communities secede because they wish to form a new state: So long as the population expresses its desire

democratically—following the procedural requirements of the plebiscite model—
its claim is a valid basis for negotiating exit from the state, without reference to
the justice of the claim, contested historical facts, or any other basis other than
the result.

This is where the new rule is radically different from most proposals for reforming self-determination. Remedial secession allows border changes solely
in response to grave harms—an ameliorative and reactive remedy, a doctrine
playing defense. Not only is this ineffective, it denies the reality that sometimes
human beings simply no longer wish to live in the states history has bequeathed
them. In this respect, remedial secession utterly fails to respond to the *logic* of
democracy and self-determination: We do not value democracy solely to achieve
material outcomes; we value autonomous decision-making in its own right.
This is completely obvious and uncontroversial when we think about politics
inside states, but mostly absent from even the most expansive efforts to rethink
external self-determination. The new rule restores democracy to the center of
the doctrine.

NO-FAULT SECESSION: NO WEIGHT FOR HISTORICAL CLAIMS The new rule's
mechanism is radically democratic and radically ahistorical: It refuses to defer
to contingent borders or historical claims. Relying on the current population's
preferences, the new rule gives no value to ancient claims of privilege or patri-
mony. It does this to resolve one of the core tensions plaguing thinking about
self-determination, evident among both separatists and states opposing them:
the tendency to reject demographic realities by making claims about historical
justice. The new rule resolves this tension decisively in favor of a focus, to the
greatest degree possible, on living human beings. Under the new rule, claims
based on past dominance, legal title, or historical injustice could not be raised
as objections to an otherwise valid plebiscite, except within very narrow limits.
The fact that the ancestors of those opposing secession once dominated the
region—as Serbs did in Kosovo—would not defeat a vote to secede. The objection that the territory is an inseparable part of an existing state would have
no force, since that is the very issue the plebiscite contests.

Obligations on the Parties

Winning the plebiscite is not the end of the process: A right to secession is
really a right to begin negotiations, which place obligations on state and seces-

sionists. These obligations vary—the new state might have to accept continuing supervision, but the existing state only has to accept monitoring of the plebiscite and negotiations—but for each, four principles are central: good-faith conduct of the plebiscite and negotiations, acceptance of populations, respect for rights protections, and international involvement.

GOOD FAITH An obligation to negotiate in good faith is difficult to enforce, but is nonetheless useful, reinforcing the principle that once a decision has been made, the process should stay within clear parameters. This has been an explicit or implicit feature of referenda in Canada and Scotland, and although in those cases postreferendum obligations were not tested—and are still being tested for Brexit—there is reason to think a good-faith framework helps maintain the civility and legitimacy of the process. This does not mean there will not be hard-fought, contested questions; even in consensual secessions, negotiations can be difficult, and if there has been violence, the negotiations can be very hard.[6]

ACCEPTANCE OF POPULATIONS Before a plebiscite, the members of the population were citizens (or residents) of a common state. If a plebiscite succeeds, some of them will be disaffected—some who opposed independence, others who might have wished to be included. The existing state should have to accept any citizen, provided he is prepared to relocate there. By contrast, the new state would only have obligations to those with legitimate ties to the plebiscite territory. This would include anyone legally resident in it at the time of the plebiscite (with narrow exceptions, such as military personnel), and could include individuals living elsewhere with defined ties to the territory: long residence, family, or the like. Either state could include others, consistent with the broad discretion states have to define citizenship.

RESPECT FOR HUMAN RIGHTS It would not be strictly necessary to require any particular level of human rights protection, but doing so would be consistent with recent practice in the Balkans and former Soviet Union, where recognition of new states was tied to rights. New states are often required to undertake more and more extensive commitments than existing states.

INTERNATIONAL INVOLVEMENT Supervision could be triggered by the plebiscite process; if the vote succeeded, supervision could continue after independence, though length of time and formal powers could vary from full administrative powers to an advisory role. Supervision could be undertaken by a UN body or on an ad hoc basis, in response to the clear signal of a valid plebiscite.

Supervision might undermine the radically self-determining aspects of the rule, but international involvement is essential to make the right meaningful; secession is unlikely to succeed without support from and integration into the community of states. Supervision is consistent with practice in places such as Kosovo and East Timor, where international administration was an important part of the transition to independence. It is also the most challenging aspect of the new rule: Existing states would have to consent to some kind of outside involvement, and they are unlikely to agree.

Iteration

A plebiscite could be called anytime a community wished to, not only in a one-off, as after the First World War, and certainly very differently from the classical rule's suspended game of musical chairs, which has been sounding the same final note since 1945. Iteration ensures that communities cannot simply invoke a right to self-determination for themselves and then deny it to others. Together with cascades, iteration helps ensure that the fit between territorial sovereignty and popular preferences is governed by a living principle, rather than the dead choices of the past. The right would only be unavailable for territories whose population fell below the minimum.

Other Rules Unaffected

Finally, let us note the new rule's *least* prominent feature: Very little would change. As much as possible, elements of the present system would be held constant. In particular, territorial integrity would hold just as it does today against aggression and the use or threat of force. The single change is to allow challenges to states' territorial integrity by internal, democratically legitimated, local majorities. Even this is not as radical as it might sound: After all, in the current system, secession is not prohibited. This proposal simply converts what is now a matter of politics into a legally cognizable right.

That is a single, small change, leaving the basic framework of the state system in place: Instead of challenging the very idea of borders or states, the new rule assumes their salience and is only concerned with the units in that system. But it is also a radical shift, a break from the decadent, dead-ended logic that has governed that whole system for three-quarters of a century.

So of course it cannot be that simple. Surely there are problems with this modest new rule that changes so little but will change everything? Well, yes, and the answers to those problems are enlightening about what we may reasonably ask, and hope for, from any system, including the one we have now.

5

People, Territory, Plebiscite: The Main Features—Objections and Answers

How does the new rule function? How well does it improve on the current rule?

It is the very process of the formation of a sovereign civil state . . . that, among other things, stimulates elements of parochialism, communalism, racialism, and so on, because it introduces into society a valuable new prize over which to fight and a frightening new force with which to contend.
Clifford Geertz[1]

THIS WARNING FROM A NOTED anthropologist seems to caution against the new rule: Making states raises the stakes, bringing out the worst and most violent in people. Much in this is true. Still, the risk is more general: It is the formation of states, not merely 'new' ones, that does this, and to the degree *existing* states engage in state-building (or, God forbid, nation-building), they are subjecting their populations to the very pressures Geertz is worried about.

It is instructive to note when he wrote, and about what. The year was 1963, his subject the newly liberated colonies—societies which, within their rigid, received borders, constituted a new prize and frightening force. Whatever human beings were then fighting over, it was not new borders, but what the existing borders contained. Geertz was in fact warning against the dangers inherent in the *classical* rule; it is hardly clear his warning applies to a rule that attempts something quite different.

But we should still take the point seriously: Might not a right of secession pro-

duce all kinds of dangers and harms? We considered this in general—looking at
the assumptions the current system rests on—but now we return to it in light of
what the new rule proposes. This chapter examines three main aspects of the
rule: people, territory, and plebiscite. It considers some objections to the new
rule and its effects—including the possibility that it would make things worse.
It answers those objections and provides a theoretical justification for the basic
intuition that democratic decision-making by local majorities is a positive good.
An important theme will emerge: In many respects, the new rule *is* flawed—in
the same ways the current rule is. And in other respects, this flawed new rule
offers us something more in keeping with our better natures.

The Self-Determining People

*[A]dherence to the principle of affinity is both distorting and dangerous,
particularly in its nationalist version. It misconceives the nature and function of law; it distorts one's thinking about cultural rights and multiculturalism; it presents as inherently problematic what we ought to regard as the
norm—namely, the movement and mingling of peoples and the dissolution
and fracturing of the boundaries of ethnic identity; and it sets us on a dangerous path towards something like ethnic cleansing, at least in circumstances where nationalist aspirations do not correspond neatly to existing
territorial and demographic realities.*

Jeremy Waldron[2]

The Sorts of Peoples This Rule Might Recognize

IS THIS DEFINITION OF A PEOPLE MORALLY OBJECTIONABLE? We saw in the
previous chapter that the heart of the new rule is a radically different definition
of a people. But what do we know about these peoples? Who are they, and what
are they like? We can predict that the peoples this rule would favor will often
be nations or ethnicities. Is this a problem? Should we be concerned about a
rule that might encourage people to organize themselves this way?

First, whatever incentives it creates, the rule doesn't *rely* on ethnicity. Unlike
Wilsonianism, it doesn't require self-determination's beneficiaries to belong to
an ascriptive group or share *any* quality: not ethnicity, language, religion, or
even shared identity; no need for a theory of nation, *Kultur,* or *'asabiyya.* It requires two things: physical proximity and a decision to create a political com-

munity—a territory and a vote. It leaves the reasons *why* people want a state in the black box of electoral deliberation.

So while ethnic groups might take advantage of this rule, that is only because they already have the kind of shared identity that makes collective decision-making more plausible, in the way we are not surprised when Frenchmen elect a president who speaks French. But it is entirely possible that a majority would form in a given place because the population shared a preference for a new state even if they don't share a language, religion, or other ethnic marker. Perhaps they all are dentists.

That is unlikely, given the economics of dentistry and the sad fact that whatever professional values they share in common, more separates dentists than unites them. But it also suggests there are reasons why political identity sometimes tracks with ethnicity. Modern states govern people on territory, and ethnicity—broadly understood—is the only ascriptive marker that distributes *unevenly* across large tracts of physical space. It is the only marker that can produce relatively high homogeneity on large territories—the only marker that most or all of a state's population can share. Relatively: There are no truly homogeneous areas. But ethnic homogeneity can be much higher across large territories than markers such as class or gender. (We shall come to how heterogeneity is to be protected.)

Occupation, class and gender don't produce similar territorial effects. There have never been large parts of the earth's surface populated only by dentists, or only millionaires, or only women, because such groups would find themselves without patients, people to clean their mansions, or the (still) most popular means of creating the next generation. But it *is* common to find areas in which most people speak French, are Muslim, have very dark skin, or the like. That's not necessarily a reason to base politics on those features—in the case of dark skin, it's a terrible reason—but that distribution is a fact, and a factor in governing people on territory, in ways dentistry and gender never are.

And in some cases, like speaking French, it's not objectionable at all, but highly functional, because people who speak the same language have a much easier time understanding each other. There are aspects of identity that express themselves differently across territory *and* make governance easier or harder. The current rule tries to pretend such differences should not matter; the new rule, by contrast, does not require, but *expects* those difference to exist and to matter.

But even if sharing language or religion can make governance easier, perhaps we should nonetheless reject this easier way as unethical. Why allow groups to form ethnicized states—based on affinity—under cover of a neutral rule? Doesn't this violate liberal sensibilities, and isn't this dangerous? After all, liberalism—the ethical template of the modern state—was a reaction to Europe's religious wars, and imagined "the possibility of a reasonably harmonious and stable pluralist society" that rejected the belief that "social unity and concord require[d] agreement on a general and comprehensive religious, philosophical, or moral doctrine."[3] Why go back? Even if homogeneous states are easier to govern, shouldn't we *prefer* diverse, pluralistic states, and structure our rules to prefer them, too?

Even if we say yes—and as we'll see, that's not a very good answer—this new rule might still pass muster. It is at least as liberal as the present rule, possibly more so, and fully accords with the logic of an inclusive, rights-respecting society. It does so in a way that—consistent with liberalism's 'empty ideal'—allows communities to achieve greater political cohesion without requiring uniformity or resorting to illiberal methods, which the current model perversely incentivizes. Let's see how, by considering the way one common marker of ethnicity interacts with and is defined by the state.

LANGUAGE AND EMPTY LIBERALISM Liberal theory can provide a rationale for a minimally decent society respectful of equality and the rights of minorities. Imagine a group of individuals agreeing to form a shared society under a "veil of ignorance"—before knowing their own position in it. They don't know if they will be rich or poor, male or female, dominant or weak; they don't know if they will be dentists or patients. In this "original position," people would choose a society committed to equality, redistribution, and a range of liberal practices, "ensur[ing] that no one is advantaged or disadvantaged in the choice of principles by the outcome of natural chance of the contingency of social circumstances."[4] People's qualities and circumstances aren't random—but this is the point: How can we act justly in a world of difference?

This principle can equally apply to the international system, providing a rationale for states to be, if not fully liberal, then at least minimally decent.[5] Qualities like language are not randomly distributed, but under the veil, no one would know if he would speak English or Inuktitut—or where he would live if he did. From this position, we can derive an argument for rights-respecting societies with protections for speakers of minority languages.

This is fine, but minority languages implies a *majority* language, and this has consequences: After all, the very idea of protecting the vulnerable implies something about the capacities of the powerful. A liberal majority can impose its language in all sorts of ways that are entirely reasonable: In places where a given language is dominant, it makes sense to organize social and political life around that language.

If we imagine ourselves in that original position, we might decide to protect minority languages—after all, we might be protecting ourselves! But it is unlikely we would give *all* languages equal status, even though we ourselves might be disadvantaged. Some countries have dozens of languages, and treating them all the same would be impractical: It would be ridiculous to require everyone in Canada to learn Inuktitut, or to require every street sign in the country to be in Inuktitut. (At least most non-Inuits would think it ridiculous, and that is almost everyone.)

And ridiculous or reasonable, it's not how we actually do things: *No* country gives equal status to every language on its territory. Instead they usually identify an official language and insist public life be conducted in it. International law completely supports this tendency: Nothing requires a state to forgo the obvious benefits of organizing life around a dominant language, so long as it is minimally nice to speakers of other languages. Nothing prevents the state from entrenching that dominance through mandatory education, monopolies of use (in public offices, street signs, rules regarding private signage, media), subsidies, and so on. States *can* be quite generous in recognizing multiple languages or in supporting nonofficial languages—but they don't have to be.

This is entirely sensible, as anyone who has met someone with whom he shares no language will know: Work on Babel stopped for a reason, because without a common language, it is hard to get much done. Linguistic pluralism requires large investment and constant management. It makes sense to pick a dominant language or two, and this is entirely consistent with liberal principles.

But 'dominant' is something we can only describe once we've put lines on a map. Qualities like language appear in clusters precisely because the ability to communicate with those with whom one is in proximity is so functional. Humans being what we are, we attach markers of social status to language use, making extraordinarily fine distinctions between accents, usages, styles, and the like. So we could speak of a language's local dominance even without reference to political units. But it is only after we have *bordered* those clusters that we can talk about majority and minority languages for purposes of policy—for the kinds of decisions any state must make.

In turn, the state powerfully shapes the linguistic space, standardizing usage, homogenizing dialects, and disfavoring smaller languages. This can be done nicely or nastily, but even the most liberal states do it, by the mere act of designating one language as the default in governance and public life.

The context in which these decisions are made is a function of borders. The delineation of a border between two territories creates two areas with different demographies and different configurations of power, which in turn shape policy. A border delineates the rough line between two demographic zones—and *will* delineate it no matter how it is drawn. Within the zone, dominance can appear almost logical, mathematical—we might even say reasonable. But it is entirely a function of those lines.

AN IMAGINARY ISLAND IN THE ORIGINAL POSITION For example, consider this map—an island with two languages spoken on it, White and Black.

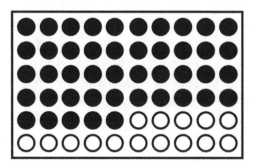

An island

If we were to imagine this island as a single country—because why impose artificial borders?—it might seem sensible and nice to adopt a policy of bilingualism. But the current rule wouldn't require that: It would be entirely possible for this country to decide that only Black is an official language, which all citizens must learn in school. Or it might choose White—nothing requires the official language to be the majority's, and perhaps White speakers hold the real power, or their language has higher status.

Even if the state adopted bilingualism, we might imagine pragmatic modifications. Would it really be necessary, or desirable, to have bilingualism on the whole island? In the south, there are no Black speakers, and in the north, no White, so maybe there could be zones with different language rights, as Finland has. Would bilingualism bind the island together—or inflame tensions between Black and White speakers, who would resent having to learn a language irrelevant to their lived experience (the language of their hated and envied superiors, or their uncultured and disdained inferiors)? Who knows, but nothing in the current system *requires* any of these particular adaptations; they are a function of politics played out within the state that governs the whole island.

But what if we made two countries? What policies would make sense then? Well, before we think about policies, we should settle on a border: You can probably think of the most sensible or obvious or best line yourself, so I haven't bothered to draw it. Instead, how about this one?

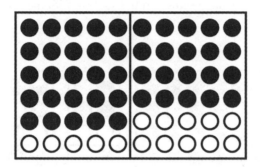

One island, two countries

This produces two countries, in each of which Black is the numerically dominant language. (Perhaps you imagined a different line?) None of the circles have moved. Since nothing in international law would require either state to give equal status to both languages, the decision, as in the single-state example above, would be a function of politics within each state. Well, good luck to White.

But if we drew the line horizontally, as in the figure at the top of the next page, White might have better luck (or seem even more threatening). Different lines produce different social and political dynamics—even under conditions of democracy.

Of course, these maps are too simple—people don't really live in such segregated fashion (although language dominance can be quite homogeneous)—but even

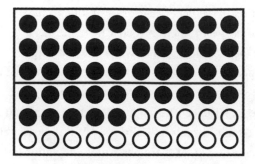

Another way to draw two countries

if we produce an even more complicated map, the point is the same. Here is the same island, the same number of White and Black Speakers, in a more realistic configuration—perhaps White speakers have migrated to cities in the north, while Black speakers have settled in the south—with the same two borders as in the earlier maps.

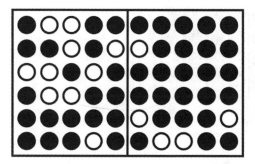   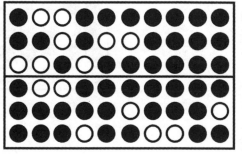

A more complicated demography . . .   . . . with a different border

We might add bilingual speakers, because some people will be fluent in both, while many will know at least a bit of the other language. But this changes very little, because although large parts of the world's population are bi- or multilingual, fewer are *equally* fluent in multiple languages, and fewer still can switch languages without some kind of social marker following them. Anyway, multiple language use is not a free-floating phenomenon; it is influenced by state policy.[6]

But whether we use the one border line or the other, or still other lines, the lesson is the same: Language policy on this island is not a natural distribution;

it is a function of line-drawing. Reasonableness is a function of the state; there are no reasonable language policies until we have drawn a border.

Over time, 'natural' demography is changed by the policies those lines enable. Speakers of less favored languages face incentives to assimilate; we would expect higher rates of bilingualism among speakers of the less dominant language, whose children would be exposed to the official language in school and need to learn it for advancement. Over time, the maps might start to look more White or more Black, starting from the same 'natural' position before the imposition of borders. We cannot actually return to such a time, any more than we can return to a state of nature or some original position. Instead, we are always in that moment: The linguistic future is being shaped by borders in the present; change them, and language changes too.

REAL PLACES, MADE BY THEIR BORDERS We can see this in the real world, not just imaginary islands. One could draw a border around a very large territory in which Kurdish constitutes the dominant language. This was briefly contemplated after the First World War in the abortive Treaty of Sèvres. Or, as actually happened, one could draw borders carving that same space up among four states, with Kurdish speakers a minority in each.

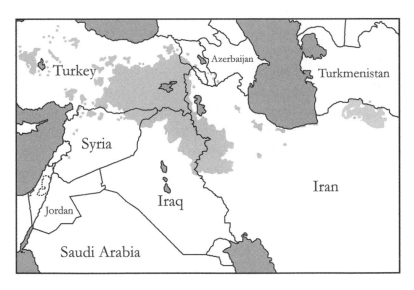

Areas with Kurdish-speaking majority, with international frontiers
(drawn with data from Central Intelligence Agency "Map of Kurdish Speakers," 1986, public domain)

Like all maps, this one obscures more than it reveals. There are speakers of Arabic, Turkish, and Farsi in the areas shaded as Kurdish-speaking—and used to be many Armenians. Many Kurdish speakers live elsewhere. Even so, a glance at the map makes it clear it would be impossible to put all Kurdish speakers in one state without also including many non–Kurdish speakers. It shows how hard it would be to fit the border just right to put as many Kurdish speakers as possible into a Kurdistan while leaving as many Arab, Turkish, and Farsi speakers as possible out.

Still, it should be clear that one *could* sketch a border that would put *most* Kurdish speakers in a majority Kurdish-speaking state, *and* that the borders actually produced after the First World War don't even try to do that. A perfect line isn't possible, but a better one is. From these choices, real consequences follow for language policy, and much besides, as any Kurd could tell you.

We could concoct even more dramatic hypotheticals—not mere border adjustments but wholesale absorptions, radical alterations in our perception of majority and minority, even of state and nation, simply by moving lines. Danish speakers are an overwhelming majority in Denmark, but if the entire country were attached to Germany, Danes would be a small minority—far smaller than Kurds in Turkey. If Denmark had been absorbed into Sweden a few hundred years ago, we could imagine Danish being a dialect of Swedish; after all, some Swedish dialects today are quite close to Danish. With a different line, an officially supported and subsidized language could be a minority language, even a dialect. Its speakers would be entitled to whatever protections they could negotiate, but not more, and human rights would offer them only the most limited support.

Most Danes will be relieved to know that Denmark isn't going to be absorbed into Germany or Sweden—the prohibition on aggression should see to that—but the same logic plays out for groups that didn't win a seat in the historical game of musical chairs that ended in 1945. This matters, because even in a rights-respecting state, it is clearly better to be part of the majority. Kurds might rather live in a state where Kurdish is the official language; Hungarians may get along fine in Serbian, but prefer to run their lives in Hungarian; and Danes definitely don't want to have to learn Swedish or German. The current system has no answer for minority communities except the ameliorative protections of human rights—and of politics within the state they happen to be in. Yet even when these work as planned, they only assure groups secondary status.

Ambazonia: Drawing Minorities into Existence

After the First World War, German Kamerun was divided into British and French mandates. A two-district plebiscite was held in British Cameroons in 1961. The northern district voted for union with Nigeria, while the southern district voted to join Cameroon, the former French mandate. (Independence was not an option.) As a result, the westernmost parts of the Republic of Cameroon have English-speaking populations that feel marginalized. The constitution guarantees a bilingual state (leaving aside Cameroon's enormous indigenous linguistic diversity), but French predominates. Laws are not translated into English, and French-speaking judges are not familiar with the region's common-law traditions. The result has been increasing frustration, protests and boycotts, government crackdowns in response, escalating violence, and calls for secession.* Union may have been the population's choice at the time, and had the region (which separatists call Ambazonia) joined Nigeria, it might have had different problems, but even so, their minority status is literally a function of line-drawing at independence.

*Searcey, "As Cameroon English Speakers Fight."

The dominant model takes a state's demography as given, even though that demography is constructed by the borders we have drawn. With different borders, different majorities and minorities would exist, to which the same liberal principles could be applied, but with very different outcomes favoring one group or the other. Liberalism aims to humanize the behavior of the majority, but it takes as given the majorities we happen to have because of the borders we happen to have drawn. Political philosophers call this the democratic boundary problem.[7]

I have been using the example of language, but all this applies to other aspects of shared life. What day shall we all take off work? Is it reasonable to make women cover their faces—or to prohibit them from doing so? Shall we have a presidential model or a parliamentary one? A secular system or one in which a particular religion plays a public role? And it extends into more-intangible realms of culture: How late is too late to come to a meeting? Is that joke funny or insulting (or blasphemous)? Should I hire my relatives? May I marry them? Some of these examples seem trivial—hardly stuff that should compel us to divide countries willy-nilly. But others go to the heart of what it means to share political space, to be a single people. Decisions about political, administrative, and electoral structures entrench and enhance the demographic dominance of a single group. Turkey has an unusually high threshold for winning seats in parliament—10 percent—which has, until recently, worked quite well to keep Kurdish parties out. Nepal's constitution adopted a combination of provincial boundaries and proportional representation that denies minorities a voice in politics.[8] Ahmadis in Pakistan are excluded from full participation in public life.[9] These are not examples from the most liberal societies, but these and other examples clearly fall within the legitimate bounds of states' discretion.

And, trivial or serious, they describe policy choices deeply patterned by demography shaped by borders. Reasonable or not, they aren't choices minorities would make if they were the majority: Kurds wouldn't adopt policies to keep themselves out of parliament! These are the kinds of choices a majority makes, however; we can expect that.

Even the trivial can become serious when communities don't have a shared understanding of their shared society. As anyone who has ever observed a relationship go slowly wrong will know, things done and said cannot be undone, cannot be unsaid, and the accumulation of small grievances—even for which no one is at fault—can alienate people enough that they cannot, or will not, agree on fundamental things. At such a point, it is difficult to talk about what is reasonable; each sees it his own way. Couples will argue viciously about the smallest things.

And so it is with collectives. It's a trope of journalism to note how much the sides in a conflict have in common, how little truly divides them. (Another equally reductive trope is to talk about primordial hatreds.) Before the war, they shared coffee and celebrated each other's holidays; the differences aren't real, and we are left in dismayed wonderment at how human beings could kill each other over such minutiae. All this is true—including the last part: we are capable of making minute distinctions, and making them matter. To outsiders, the differences between Hutu and Tutsi, Nuer and Dinka, Serb and Croat, Catholic and Protestant seem obscure; inside, those differences can be clear and consequential. It is no reply to say they are socially constructed; that's true, just as it's true people can feel differences in passionate, even fatal ways—not ancient hatreds: current hatreds anciently felt.

Communities share narratives about themselves, about history; they have par-

ticular grievances or points of pride, and these can be in tension with the grievances and the pride of others. Each May, Israeli Jews celebrate Yom Ha'atzmaut,
Independence Day, but Palestinians commemorate Yawm an-Nakba, the Day
of Catastrophe. Stories about the past, about identity, are filters through which
statements about the present and plans for the future are screened, and their reasonableness too.

Communities are not monolithic: Members have complex, plural understandings of their shared community, and each may belong to multiple groups. No
one is just one thing. But this is also true for that community we call the state:
Its members are complex, belong to different groups, with plural identities: No
one is just a citizen. No people is monolithic, or ever could be, and no border
produces a truly uniform community: There is always diversity within. And
that's the point: Different borders create different combinations, which have
consequences for politics. The inevitable internal diversity of any community
can take various forms; it can be trivial or an overwhelming fact.

This does not arise out of disregard for the interests of minorities; in fact,
liberal theory expressly tries to account for this diversity:

> Our exercise of political power is fully proper only when it is exercised in accor-
> dance with a constitution the essentials of which all citizens as free and equal may
> reasonably be expected to endorse in the light of principles and ideals acceptable
> to their common human reason. This is the liberal principle of legitimacy.[10]

The problem is that the constitution, laws, and institutions of societies aren't
negotiated under some veil of ignorance but in particular historical and social
contexts, whose shaping influence reflects the interests of the majority. Even if
the constitution meets some general standard of reasonableness, it will land at
a different place on the spectrum of reasonableness than it might have with different demography: a different state language, a different day of rest, a different
way of being.

Determining what is reasonable—"mak[ing] mutually acceptable to one another their shared institutions and basic arrangements, by citing what are pub-
licly recognized as sufficient reasons"[11]—is a process whose particular outcomes
are determined by demography. Liberal theory might identify a range of possible constitutions, but it cannot determine the particular constitution a society
will settle upon. Principles of public reason assure that no one group's prefer-

ences totally *dominate*, but the majority's do *prevail*, so long as no fundamental liberal principle is at stake. Even those principles will reflect the majority's view of what is reasonable, because reasonableness is in the eye of the holder of power.

The effect is that public reason in a given society will conform to the perspective of the dominant community. The expectation that even a highly pluralistic society must share a single public reason is a demanding standard, and particularly difficult if its pluralism is geographically distributed, as when there is a territorially concentrated minority. People's proximity to each other matters in deciding about public reasonableness. We can recall our island maps and intuitively understand that some configurations will produce different politics; dispersed communities will be treated quite differently from compact ones. Suppose we added a third language group constituting 3 percent of the population; what policy should the state adopt? The answer might depend on their distribution: If spread uniformly around, they might get no rights; if concentrated, they might get local rights, such as signs in their language. Either is reasonable, either possible under existing international law. Each relies on the fiction that there is a single public reason; but as a local majority becomes larger—when there are whole provinces in which no one speaks the state language—that fiction comes under greater strain.

Every attempt to identify a reasonable basis for a community's decisions—to identify the scope of its public reason—will be shaped by that community's demography, which is a function of the state's shape. What groups are included, in what proportions? Are they central or marginal? Borders shape the community and its policies: Which social, cultural, and economic practices will be favored, subsidized, and supported, and which merely tolerated, marginalized, even suppressed? Robust versions of liberalism prescribe limits to what is reasonable but ultimately offer no guide to the answers a *particular* community will reach. We accept the state as it is, with the people it already has.

CHOOSING A SPHERE TO SHAPE THE PUBLIC: DELIBERATION AND AUTHORITY Nor is this just a function of 'original ignorance.' Even if we focus on *how* to govern difference, we find a similar empty space. Democracy isn't just about tabulating votes, but informed, authentic deliberation. That implies some equal power within the system, so that rational discourse rather than wealth or position determines outcomes. All citizens should have access to the space in which public opinion forms: Status distinctions should be disregarded so the public sphere is inclusive.[12]

Yet, just as with public reason, the contours of the rational and authentic are not neutral but patterned by social expectations, position, and privilege. Deliberation has a shape responding to society's contours, and if consensus proves impossible, a majority can decide: Deliberation is process, not end point. The incentives such norms create are obvious. A supposedly universal public sphere in fact excludes marginalized groups—women, the poor and unpropertied, minorities—some of which could form their own "subaltern counterpublics."[13] Even included groups have to bracket their differences in ways that favor the dominant group's perspectives. We might recall how we reasonably deny small languages equal status, but bracketing also involves concepts, values, and cultural preferences. Some marginalizations reflect broader patterns of dominance common across societies (such as gender) but some—especially of linguistic, religious, or national communities—are almost entirely a function of existing frontiers, within which dominant groups can exclude others by acting reasonably.

Similarly, the need to coordinate among plural communities makes it necessary to have some common authority: a liberal state.[14] But this increases the importance of real access to state power: A minority may not win the contest and find its alternatives consistently voted (or shouted) down. Relying on a common authority proves no better than public reason or the public sphere in ensuring that minority views are heard and preferred: A leader devoted to the common good is better than an extractive dictator; but if that leader isn't you, it can still be unpleasant to have someone else's authority applied to you, even for your own good.

Each of these philosophical approaches shares a common, curious blind spot: the state. Despite intently focusing on governance *of* the state, they are strangely unable to get *outside* it, to develop arguments that do not take the states we have as the default: "classic liberalism never really theorized the distinction of the world into separate *territorial* political communities at all."[15] The liberal tradition generates powerful claims about how states and the societies within them ought to behave, but is unable to explain why *these* states ought to be the ones behaving.

Although post–Cold War liberal theory has been much hollowed out, it still exhibits a Potemkin-esque triumphalism. And the more that theory identifies nonnegotiable, irreducibly reasonable practices—like thick rule of law and fundamental rights—the more it demands homogeneity both *among* and *within* states. The result, curiously, is increasing disconnection between the states we happen to have and the justification for them—an inability to explain why we have exactly *these* states. Here we see the ethical and emotional hollowness of *Verfassungspatriotismus*—constitutional patriotism. Enmeshed in a web of liberal desiderata, a modern constitution has a hard time expressing aspects of culture or identity that would justify *its* community. We can see this in the call in postconflict situations to create states 'for all their citizens'—an anodyne formulation that begs the question of why *these* human ought to share citizenship. No true particularism is possible, with the (un)surprising result that it is hard to come up with reasons to commit to *this* state as opposed to some other. In a liberal world, all constitutions would be much the same—but then what's the point of different states?

Yet it is precisely this aspiration for democratic, liberal constitutionalism—and the universalist echoes hanging about it—that makes national identity paradoxically more relevant. If all states were liberal and rights-protecting, why not have a state including, say, northeastern France and western Germany? Shall we include parts of the Netherlands, since the Rhine (Rhein, le Rhin, Rijn) flows through them all? Why not append Quebec to the eastern United States, since this would create a more efficient market for hydropower, and what could be more important than that? Why not merge landlocked Armenia into Turkey, to give it access to the sea? Surely the Armenians would be grateful!

THERE IS NOTHING WRONG WITH CREATING A NEW MAJORITY We have good answers for why we shouldn't do these things, even without embracing crude nationalism or Herderian metaphysics about the mystic continuity of *Sprache* and *Volk*. The answers have to do with administrative efficiency and practicality: It simply makes sense not to configure states that way, since it would raise unnecessary social difficulties. If we inquire into the source of those difficulties, we find different identities and preferences—not primordial emanations, but practical problems of lived politics. Some territorial configurations make more sense *because of* identity. France is an administrative convenience for the great majority of its citizens who—whatever other identities they have—consider themselves culturally French. France is also convenient for Spaniards,

Andorrans, Belgians, Luxembourgers, Germans, Swiss, Italians, Monégasques, British, Surinamese, and Brazilians (bordering French Guinea, an overseas department and region)—all neighbors not compelled to compete with Frenchmen in a single unit.

It seems like a truism, but that's the point: Even liberal, cosmopolitan people do many things that are nationally inflected. There are no humans without a culture; there is no *particular instance* of public reason not marked by a context. Pretending otherwise simply masks the normalization of some group's hegemony: "the apparently 'neutral' stance of indifference towards ethnic identity, of reducing all members of a state to mere abstract citizens, in fact favours the largest ethnic group."[16]

When groups within a state dominated by another group say they would like to opt out, they are not necessarily disagreeing with liberal values. When they frame their dissatisfaction as nationalism, they may be out of step with contemporary rhetoric, but not with the basic contours of the contemporary, democratic state, in which dominance is demographic. They are simply saying they *too* would like the benefits that come with being a majority. So long as they apply the same liberal principles, their claims can be understood as a wish simply to have the same thing we already divide the world into: states.

So, what's wrong with a secession that produces a new majority? Nothing: A new border creates a new demographic dominance no more problematic than the existing demography that current borders create. That new bordered demography is equally amenable to the demands of liberal reasonableness and equally capable of acting as a community whose democratic approval legitimates the state's authority over that particular people and their territory.[17] This new majority will have qualities, but *every* unit creates a demography. Indeed, if we are concerned about dominance of one group by another, then on utilitarian grounds new borders that subject *fewer* people to unwelcome dominance should seem attractive. By definition, democratic secession achieves that.

Purposive Change in Demography and Discriminatory Intent

But is it perhaps a problem if that dominance is *purposive*—if a group establishes a new state in order to dominate others? States aren't supposed to exist solely to validate the main group's power. Many have names suggesting their origins in an ethnic community—Deutschland, Türkiye, Muang Lao, Prathet

Thai—but that doesn't mean they only benefit one group and disadvantage others.[18] We might reasonably worry about new states doing that. You know what they say about two wrongs: Today's states may have troubling origins, but we cannot go back in time, and that doesn't mean we should support another round of wrongdoing.

So even though the new rule operates neutrally, we can expect ethnic groups will use it to their advantage to create new units they can dominate. Is this something we should accept? The answer depends, but not in a way that should make us question the rule itself. Unless there is some objection to change as such, it is hard to see why any given group should not aspire to political dominance of the type that normally occurs in any state—why they should have to accept being a permanent political minority. So is there any objection to the act itself—to peaceful change that aims to create a new dominant group—or even to change in borders as such?

Assuming that the status quo is morally superior is a dubious proposition, but in any case the status quo does not maintain itself automatically in a cost-free way; it often takes coercion and violence. States enforce criminal penalties for separatism, and forbid or limit political advocacy for it; they shape the educational and social environment to discourage it. And, as we have seen, the violence accompanying secession is often attributable to the state's resistance, not the attempt. All this maintains a particular demographic dominance within existing borders.

Objecting that a separatist group wishes to become dominant—to be a majority rather than a minority—ignores the reality that maintaining existing states simply favors other groups in this contest, without providing any justification apart from status quo for why those groups ought to be privileged. In a world in which, in the normal course of things, there are majorities and minorities, why would it be immoral for any group to aspire to majority status, if it can do so peaceably and with respect for the rights of others? This a secessionist group can surely do.

Certainly the *manner* in which change occurs can be relevant. We should not normally approve violent change or change that produces invidious discrimination, but by this same logic we should not approve violent or discriminatory *maintenance* of the status quo, either. Nothing prevents a new state from applying the full range of liberal protections, and nothing prevents us from insisting on specific, substantive commitments as the price of recognizing their independence. Existing states are supposed to apply them, after all, and the new state would be just another state. (Actually, this would hold new states to a higher standard, but there is precedent for this. The EU issued guidelines for recognizing new states in the former Soviet Union and Yugoslavia that required them to adhere to rights treaties, and insisted applicants for membership join treaties existing member states didn't have to.)[19]

We might object if the intent were to discriminate as such—to actively harm some other group. But political dominance isn't a harm of that kind. Wishing to enjoy the benefits of being the majority in a liberal, democratic polity is different from wishing to harm others. The normal operations of states themselves produce benefits for the majority that any group could desire. If a group can capture those benefits by legitimate means—through political organization, elections, natural shifts in demography, or changes in the shape of the state—there can be no objection.

Determining the People That Determines Itself

Even if there's nothing objectionable to a people imagined this way, how are we to know who the people is? Historically, a key objection to secession has been the impossibility of identifying the self-determining unit; it "begs the question of who is the 'political self' that has the right to determine whether or not the historical nation—even if composed of several peoples—will be broken up and secession allowed. . . . There is no self-evident answer to this question."[20] But often the group's identity is clear, or there's a preexisting territory; even in more-fluid situations, humans are quite good at asserting identities and selecting authorities to represent them.

Often it is easy to identify the political self, because a unit already exists. A federal unit or autonomous territory can act as focal point, doing much of the work a state does in identity formation. This is true for Quebec, Scotland, Kosovo, and also Catalonia and Tibet; in each, a unit already exists inside the state's constitutional architecture, reinforcing and promoting political identity.[21] When the parent state or others actors agree to consider a unit relevant—as Canada and the United Kingdom did, and as many states have for Kosovo—a self-determining people can be identified with that unit's population.

Units can create peoples that had no shared identity beforehand. This is the logic of 'imagined communities,' formed within bordered territories that create bureaucratic, economic, and social circuits, share information, and invoke the imaginative power of maps.[22] It would have been meaningless to speak of 'Indonesians' before the Dutch united the archipelago; Indonesians are a product of Dutch colonialism, Andersonian imagination, and the idiot rule of postwar self-determination. And not only in the postcolonial space: In the heartland of the national state, the same logic is embedded in Massimo d'Azeglio's lapidary utterance, "*L'Italia è fatta. Restano da fare gli italiani*": "We have made Italy. Now we must make Italians."[23]

Sometimes the causality runs the other way: The construction of the people occurs first. Often a unit is created to accommodate an existing "social and demographic reality[,]"[24] which means it was possible to approximate the community's contours *before* a fixed boundary defined it. Wilson called for a restored Poland because he believed Poles already existed. The causal sequence is unimportant: Political communities are social constructions; the point is simply that they can and do come into being in ways that the members themselves— and the rest of us—can readily recognize.

There will never be a perfect match between unit and people, often not even a very good one. Some inside will not identify with the group; others who do won't be inside. Having a unit can even work at cross-purposes to separatists' aspirations, since pro-independence sentiment may not be evenly spread across the territory. In three recent efforts at democratic secession involving a preexisting unit, large populations unsympathetic to secession were unavoidably included. English-speaking parts of Quebec and its Cree-populated north opposed secession; in Scotland, the Orkneys and Shetlands strongly opposed secession; and in Catalonia, independence sentiment is stronger in the north than in Barcelona, with its larger Spanish-speaking and immigrant populations.

Group members can also be excluded by existing boundaries. Catalan speakers also live in Valencia, eastern Aragon, southern France, Andorra, and the Balearic Islands; Tibetans don't only live in the Tibet Autonomous Region. Secessionists face a choice: Pursue unity for the whole group or take advantage of the unit and leave some behind. States sometimes draw subunits in order to divide ethnic or national communities; the complex Soviet borders in the Fergana Valley are an example.

The point is that preexisting units can provide a source of legitimation not based solely on ethnicity. Thus, in Catalonia, a robust secession movement focuses on the existing province, marginalizing calls for a linguistic Greater Catalan state. The new rule would allow Catalans to pursue a broader claim, but does not require it, since it does not require any link to ethnicity; if Catalans see advantage in relying on an existing unit to legitimate a claim, nothing prevents that.

Existing units can solve much of the supposed problem of identifying a self-determining people. But even without a unit, the question isn't so difficult to answer. Political communities constitute themselves in many ways, often quite quickly, and there's no reason why a people can't. Individuals in diverse circumstances form associations to take part in governance. Parties, trade unions and civil society organizations form spontaneously and interact with official authority; effective organizations even form in the face of state opposition, as the Solidarity trade union did in Poland. Within months of the collapse of the Iron Curtain, political parties sprang up—new parties, parties suppressed decades earlier, rebranded Communist parties. Insurgents can acquire considerable authority and prestige, even becoming recognized interlocutors with the state. Groups purporting to represent a self-determining people commonly appear, as well, and can have considerable internal and international legitimacy, such as the Palestinian Liberation Organization, the Tamil Tigers, Ibrahim Rugova's Democratic League of Kosovo, and many others.

There are real questions about representation and inclusion when some individual or institution claims to speak for a people. Leaders sometimes maintain authority through coercion and violence, or claim legitimacy they don't possess. But these questions do not change the core point: Locally legitimated authority is possible and can be recognized. The claim that some community is a self-determining people can plausibly be made by actors speaking on behalf of that community, and their legitimacy comes from acknowledgment by the community itself. The best answer to the objection about identifying a people is an Alexandrian one, cutting the Gordian knot of proof: The self that determines, determines itself. The new rule provides a mechanism for testing claimants' bona fides: a plebiscite.

Besides, it is unsatisfying to say, simply because there is no self-evident answer to how to identify a self-determining people, that we should prefer whatever communities happen to be lying about beneath the angel's wings in the detritus of history. Are there not also real questions about authority, representation, and inclusion when one assumes that a *state* speaks for its people? Don't many states—how did I just put it?—"maintain authority through coercion and violence, or claim legitimacy they don't possess"? The objection is unsatisfactory because its implication—the apotheosis of the status quo—treats the existing distribution as a moral given, and perpetuates unsatisfying conditions for large numbers of structural minorities.[25] Those conditions require their own justification.

Far from being retrograde, the new rule's definition of a people is fit to contemporary sensibilities: sensitive to identity, respectful of subjectivity, but suspicious of immanent truths. Its identities are politically potent: Arising from the perspectives of those who assert them, rather than being imposed, they are imbued with agency. But not static: They are fluid, dynamic, malleable. The idea that a people defines itself—constitutes itself, with no referent outside the self-creating act—is both unsettling and fully consistent with liberal understandings of how humans are and act in their shared world. This is not the nationalism of our forefathers, not of Wilson, but a thoroughly postmodern—let us say, postclassical—understanding of identity fit for that still-unavoidable unit of political organization, the state.

A Territorial Definition of State, People, and Democracy

A people defines itself, but it does not define itself anywhere it pleases. The new rule requires a people to be a majority in some place. A people is, therefore, a territorial concept, just like the state. It is possible to imagine nonterritorial polities—they were once quite common[26]—but they are rare in the modern world, and there are compelling (if not necessarily good) reasons for this. The territorial state is a highly effective technology for mobilizing resources, and it usually wins political or military competitions with differently organized communities, in the way men with assault rifles usually kill men with spears.

The rise of global governance notwithstanding, there is little reason to believe territorial states will disappear, so it is imperative to structure the ones we have rightly. The new rule follows that logic, making it easier to create new states that are otherwise like existing ones. In a sense, of course, the rule does create a different kind of state—or conceives of all states in a different way. Its conceptual innovation is to invert the postwar logic of how population and territory relate. Under the current rule, a unit exists, and those in it are a people. Under the new rule, a people has a relationship to some place, which provides the justification for creating a unit there. So groups must vindicate their claim by prevailing in a vote by the whole population of a defined territory; thus, by the very act of making their claim, the new community's potential sovereignty claim is territorially delimited.

So territory is central to the new rule. Members of self-determining communities need not share any intrinsic qualities, but they do have to share a place. Proximity is central both to the operation of the rule and its justification. Proximity underpins the democratic foundations of the rule and justifies the group's claim to form a new state, since the self-determining community constitutes a numerical majority on some territory. We must consider two closely related questions here:

- Why should territorial proximity matter in forming a self-determining people?
- Why should a local majority matter more than the majority in the entire state? Why should a minority trump a majority?

Proximity's Priority: The Right to Secession as a Right of Place

Many of the features of our "information age" make us resemble the most primitive of social and political forms: the hunting and gathering society. As nomadic peoples, hunters and gatherers have no loyal relationship to territory. They, too, have little "sense of place." . . . The lack of boundaries both in hunting and gathering and in electronic societies leads to many striking parallels. Of all known social types before our own, hunting and gathering societies have tended to be the most egalitarian.

Joshua Meyrowitz[27]

This view, which the German philosopher Jürgen Habermas cites with approval (even if calling it "somewhat overblown"[28]) seems romantically detached from reality. Many nomads travel precise circuits that suggest a close relationship to place and are acutely more attentive to the physical world than 'less primitive' moderns. The idea that the Information Age has made 'us' resemble hunter-gatherers seems more precious than plausible; the differences are profound, the parallels superficial. Telecommuting from Starbucks and having Gold Status in the Star Alliance don't constitute the life nomadic.

Still, whatever the dubious value of this description, it is useful for suggesting something obvious: Our forms of political organization are not immutable. The territorial, bureaucratic state is not inevitable but is a function of material conditions, technologies, and ideology. It is itself a technology and an ideology— and when those conditions change, the state will, too. Not so much that we are likely to adopt the mores of the Kalahari !Kung, but it will change nonetheless. This raises a question: If the *current* rule is problematically premised on territory, why focus the new rule on territory, too?

WHY PROXIMITY MATTERS FOR MAKING A PEOPLE

> *It is long past the time when ethnic kinship could form the foundation for homogeneous communities. Territorial proximity is now an inescapable basis for political community.*
>
>   Donald Horowitz[29]

Self-determination is a territorial principle, but not the way the classical rule is, in which first we draw the territory and then look who's inside. Instead, it is territorial in a more open-textured way, recognizing that people live in places that matter in particular ways to them more than to others. Proximity makes community—and communities make claims that deserve political priority.

Other things can make community too, but contingently, whereas proximity always is relevant. There is an irreducibly physical aspect to politics, which at its heart is about governing people in relation to each other and to resources. Human beings are biological beings, existing in physical space, with persistent, even immediate physical needs: food, water, security, warmth, air. Restrict the supply of any—go a week without eating, a day without drinking; see a stranger unexpectedly brandish a large knife; step outside naked in winter; let someone thrust your head underwater—and you will quickly discover how intimately, intensely physical even the most transnational, networked individual actually is: how much we are all citizens, not of the world, but of our bodies.

However enthusiastic one might be about cyberspace, it is difficult to actually live there; even the most intrepid netizen finds that a supply of junk food and access to the facilities eventually matter. "Difficult" actually understates the matter: *Nobody* lives there. Instead, everyone lives here, on earth. And, as it happens, in particular places: our physicality is typically linked to specific locations with which we become intimately familiar in ways we are not with other places. We are marked, socially, by the fact and effects of proximity. People live in places, and this has consequences for our politics.

People also move. In the past, people went on foot, horseback, or ships, yet that didn't prevent them moving vast distances or setting up complex trade networks spanning thousands of miles. History's largest land empire was governed on horseback—a fact we do well to remember when we suppose modern technologies fundamentally alter the deepest patterns of human experience. We are a traveling species as well as a sedentary one, and always have been. But few populations *only* travel, and most are quite sedentary. Human beings travel and then come home to where they live.

This is true even under the supposedly novel, disruptive conditions of globalization. Most people lead lives centered in a particular place. (Do you know what percentage of people lives in a country other than that of their birth?)[30] Even the most cosmopolitan among us have a limited number of places of relevance to our personal, social, economic, and political lives. The idea of transnational citizenship projects an image with little relationship to the lived experience of most humans.

A Typical Global Citizen in His Habitat: I'll use myself as an example. Someone reading this book might wonder if I qualify as a cosmopolitan given my obsession with borders and states, but I have lived in a half dozen countries, visited 60, and often travel internationally; this puts me toward one end of the spectrum of human peripateticism. If there were such a thing as global citizenship, I'd probably qualify.

But visiting 60 countries means I have *never* visited 135—nowhere in South America or Australia, never China, India, or most of Africa—and some of those 60 were short jaunts twenty-five years ago, now hazy memories. These days I am part of the 97 percent, living in the land of my birth. I can tell a similar story inside my country. I've visited most US states but mostly lived in three towns: six years in Boston, twelve years and counting in Bloomington, Indiana, and the first, formative twenty years in Los Angeles. I still have family there, a few things squirreled away at my mother's house. I kept a California driver's license for twenty more years after I left (until Indiana made me surrender it), and still remember the number: C3001816. But that's it. I've barely visited most states: three days in Texas, never Alaska. We might ask what my relationship to those places is or ought to be. In answering, we'll see that political relationships get created in two ways: through proximity and the abstraction of the state.

Let's start with my relationship to foreign countries; say, Norway. I have been there several times, traveled the length of the country—nearly to Nordkapp— and once lived in Oslo for three months, looking illegally and unsuccessfully for a job. I speak Swedish (proximity again, since I lived there for a year), so I understand Norwegian; the last time I was there, I used a bastardized mix of Norwegian and Swedish. I have real, personal links to Norway. But I don't have a *political* and *legal* relationship to Norway or Norwegians. I have no right to live there, or even visit, except at the sufferance of the Norwegian state. If I do go, I am subject to Norwegian law; I am protected by international human rights, but that is about it. My relationship to Norway is the same as it is to 193 other countries that aren't the United States.

What about Alaska? As an American citizen, I have a perfect right to go there; I could move tomorrow, get a job, draw benefits. I share a legal and po- litical space with Alaskans: We live under the same constitution; the federal officials for whom I vote make laws for me and Alaskans, and the ones they vote for do, too. Many things there would be familiar: language, goods and services, culture. But I have never been. The connections I share with Alaskans are en- tirely a function of the United States' existence—of a shared political, admin- istrative, legal, and economic space. I have no personal relationship to that distant place. We share citizenship, and a shared culture has developed *because of* that citizenship.

As for Indiana: I have connections for both reasons—proximity and the state. All the connections to Alaska were true for Indiana the day before I arrived; but in the last decade, I have developed personal links to the place and its people. I own a house; my children go to school; I work at a university—a state em- ployee. I live here. I vote in Indiana: It would hardly be fair if I couldn't, since I'm a citizen and what happens here affects me. These relationships arise out of lived experience and a political construct. One part arises out of immediate in- teractions, the other out of abstract, formal, legal relationships. But we should not call one natural and the other artificial: Both are social, constructed, and, as Aristotle reminds us, political; both are interactions human beings engage in by their nature.

The Shared Politics of Place: This is how one Hong Kong independence ac- tivist expressed his alienation from China:

Hong Kong is a place, and China is a country.[31]

States can create relationships that are often abstract, but proximity can create commonalities that arise because of the shared material conditions in which humans find themselves. You probably check the weather where you live, and would certainly be interested if someone was murdered on your block. If an infectious disease struck where you live, you'd be concerned in a different way than if you read about people dying halfway around the world.

This doesn't mean people in proximity necessarily share values: Proximity can breed conflict—after all, it's hard to fight with people to whom you have *no* connection! Proximity creates cooperation or contestation, or both, but does create them; it summons forth communities—functional or feuding—of necessity. Proximity creates the need for human beings to relate to each other in and about their shared space. Other forms of association *can* do that, but proximity does it in ways that relate to our irreducible physicality, the fact that we are biological beings present in particular places. Other processes can modify the effects of proximity: Social distinctions can produce such nuanced layering that people in the same place have almost no interaction; in segregated societies, one group may ride public buses, another cruise in SUVs, and they will view the politics of their shared space quite differently. But they still will be related, if only in their efforts to construct parallel systems: Gated communities don't overcome proximity, they confirm its salience. There is no escaping certain shared experiences; when it rains, it rains on everyone, even if some shelter under bridges and others beneath their chauffeurs' umbrellas. Nor can conflict be avoided when it comes: It was a half day's walk from the slums of Paris to the gates of Versailles, and as Louis XVI learned, on the day the downtrodden had had enough of not having enough, proximity mattered a great deal.

Whatever other communities technology and ideology may encourage, we will always need to organize ourselves in physical space, so proximity will always matter. That is the bare minimum: The social and cultural qualities of community reinforce the imperative of proximity in much thicker ways. We've seen this with language, but it's equally true for religious observance, folkways, and the like: Some religion's processions will get right of way, its bells or muezzins accorded priority, its day of rest respected, its laws made The Law. Or not, if there is an ethic of tolerance—but even that is a social practice whose very purpose is to accommodate differences in jostling proximity in a common order. There is no escaping the need to regulate the physical aspect of our shared existence.

The effects of proximity extend beyond the practical. Kant promotes a universal ethical ideal, but Adam Smith gives us a more realistic portrait of how moral relationships are mediated by proximity: "If [a man would] lose his little finger tomorrow, he would not sleep tonight; but, provided he never saw them, he will snore with the most profound security over the ruin of a hundred millions of his brethren[.]"[32] We may regret this, but it's every bit as true as in Smith's day: Proximity matters in ordering morality. Political community naturally forms in relation to local circumstances—with good reason:

> [H]umans cluster together in particular areas; endemic and entangled disputes are likely to arise in these areas. For reasons of efficiency, reasons of integrity, and reasons of justice, it is important that these thickets of disputes be addressed by a political community taking responsibility for the administration of the centralized array of legal arrangements we call a state.[33]

Citizenship in the Global Order: Proximity's priority informs the existing system's norms of citizenship, although this is poorly recognized. There is a famous case in international law, *Nottebohm (Liechtenstein v. Guatemala)*, which describes citizenship norms. States can grant citizenship to whomever they please, but in this case, the question was whether *other* states have to recognize that grant. The answer suggests the relationship between person and state is rooted in a contingent logic of place.

Nottebohm, a German national resident in Guatemala, hastily acquired citizenship in Liechtenstein early in the Second World War to avoid expropriation as an 'enemy national'—unsuccessfully, because after the war he brought a claim to recover his property. The case ended up at the International Court of Justice. The ICJ found that, although Liechtenstein considered Nottebohm a citizen, Guatemala wasn't obliged to recognize that relationship, because Nottebohm's links to Liechtenstein were so tenuous. It's the court's reasoning that's interesting: States have to recognize citizenship based on a "genuine and effective link" determined by the "habitual residence of the individual concerned but also the centre of interests, his family ties, his participation in family life, attachment shown by him for a given country and inculcated in his children, etc."[34] The essential link between individual and state depends not on formal ties or presence within arbitrary borders but on shared values or identity.

Although still the basis of international law on citizenship, *Nottebohm* is shockingly out of sync with contemporary mores, since it suggests *political community* is grounded on *national* or *ethnic* identity. We needn't go so far, but something other than the incident of birth actually underpins our belief that people ought to share political community. As a matter of convenience, we assign citizenship based on formal categories, but the logic behind citizenship has to do with real connections. If we read *Nottebohm* backward, we arrive at an intriguing possibility. *Inside* the state, there are different relationships between different parts of the population. All citizens share an abstract relationship to the state, but their relationships vary, just as my relationship to Americans in Indiana is quite different from my relationship to Americans in Alaska. Perhaps those differences matter, or should, when the state changes.

> But submitting to the laws of any country, living quietly and enjoying priv-
> ileges and protection under them, makes not a man a member of that soci-
> ety; it is only a local protection and homage due to and from all those who,
> not being in a state of war, come within the territories belonging to any
> government, to all parts whereof the force of its law extends.
>
> John Locke[35]

Citizenship and Place: What Happens to the People When the State Ends: We can see how those different relationships matter in the rules that govern states when they break up. Because it turns out that even in the current system, place matters at the moment a state divides.

One of the seemingly strongest objections to secession is the effect it has on citizenship and rights. Normally people acquire citizenship one of two ways, both related to territory. Under the *jus soli* principle, you acquire citizenship by birth in a state's territory. You are born in a place that belongs to a state, so you have that state's citizenship. People also acquire citizenship through descent— the principle of *jus sanguinis*. Even then, the parents typically have or had some physical relationship to the state, and many states revoke citizenship for people who have never lived in the state or permanently reside elsewhere; a continuing relationship mediated through physical presence matters.[36]

Modern citizenship is usually a general category, the same for all possessing it. Citizens can move about the state, living and working in different places, making new connections, all under the overarching, abstract umbrella of shared citizenship. And this is why secession is seen as a challenge, because it breaks a legal people in two. The harm seems especially onerous for those forced to change citizenship against their will, but it affects the whole population: Shared citizenship is shattered, and with it the benefits citizens enjoyed in common. This can be traumatic—it is harmful in that sense—but is there a human right not to be deprived of citizenship?

There are legal obligations to avoid statelessness, but people don't have an absolute right to their existing relationship to a particular state. States actually can swap land and people—the Statelessness Convention clearly contemplates transfer of populated territory:

> Every treaty . . . providing for the transfer of territory shall include provisions de-signed to secure that no person shall become stateless as a result. . . . [A] Contract-ing State to which territory is transferred or which otherwise acquires territory shall confer its nationality on such persons as would otherwise become stateless.[37]

This would make no sense if transfers of populated territory were illegal. (The text refers to treaties, not secessions, but there is little reason to treat them dif-ferently, and secessions often include treaties.)

When states divide, dissolve, or change their borders, they also divide their citizenry. (Technically, in dissolution, the entire population acquires new citi-zenships, whereas when part of a state secedes, the population of the continua-tor state maintains its citizenship. Either way, one people is divided.) This has happened with all the post–Cold War cases, each of which assigned citizenship based on individuals' primary ties of descent or geography. In most cases, in-ternal boundaries determined the assignment: Former Soviet citizens generally acquired the nationality of the republic in which they were resident or regis-tered; they didn't retain some general citizenship applicable in all fifteen states, and most didn't get to choose.[38] Even when entirely novel frontiers have been drawn—as after the First World War—citizenship has followed this principle.

Some scholars argue that a customary 'right of option' has developed, such that a "transferring state must allow its citizens to choose between retaining their citizenship and/or choosing to move to territory remaining under the sover-eignty of the state, in order to keep the social rights they previously enjoyed."[39] The Venice Commission recommends that "when the predecessor State contin-ues to exist, the successor State(s) shall grant the right of option in favour of the nationality of the predecessor State."[40] This view, while humane and sensible, is almost universally ignored. When states divide, individuals generally get the citizenship of the unit to which they have the strongest links, and in the overwhelming majority of cases "lose the nationality of the predecessor State and become ipso facto nationals of the successor State."[41] There are *no* instances in the postwar era of a dividing state's entire population choosing which citizenship they would prefer.

This has real consequences. Division prevents citizens from doing things they used to do as a matter of right, like move about to take a job. Yet in *no* case have these restrictions been a reason to reject the division of a country or condemn it as a violation of human rights. On the contrary, divided citizenship is the presumption: The International Law Commission recommends that "persons . . . having their habitual residence in the territory affected by the succession of States are presumed to acquire the nationality of the successor State on the date of such succession[.]"[42] Residence in a particular place—not citizenship or residence anywhere in the state—is decisive.

In none of these cases has reassignment been subject to approval by the affected population or the population left behind.[43] This is true whether a state divides voluntarily or a part secedes, as Kosovo did (Serbs from Belgrade don't have citizenship in Kosovo, as far as Pristina is concerned). Division reassigns sovereignty over territory *and* people, whose citizenship follows the land they live on. Affected individuals cannot be left stateless, but so long as they are assigned to a new sovereign, there's no objection in law or practice. People simply do not get to choose.

And there is a logic behind this, which shows, as if in a photographic negative, the influence of proximity. When things run normally, citizenship functions like an abstract relationship among all citizens, but that relationship is mediated through place: Citizenship depends not simply on a relationship to a state, but to a place that *happens to be* in a state. If the place to which one is affiliated no longer is part of the state's territory, the relationship changes. We then ask difficult but logical questions about affiliations that have to do with relationship to place. That is not the *proposed* rule; it's how we treat citizenship *today*—the logic of *Nottebohm*. It's not a pretty process, but it's how we respond when states divide. For all our rhetorical commitment to citizenship as something mystically indivisible, it depends upon a deeper relationship to place. Proximity and identity already play a determinative role in the construction of citizenship; the new rule merely makes that logic visible. Requiring a connection to territory "is not to revert to forms of feudalism but to recognize a human and political reality, which underlies modern territorial settlements[.]"[44]

Focusing on the territorial aspects of human experience may seem disappointingly (or refreshingly!) retrograde. Yet the popular notion that we live in a globally connected village is, in many respects, simply an extension of this logic. We have technologies that let us trade more intensively with distant places and watch events there in real time, and therefore, just as Adam Smith supposed, those places matter more; it is simply a more complicated social geography. Globalization supplements but does not supplant the logic of physical proximity. As with those notional nomads of the Information Age, technology binds us into new relationships but doesn't replace the persistent, insistent intensity of the proximate. We trade and travel, *and* still need to govern ourselves in the places we live.

People live in places; they have particular locations, circuits, associations that matter much more to them than others—a commonsensical observation that actually has effects when we make new states. But why actually embrace that, as the new rule would? After all, each state is already a self-determining people, so why would we allow a part of that people to take a different path—even against the majority's will? Why *should* we? That is our next question. The answer, as we'll see, is that proximity is not only a fact; it has a normative logic, too.

WHY SHOULD A LOCAL MAJORITY TRUMP THE LARGER MAJORITY? We saw that communities form around interests and identities that proximity creates. And we saw that there is no reason to privilege one majority over another—no reason to let the historical incident of where borders formed determine where borders should be. But if we are skeptical of majorities, why privilege the *minority?* Even if we call it a 'local majority,' why should it have priority over the whole? Recognizing that these categories are functions of borders may undermine the majority's claim to deference, but how does it support the minority's claim? It would seem to leave us with no way to prefer either.

This is a collision of models. Recent secessions would have gone differently if the question had been put to the whole population. Independence declarations in Slovenia, Croatia, Macedonia, and Bosnia would have failed in a Yugoslavia-wide vote. Montenegro, which voted 55 percent for independence, was just 6 percent of the population of the State Union of Serbia and Montenegro. Even overwhelming votes would fail if put to the entire population: Over 78 percent of East Timor's voters chose independence, but its voters were less than 1 percent of Indonesia's population; South Sudan, where the independence vote was over 98 percent, was under one-third of Sudan's population. Submitting secession to the whole state practically guarantees its failure. The problem is even larger, since a secessionist 'local majority' shares space with a 'local minority'— which is really part of the *state's* majority—that doesn't wish to leave. The new rule compels them to accept a new state. How can that be right?

The answer lies in the normative implications of proximity. People living in a place have a different relationship to it than other citizens. We saw that when states cede territory, the whole population is affected, but those actually living there are affected in a special way. For this reason people living there are sometimes given a special say in the decision, even a veto, as in the French constitution. (International law doesn't actually require this.) We care about the directly affected group's preferences in a different way than we do about those of the general population, because of their relationship to place. That same logic applies to a secession: It specially affects some people differently.

Many states describe themselves as indissoluble, with an indivisible people. Assuming the moral priority of a unitary people is plausible for governing a shared community—the Kantian view that, in "ordinary moments," so long as a state is minimally decent and respectful of people's fundamental rights, "we ought to see its laws as making moral demands on its subjects."[45] But it is not a useful framework for evaluating claims that *challenge the existence* of the community. Then the question is not simply one of decent governance, but identification with the relevant unit.[46] By seceding, a minority compels a significant change in the state's future. That is only undemocratic if we accept a priori the validity of the whole population as a *demos,* which is precisely the thing at issue.

People live in places and have a special relationship to those places. They also have a relationship to the broader community, which we call citizenship, because the place to which they have a relationship is part of a state. But when that changes—when the union of those places is the very thing at issue—then people have a natural priority in deciding about the governance of the places where they actually live. That priority is submerged within the larger unit for everyday governance, but it necessarily and properly reasserts itself whenever the question arises: Shall this community continue to be?

This priority arises because there is a difference between ruling oneself and ruling others. Secession alters the whole community's circumstances, which is an imposition, but the result is that more individuals rule themselves, in communities reflecting their preferences. The secession of, say, Oregon would affect all Americans, who might no longer be able to travel or move there, and whose taxes might be collected and spent differently. But people in Oregon would be much *more* affected than people in Vermont, who may share nothing with them other than citizenship. Some Americans would be affected more than others: People with links to Oregon—family, business, plans to visit Portland— would be specially affected. People in southern Washington would suddenly live on an international frontier; perhaps those connections should matter in the calculation: Here, as in all rules, there is an element of line drawing. But for all, the basic principle applies: Claiming a right to leave is different than demanding that others stay. If Oregonians sincerely wanted to go, why would we interpret that as an imposition *on* other Americans, rather than a desire to escape imposition *by* other Americans?[47]

This local priority is limited: It applies only to questions about the state's existence, not its governance. Treating the state as a given makes sense for deciding what tax rates should be, which side of the road to drive on, when to go to war—and allowing a minority to override those decisions would violate democratic principles. So the rule is not a right of nullification: The state can compel obedience. But when the question concerns the state's existence, it is unsatisfactory to 'assume the state' in answering.[48] Proximity provides a reason for overcoming the inertial authority of the existing state; it provides what theorists have supposed was missing from plebiscitary theories of secession—an "account of the normative implications of the occupancy of territory."[49]

It is the difference between the logic of marriage and divorce. Rules governing marriage are oriented toward joint decisions; but rules for divorce allow each party to decide if the marriage shall continue. The choice is not entirely free—there may be costs, and it will be hard on the kids—but it is each individual's to make; that is the logic of no-fault divorce. An imperfect analogy, as all analogies are, but it goes a long way before it fails. And that's no coincidence, for self-determination is as much concerned with individuals as nations; its logic is deeply rooted in each human's autonomous responsibility for his own person and for the community of which he feels, and chooses to be, a part.

Shaping the Plebiscite

A referendum magnifies the worst aspects of an already imperfect system—democracy—channeling a dazzling variety of issues through a very narrow gate. It has the appearance of intensification—Ultimate democracy! Thumbs up or thumbs down!—but in practice delivers a dangerously misleading reduction . . . a very ineffective hammer for a thousand crooked nails.

Zadie Smith[50]

This recommendation will bring a smile to the lips of the transcendants of politics, these infallible beings who . . . take pity upon our mundane concerns. "Consult the populations, for heaven's sake! How naive! A fine example of those wretched French ideas which claim to replace diplomacy and war by childishly simple methods." Wait a while, Gentlemen . . .

Ernest Renan[51]

People form political communities that relate to their shared environment. This fact underpins the intuition that people *ought* to be able to form political communities to govern the places they live. This suggests a third element we must consider along with people and territory: a process—a plebiscite.

Controlling the Process

There's a joke from the Yugoslav wars. Croatian President Tuđman and Serbian President Milošević agree to meet on the border but miss each other by a hundred kilometers, each on the edge of his own fantasy map. The joke would be funnier if it weren't for all the dead people in between.

Groups sometimes want more, not less. History is filled with state-formative projects with hubristic ambitions: *Megáli Idéa, Lebensraum,* Greater This and Greater That. Even being a victim doesn't ensure good behavior; oppressed groups can be shockingly oppressive when their turn comes around. So if groups define themselves and their territory, what's to prevent them from claiming too much?

The first line of defense is the new rule's logic. A separatist community must define a territory on which it can win a vote. This introduces self-regulating incentives rarely seen in a negotiating context:

Curiously, the prospect of a plebiscite tends to encourage the parties to reduce their more exaggerated claims to territory. This is because an unreasonable boundary claim would include greater numbers of other nationalities or factions and thereby lessen the likelihood of electoral victory. . . . Thus, unlike nearly every form of inter-state negotiations—where exaggerated claims are the norm—the plebiscite encourages modest claims, claims that stand a chance of being upheld by the people in the territory at issue.[52]

Still, a separatist community *could* claim an expansive territory on which it constitutes a narrow majority. (Thinking back to our island, imagine the White language zone, to which one could attach a sizable part of the Black zone.) To forestall this risk, plebiscites could have several features to limit overreach: supermajority, cascades, limits on population and shape, and iteration.

SUPERMAJORITY If the threshold for victory were set at, say, 70 percent, secessionists would have to choose a territory in which they could confidently secure that level of support. The higher the threshold, the more homogeneous sentiment in the territory has to be, incentivizing groups to exclude areas whose population is unsympathetic. Indeed, a supermajority reinforces the intuition that the value of local priority will be strongest in cases in which the sentiments of a local population are highly homogeneous.

The advantage of supermajority also shows up in close outcomes. A close vote with a bare majority raises the prospect of revision, especially if there is evidence of voters' remorse, as after Brexit. A supermajority requirement reduces these tensions. Technically the problem still arises—whatever the threshold, a close victory will tempt opponents to challenge the outcome—but with a supermajority, even a close vote shows strong support.

This is also a cost. With a bare majority, if a vote fails, it's clear it doesn't have majority support. But falling short of a supermajority still means a local majority in favor. If the requirement were very high—say, 90 percent—even popular movements would fail. That seems unsatisfying and could heighten tensions. Still, the result could also act as a signal, spurring states to respond: In Canada and the United Kingdom, even failed referenda prompted serious negotiations for more generous devolution. In any case, this cost is no worse than in other cases of supermajority decision-making: Constitutional amendments requiring supermajorities can also fall short, producing majorities for change that does not happen.

There are two basic models—actual voters, or voting-age population. Each has disadvantages. A supermajority of voters can create false positives if opponents boycott. In Catalonia's contested 2017 referendum, the vote was strongly in favor of independence, but turnout was very low. Similarly, in Bosnia in 1992, almost all Serbs boycotted, resulting in an overwhelming pro-independence vote. By contrast, relying on the eligible voting population avoids this problem but creates a different challenge: It is harder to know with certainty what the population is, so close results will be contested.

On balance, the better model is probably the zone's potential voters. Getting a majority of an area's population to affirmatively support independence is a formidable accomplishment; in regular elections, parties rarely achieve a majority of potential voters. (With 75 percent participation, separatists would need two-thirds of votes to reach 50 percent of the whole population.) That's a high hurdle—but for that reason, it signals seriousness and broad popular sentiment. Nothing would prevent a state from recognizing lower standards, as the United Kingdom did. But a common international standard would signal that this isn't something a state can reserve to its domestic sphere, effectively making secession impossible.

CASCADING PLEBISCITES Whatever mechanism is used, some dissatisfied individuals will be caught up in the plebiscite. How might we reduce their numbers? A cascade encourages secessionists to moderate their claim by providing a corrective: Dissatisfied groups within the zone can set up a counter-plebiscite; victory in *that* vote would allow them to remain in the original state. Residents of the second zone also vote in the main plebiscite, so they can help defeat it. If the main vote fails, a cascade is moot; but if it succeeds, the population in the second zone has a chance to adjust the contours of secession.

This was the model used in the Polish-German and Yugoslav-Austrian plebiscites after the First World War. Following the top-down logic of Wilsonian self-determination, zones were identified by outsiders. Under the new rule, zones would be determined by the communities themselves; if a group wishes to remain, it has to mobilize. (This is actually happening in Catalonia: A partly ironic movement for Tabàrnia—the coastal strip including Tarragona and Barcelona, where separatist sentiment is weakest—has arisen, calling for continued union with Spain. It looks very much like a cascading plebiscite.) Another model would demarcate districts, which secede or remain depending on the outcome in each. This was used in the Schleswig plebiscite, and although in that case district designations were quite biased, the principle is plausible.

Jurassic Partition: The Plausible Mechanics of Ongoing Secession

The plebiscites after the First World War included cascades, but there's a more recent example: the slow division of a Swiss canton. Bern was confessionally and linguistically mixed, and after the Second World War, a cantonal secessionist movement developed. In 1978, a Switzerland-wide referendum approved the division: Three French-speaking Catholic districts formed the new canton Jura, while four French-speaking Protestant areas remained in German-speaking Protestant Bern.

The process wasn't over. The departure of the French districts left German Laufen an isolated exclave of Bern. After a 1989 vote, it seceded and joined Basel (not Jura) in 1994. Vellerat had also remained part of Bern but was accessible only from the new canton; it joined Jura in 1996. As linguistic divisions became more salient than religious ones, the rationale for separation changed, and there have been further plebiscites. In 2013, Bernese Jura as a whole voted to remain in Bern, but one district, Moutier, voted to join the new canton. In 2017, Moutier voted again in a separate plebiscite to join Jura, while the village of Sorvilier voted to remain in Bern.

The Jura secession has played out within a single, cooperative state, so its experience isn't always apposite to the international context. But it shows how some important mechanics can actually work—cascades, iteration, transition periods—and how the motives for secession can be separated from the mechanics of democratic decision-making. As for that cooperative state, like Scotland, it simply shows what is possible.

These alternatives present their own problems. Districts and sequencing require negotiation in advance and over how to interpret results. They require more intrusive supervision and therefore risk departing from the basic democratic principle animating the rule.

Diamond Mines and Offshore Platforms: Regulating Size and Shape

Supermajorities and cascades discourage separatists from claiming too much. But what about communities that want less—that are trying to exclude as many people as possible? The risk of encouraging microstates with sovereignty over valuable resources is a serious challenge for the new rule—more serious than the creation of large units.

There is no *natural* lower limit to the logic of self-determination. What's to prevent a village or the employees of a corporation from seceding with a country's only diamond mine? Or, indeed, why couldn't an individual "just stand still and draw a circle around [his] feet and name that Selfistan?"[53] The Sovereign Citizen movement in the United States and occasional efforts to declare some derelict oil rig a state are testimony to two persistent qualities of our species: the desire for autonomy and willful disregard for reality. A right of secession would attract all manner of claimants, from warlords to lunatics who take the pleasures of home ownership too seriously. This is both a practical concern and, for some, a sign of deeper conceptual problems. But there are practical answers, and the concept is governed by a sensible principle: not to let the perfect be the enemy of the good. There are ways to limit the risk of micro-states.

First, the imperatives of economics and security will cause most communities to self-regulate. Having one's own state sounds attractive, but the practical challenges of governing a micro-state in a dangerous world will dissuade most claimants. Several islands with the right to independence have not exercised it because the advantages of remaining linked to the colonial metropole outweigh independence. Most are not sitting on enormous physical wealth, but even if they were, they would still have a right to independence. We don't have any *principled* objection to areas with highly concentrated resource wealth becoming independent—if they are colonies. It's not clear we should treat some richly endowed area less favorably just because it happens to be part of an existing state.[54]

Small states have to survive and prosper in the real world. It is a mark of the new rule's realism that it assumes the laws of physics, economics, and politics continue to operate: Power and wealth still matter, risk and insecurity still exist; states will use the means at their disposal to compel weaker neighbors to accommodate their interests, and will not tolerate dysfunctional neighbors. The risk of violence is real and ever-present; we may have outlawed war, but states still worry about intervention and domination. This corrective mechanism isn't pretty but would function under the new rule just as it does today.

Even below this threshold, states could still make their preferences clear. The United States didn't object to the Scottish referendum but made it clear that it hoped Scots would stay. (President Obama also encouraged the United Kingdom to stay in the EU.) The United States supports a One-Iraq policy, and its opposition (along with Turkey's and Iran's) has long dissuaded Iraqi Kurds from seceding. Acknowledging a right and supporting its exercise are different things, and we could expect major actors to discourage many secessions.

Self-regulation won't always work. The attractions of independence would surely lure some dubious claimants: To hell with what the neighbors say, my sons will be ambassadors! A brief perusal of the Internet's more-marginal corners reveals any number of aspirational mini-states declared under the most questionable circumstances—Sealand, Liberland, Hutt River, and the admirably named Wy. Ridiculous claims, but at least current doctrine rejects their ridiculousness. What would happen if we appeared to actually encourage such foolishness, not simply in the privacy of people's backyards—for that is the size of some of these states—but in combination with a few thousand of their neighbors? For cases not amenable to self-regulation or the general system's cautionary suasions, the new rule could include rough-and-ready limits to discourage micro-states: minimum population, limits on shape, and conditions under which a plebiscite could be called.

Minimum Population

There are strong prudential grounds to limit the right of secession to groups of a certain size. Requiring a minimum population reinforces democratic legitimacy: Practically, a larger population suggests a more important claim. A population minimum is analogous to electoral thresholds for winning seats in a legislature or getting signatures for a referendum, which limit the influence of *de minimis* groups, whose views are not necessarily less valid, simply less popular.

How should the limit be determined? There are two principal models: a percentage of the population, or an absolute number. Each has advantages and disadvantages. A percentage would yield wildly variable outcomes. The secession of 1 percent of China's population would produce a country more populous than 120 existing states. Even a compact, homogeneous community of 10 million inside China would be barred from seceding by a 1 percent rule. (It would need 13.5 million.)

The effects in smaller countries would be quite different. A 1-percent rule applied to Mongolia would allow 28,390 people to secede—and Mongolia is by no means the smallest. And because the right of secession would be iterative, that tiny state would also be subject to the percentage rule, rapidly yielding village-states. A percentage produces problems on both ends of the demographic spectrum, leaving enormous populations without recourse at one end, legitimizing micro-secessions on the other.

A percentage also makes the right of self-determination dependent upon the demographics of the existing country. A group is only a minority by virtue of its enclosure within a state's borders, so defining the group's right in relation to the whole population replicates the dilemma the rule is designed to redress. If we otherwise believed that a group has a valid basis to form a political community, we should not dismiss its claim simply because it happens to be embedded within a large state instead of a small one. Either 7.5 million Tibetans deserve independence or they don't, but the answer shouldn't depend on how many Han Chinese there are elsewhere in China.

The alternative is an absolute number. A group wishing to secede would have to identify a territory with at least, say, 1 million people, with progressively smaller thresholds for cascading districts. If we imagined a process with three stages, it might look like this:

- Initial plebiscite (to secede)—minimum 1 million
- Cascade 1 (to remain in state)—minimum 100,000
- Cascade 2 (to join the secession, withdrawing from Cascade 1)—minimum 10,000
- Further adjustments by negotiation

There could be a lower limit for isolated communities, such as island populations. (Islands already have different status in international law, and today's micro-states are mostly islands.) Nothing would prevent states from voluntarily recognizing lower thresholds or letting a defined territory exercise the right of secession. Denmark, which acknowledges Greenlanders' right of self-determination,[55] could recognize Greenland's independence without waiting for the population to increase by 930,000.

These are arbitrary numbers; why is this acceptable? Why should 1 million people have the right to form a state, but 900,000 not? A limit of 1 million would be extremely unattractive to, say, South Ossetians, who number less than 70,000. It would have disappointed pro-independence Montenegrins. Why is it okay to say to a group with 850,000 members all committed to independence, "Sorry, you need 150,000 more"? There is no principled answer: By their nature, arbitrary rules are *not* principled. But an absolute number is practical and responds to the most common objections.

A threshold makes the rule quite conservative. It eliminates micro-state risk: a 1-million threshold produces a population larger than forty UN members. It helps ensure the reasons for secession are ones we might accept, because large groups inevitably have complex, disparate motives. A rogue corporation or war-lord could bribe or bully some people, but at 1 million, it gets harder, making it more plausible that we are dealing with popular sentiment. (Later we'll consider why crass economic reasons are no objection to secession.)

A threshold is arbitrary, but the existing rule is no better: It says *no* group, however numerous, has a right to secede—not 850,000, not 1 million, not *any* number. The current arbitrary limit only benefits those who already have a state. That's consistent, but little consolation to those it excludes. Consistency is not the only or even chief virtue of a just society; it is better to help some than none. The new rule is at least as coherent as the current rule, and with better outcomes. An arbitrary limit that expands the opportunity for some groups to claim statehood while preventing micro-claims would be an improvement. And since the rule doesn't require shared identity, almost any group could meet the threshold by persuading others to join.

Still, this is one of the core challenges the new rule must overcome: The fact that it opens the global system to new states creates a need to limit that process. This is a complex challenge—because the new rule is responding to a complex world. The concern with micro-states isn't their size—there are many viable small states today—but the belief that they aren't genuine political communities. We *should* be suspicious of manufactured democratic sentiment, but there are clearly claims that reflect a genuine, democratic desire; when we find them, we should take them seriously. In the present system with its gloriously simple idiot rule, the problem doesn't arise, because *nobody* has the right to try.

Territorial Limits

There are pragmatic reasons for a minimum population. What about minimum territory? The new rule is territorial, but its motive force and moral impulse are humans' relationship to territory, not the territory itself. Still, we might want to insist on certain features, such as limiting gerrymandering and regulating contiguity; at least, these are issues we would have to address in crafting the new rule.

GERRYMANDERING Separatists have incentives to include people sympathetic to independence while excluding opponents. But populations are never homogeneous. Demography is complex within and among settlements. Even when a population is homogeneous on one measure—everyone is Muslim, for example—it will be diverse in other ways: wealth, education, political preferences. Any quest to describe a homogeneous map faces real challenges. One way to meet them is to do what is done in some democracies: gerrymander the territory. The new rule both harnesses this strategy and places limits on it.

Gerrymandering refers to creative map-drawing designed to produce electoral districts that advantage one party, either by aggregating like-minded voters into safe districts or breaking clusters apart to weaken their voting power. American congressional districts—where the term originated—provide striking examples of the possibilities and risks of computer-driven gerrymandering. Using data about identity, attitudes, and voting, cartographers can engineer precise outcomes by producing bizarrely shaped districts. A strategically minded separatist could do this, capturing sympathetic populations while avoiding clusters opposing independence. (On our island, the White population could draw a line around all its members, while bringing in a smaller number of Black speakers.)

But the extended arms of a gerrymandered district also pose the opposite possibility: Opponents of secession could design a cascade to dismember the plebiscite zone, the way Israeli settlements in the West Bank limit the viability of a Palestinian state. Two groups trying to maximize inclusion of their members will produce claims cutting into each other's population. This suggests the need for limits.

Of course, that assumes this is a problem rather than a solution. Engineering a plebiscite means more people wishing to secede would be able to, while more wishing to stay could stay. It is a way to avoid the exact problem we considered earlier, that a secessionist movement might take a lot of unwilling people with it; instead, it can cut the border carefully around them. Seen that way, it sounds far better.

The distribution of Hungarians and Romanians in Transylvania illustrates the problem and the possibility. On a map of Romania, one sees a concentration of Hungarians at the southeastern crux of the Carpathians, separated from another zone on the border by an area of Romanian settlement.

Romania's annexation of Transylvania after the First World War absorbed these Hungarian populations along with much larger Romanian ones. In 1938, the Second Vienna Award, negotiated by Hitler, transferred the pocket of homogeneous settlement to Hungary but included a corridor of predominantly Romanian settlement; at the war's end, the interwar arrangement was restored.

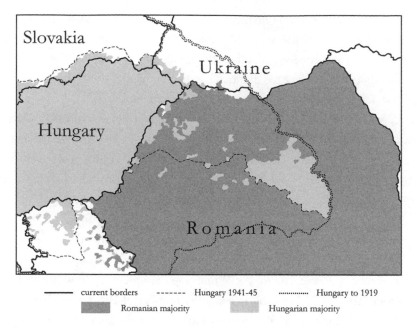

current borders ------- Hungary 1941-45 ············· Hungary to 1919

Romanian majority   Hungarian majority

Hungarians and Romanians
(drawn with data from Platon, "Ethnic Map of WW2 Hungary"; "Magyarország Hegy- és
Vízrajzi Térképe"; and László, "Nationality Map of East Central and Southeast Europe")

There is no way to draw lines to avoid both results. No plausible line around the Hungarians in the heart of Transylvania could link them to those on the border (or to Hungary) without including a corridor of Romanians. But, equally, a state incorporating all large Romanian populations necessarily includes territories populated by Hungarians.

The problem is unavoidable but can be minimized by gerrymandering: carving out ganglia that snorkel out from Hungarian settlements on the border toward the center, bypassing most Romanian settlements. One could in theory draw a pencil-thin strip to bypass areas of Romanian population—something actually done in American congressional districts, which have sections linked only by unpopulated highway medians.[56] That would effectively cut Romania in half, with a tiny sovereign strip bisecting the state.

That would be an extreme solution, but even less extreme models can minimize the dual problems of capturing unwilling populations and leaving willing populations behind. The price is oddly shaped territories, but those shapes are not random; rather, they respond to demography. There are complex logistical and strategic issues surrounding any districting exercise—and indeed, gerry-mandering is just an extreme variant of that otherwise respectable activity. Ger-rymandering has a bad reputation, but it shows that precise divisions based on salient criteria are possible: It is not true that such things *cannot* be done. Usu-ally, that claim is a proxy for saying such things *shouldn't* be done because they are illiberal; but as we have seen, the belief that secession tends to illiberalism is not empirically justified.

The first step is to see that those issues are worth grappling with—that the exercise is actually a good idea that arises from legitimate impulses, like the reform of England's 'rotten boroughs.' Redistricting is a useful part of demo-cratic process: Done correctly, it serves goals of demographic justice, helping to ensure that units don't undercut discrete constituencies' enfranchisement. There are challenges with any districting model. But the real problem with the current global system is that it doesn't allow *any* redistricting. The units—states—were 'districted' in 1945 and have remained largely unaltered, despite enormous changes in their demography. It is as if we engaged in a single, global gerry-mander, and then froze the units in place. Seen that way, the idea that we might intentionally reshape units to fit the populations living within them sounds not like a perversion of democratic participation, but its very essence.

NONCONTIGUOUS ZONES That strip is a problem, so why not cut it? One way to maximize desired exit while minimizing unwilling exit is to not insist on territory contiguity. But noncontiguity introduces other challenges.

Consolidation of territory is part of the standard narrative of modernity: With the rise of the centralized state, noncontiguous territories largely disappeared from the map. There are reasons for contiguity: It simplifies administration, security, and distribution of goods and services. Noncontiguous territory is vul-nerable to interference by other states, which can blockade enclaves. Indeed, the theory of proximity on which the new rule relies assumes contiguity is simpler.

But contiguity isn't essential, and many borders are complex. Many states are divided by water: Malaysia's two landmasses are connected to other states but separated from each other by hundreds of miles of open sea. There are many enclaves surrounded by other states: bits of Germany within Switzerland, part of the United Arab Emirates inside an exclave of Oman inside the UAE, en-claves of India and Bangladesh within each other.[57]

Plebiscite zones could be noncontiguous, too. Each section might have to

A Fractured, Peaceful Border

It is instructive to look at the Dutch-Belgian border. What looks like a classi-
cally solid line is actually a fractured mosaic, with tiny enclaves of Belgium inside Dutch territory—and tinier enclaves of the Netherlands inside *those*.

Baarle-Hertog and Baarle-Nassau (Drawn by author)

Individual properties—including a café—are bisected by the border. This may
seem like a comically irrelevant example—of course it works, because two wealthy,
culturally similar neighbors can afford to tolerate archaic feudal holdovers on
their peaceful border. But that's the point: Good relations between states and
populations are more important than contiguity. Contiguity can become a liabil-
ity: If communities are in conflict with each other, even complex separation can
be better.

meet a lower population minimum—say 100,000 or 250,000—and together
must meet the overall threshold. This presents its own problems: High limits
would ensure that either sizable populations will be left behind or large, unwilling populations carried out. But low thresholds greatly increase the complexity
of the territory, producing interlocked Swiss cheese states. Whether it would be
better to have a ragged line of small noncontiguous territories or to leave large

numbers on the wrong side might depend on the particular relationship of groups in the area. Determining whether a district should be treated as a whole or as several parts could be part of negotiations between the claiming community and the state, or entirely within the control of the seceding community (subject to cascades). In some cases it might require assessment by a supervisory mechanism, parts of which would have to be done before the vote.[58]

Whatever the model, however, we can expect that all sides will try to game the rules: Secessionists will try to draw in isolated supporters or exclude pockets of the majority, while the state will object to whatever map is proposed. Other states will naturally seek to influence these processes, too. Even if we could imagine negotiating these territorial moves without outside supervision, the bare fact of imposing limitations is in tension with the radically democratic aspects of the rule.

Still, insisting on territorial contiguity requires more people to live in a state other than the one they might wish; as Transylvania shows, the issue is not only one of tiny enclaves, but sizable areas. Noncontiguity requires states to cooperate in administering divided units. This can be challenging, especially if the remainder state is angry about the loss of territory. But if cooperation is impossible, at least above the level of trivial examples like Baarle-Nassau, what does this say about the belief that these kinds of differences shouldn't matter? Focusing only on the challenges noncontiguity presents distracts us from the problems that insisting on unchanging frontiers creates—or hides.

Border Adjustments

The new rule aligns territory with the wishes of those living on it, but even so, people will end up on the wrong side. A final correction might be needed: border revisions. The new and old states could negotiate to account for small populations, or make adjustments on administrative, economic, or security grounds. Adjustments could be subject to approval by the affected population or not.

Two sovereigns bartering over the fate of populations might seem contrary to the spirit of the new rule, just as letting economic or security interests override a plebiscite might seem contrary. But the rule is not the only one on which the system is built. It doesn't pretend to 100 percent accuracy: Even a supermajority supposes that many people will not be happy. This is another example of the rule's minimalism, since in relying on border adjustments to fine-tune the outcome, it merely does something already possible under the current model.[59]

Adjusting Borders in Kosovo

An untaken path for Kosovo shows how border adjustments could work, consistent with the principles underlying the new rule. Kosovo won independence, a rare case of remedial secession. But significant areas in the north are populated by Serbs opposed to living in an independent Kosovo. Yet because the current rule defaults to existing units—in former Yugoslavia, republican and provincial borders—those areas were included in the new state. Remedial secession was overdetermined: It helped Albanians but also 'helped' everyone else in the predetermined unit.

Imagine a different approach. Kosovo as a whole could easily have met the new rule's thresholds: With two million people, it has a large enough population. The Serb-populated north would have voted against independence, but Albanians, who make up over 90 percent of the population, could have included the north anyway, knowing they could still meet the threshold. Serbs there could organize a cascading counter-plebiscite, which they would easily win. There are Albanians in the north, but quickly the numbers would get too small to meet the thresholds.

Here is where border adjustments could help correct the line even after the cascades ended. Albanian enclaves in the Serb-populated area north of the Ibar River could be (re-)attached to the independent south. The mechanics for such adjustments exist in the contemporary system, but their use would seem more plausible to finalize the results of a plebiscite, rather than as a departure from the norm of territorial integrity. A recalcitrant Serbia might accept a deal that, after all, gave it a chance to retain some areas in exchange for recognizing Kosovo. (We are imagining the rule generally if grudgingly recognized, leaving the politics of how that might happen for chapter 7.)

Allowing adjustments ameliorates the inevitable imperfection of any border delimitation.

In any case, the imperfection of the process is not an excuse for leaving even *more* people on the wrong side—whether of existing lines that have a cruel continuing effect, or entirely new lines suddenly given international status, as happened in the former Soviet Union, Yugoslavia, and much of the colonial world. The new rule is not perfect, but it does a *better* job of fitting lines to people's preferences.

We've seen that one theoretical objection to secession is its potential for frac-

> ### Empty Places
>
> It's often easier to decide about crowded places than empty ones. Sparse, heterogeneous populations present special challenges of overreach. Still, this is not so much a problem as a description: Sparsely populated areas are just that, and yet we have no problem conceptualizing sovereignty over them in the current system. There is nothing different in the proposed rule—it is a rule for changing sovereigns, but it assumes sovereignty otherwise has the same qualities it does now.
>
> Truly empty areas present a peculiar challenge—the problem of the last house before the national park. Where does one draw the line in a vast, unpopulated wilderness? Does it belong to the people living east of it or west? The self-regulating mechanisms of population thresholds and supermajority will not serve as well to constrain claims over valuable but empty lands, since there is no population to alter the plebiscite's electoral calculus. Perhaps it is best left to negotiation between the secessionist and the state, as a border dispute of the kind the current system is already capable of dealing with.

ture *ad infinitum et absurdum.* But the response is an eminently nontheoretical one, familiar to lawyers since time immemorial: the setting of limits. There is no *principled* reason why cascades could not continue until they clear—until there is no area left in which a population wishes to mount a counterclaim (or counter-counter-counterclaim)—but also no *practical* obstacle to simply declaring an end, after which the matter is treated not as one of right, but of politics.

The Basic Territorial Limit: No Cross-Border Plebiscites

One additional restriction animates this new rule: A plebiscite may never cross existing frontiers. This feature runs directly counter to the common intuition that we should fear the fracturing potential of secession—it keeps seceding units smaller!—but to a purpose: to discourage foreign intervention.

If a group in one state claimed territory straddling an international frontier, the other state would have a plausible claim to concern itself with the threat from across the frontier (even if that threat were in fact a welcome opportunity for revanchism). But an internal group making a claim against its own state does not necessarily implicate any other state's territorial integrity. For this reason— to minimize the risk for pretextual interventions—any plebiscite could only be conducted within one state.

So if Kurds living in Turkey, Syria, Iraq, and Iran wished to form a common state, they would have to conduct four separate plebiscites. Each would have to succeed, form a new state, and then agree to union. The last phase is already possible under the current system, since sovereign states are free to merge. Revanchists would have to pursue this two-stage process: Macedonian Albanians could unite with Albania, Italian Germans with Austria, Kashmiris with Pakistan, only by first achieving their own independence, then negotiating a merger with the neighbors. This seems like an exercise in formalism, but formalism is the point: It slows down nationalist claims, subjecting those claims to a multistage process subject to international norms, reducing the risk of intervention and cross-border conflict.

Revanchism has a bad name, but often it is the sentiment of two communities that they share a political identity—ironically, a sentiment of integration, and when put that way, it sounds much more benign, like the 1990 reunification of Germany. There is nothing wrong with it so long as it's done peaceably with respect for the interests of others. That is what the rule aims to ensure: Even if the end of the process is unification, the interim stages are subject to democratic process, shaped by human rights.

Iteration

Finally, secession can be repeated. This introduces uncertainty. Although *interstate* norms of territorial integrity and nonaggression would remain in place, states could no longer take their own population's loyalties for granted, and other states would have to decide when to recognize a secession. To some, any uncertainty is bad, but there are advantages to treating secession as a permanent possibility. The history of the classical period is one of colonies claiming independence and then slamming the door shut on their own people; iteration forces secession's beneficiaries to give their own populations the same right. And iteration responds to the reality of changing demographics: Populations and their preferences change. Identities are malleable, so why would one historically determined set of frontiers suit those identities for all time?

An open-ended right would tend to create more units, but as we've seen, there are countervailing incentives to integrate. Most of all, we've seen how problematic assumptions about fracture are, both as empirical predictions and normative preferences. Some kinds of certainty are overrated: The idea that states might have to earn their people's loyalty, far from being a problem, might be a virtue.

REPEATING PLEBISCITES Plebiscites sometimes fail. What then? Can a community try again and again, as the Quebecois have done? Because the right is iterative, communities are not limited to a single attempt. Some limits might make sense, given the serious, quasi-constitutional nature of secession. One might set a cooling-off period of, say, five years between plebiscites, in which parties could pursue their agendas outside the heightened atmosphere of a referendum. Supervision could help mitigate the uncertainty through braking procedures, such as requirements to reconfirm an outcome. Just such concepts have appeared in actual referenda, such as the final vote in South Sudan at the end of a five-year transition.

But it would be difficult to impose an absolute standard. It would be hard to say if two plebiscites were actually repeating. Either side could game a rigid rule: Secessionists could evade a suspension by varying the territory, opponents could hold a pretextual plebiscite on a large-enough part of the state to ensure it would vote to remain, preempting a smaller, pro-secession territory. Better, therefore, to make no formal restriction and trust to politics to regulate their frequency. Repeated plebiscites might increase instability, but freezes have costs, too: If the state knows secession is blocked for a generation, it might be less willing to make concessions. On this question, as on so many, we may expect self-regulation, since voters can suffer plebiscite fatigue, and secessionists will take this into account.

The best reason to leave repetition unregulated is that there is no principled reason why a plebiscite shouldn't be held as often as enough people wish it. Scotland's referendum was supposed to be "once in a generation," but Brexit has encouraged calls for a second effort. It is precisely that sort of thing—events, whose significance is understood by the humans living through them—that increases or reduces separatist sentiment, and events do not occur on a timetable.

The Plebiscite Question

People can call a plebiscite, but what will they ask? In most cases a simply phrased question in isolation works best. But in practice, the question is often complicated and asking politically fraught.[60]

The Canadian Supreme Court's *Quebec Reference* declared that starting negotiations required a clear majority answering a clear question.[61] In the 1995
referendum, the question had been anything but:

> Do you agree that Quebec should become sovereign after having made a formal
> offer to Canada for a new economic and political partnership within the scope of
> the bill respecting the future of Quebec and of the agreement signed on June 12,
> 1995?[62]

That question was criticized for its vagueness and complexity: Mentioning
sovereignty, but not independence or a country; and with references to other
documents, it was difficult to know what exactly one was agreeing to.

The Crimean referendum was even more defective. Organized on short notice under Russian occupation, the ballot offered two choices—restoration of
autonomy under the 1992 constitution, or union with Russia—but no option for
the status quo. This made it impossible to know if voters' preference for change
was meaningful, even if the context had allowed a free vote.

Catalonia demonstrates the problems of ambiguity, not only in the question,
but its context. After the Spanish state quashed the Catalan government's referendum in 2014, secessionists devised a creative work-around. In 2015, pro-
independence parties won parliamentary elections on a platform promising to
build institutions for independence in eighteen months. The election was for a
new Catalan government, so Spain couldn't prevent it. But although a clever
way to bypass Spain's objections, this stratagem did not actually produce a clear
answer to a clear question. The coalition parties had a common independence
platform, but differed on other policies. The mandate was ambiguous: There is
no way to know if individuals were voting for secession or for their choice to
govern Catalonia *within* Spain.

By contrast, the Scottish referendum was clear and decisive. The final question
was straightforward: "Should Scotland be an independent country? Yes/No."
The question posed a binary choice, one prong of which was the status quo, the
other independence. It was asked in a stand-alone referendum.

There is no reason why questions must follow a rote form—and good reason, given varying circumstances, why they won't. Yet the new rule suggests
a binary choice. Its purpose is to decide about independence, so a formulation
authorizing an independent state makes sense. The rest—the issues of utmost

---

A Simple Question's Complicated Path

The Scottish referendum question was the result of hard negotiation, and the process is instructive. London and Edinburgh agreed the "question must be fair, easy to understand and capable of producing a result that is accepted and commands confidence."* Beyond that there was considerable disagreement, based on political calculations. The Scottish National Party, recognizing the weakness of support for independence, originally favored including an option for increased devolution, known as 'devo-max.' But the UK government insisted on an in-or-out question—calculating that a stark choice would encourage voters to reject independence.

Under the terms of Scotland's devolution statute, the Scottish Parliament determined the wording, subject to review by the UK Electoral Commission. The SNP wanted the question to read "Do you agree that Scotland should be an independent country?" but the commission said that implicitly solicited a positive response, and the SNP accepted this. The decision was embedded in an administrative and political process that gave the state's institutions considerable influence. The result was a clear question that—given the United Kingdom's commitment to respect the outcome—could produce a consequential decision.

*Memorandum of Agreement (United Kingdom–Scotland), ¶ 5.
**Black, "Scottish Independence."

---

importance—is left to politics under the shadow of a vote made on a single, simple question.

The challenges to a straightforward question are not linguistic but political. There is considerable ambiguity in politics, but that needn't be reflected in the question:

> The wording of the referendum question must be clear and should leave no room for ambiguity. The question must not be misleading, must not suggest an answer, especially by mentioning the presumed consequences of approving or rejecting the proposal and it must not ask an open question.[63]

As is often the case with plebiscites, it is instructive to think how regular elections work. The politics of a general election can be complex, and voters' motives complicated, even contradictory; yet the actual vote is a bracingly straight-

The Name Is Not the Territory

A complication arises in formulating the question: What should the territory be called? For existing units, like Quebec, it was possible to fill in the formula with a clear name. But sometimes the territory doesn't exist, and it can be problematic to appropriate some historical name or ethnonym. Where exactly is 'Kurdistan'? In Turkey, it includes areas secessionists couldn't possibly win, but applying the term to a smaller area might confuse those inside and out about what's being voted on. In Iraq, there is an identified Kurdistan, but also areas subject to a much-deferred referendum under Iraq's constitution, and other areas Kurds consider traditionally Kurdish. So what did the September 2017 referendum question—"Do you want the Kurdistan region and the Kurdistani areas outside the region's administration to become an independent state?"—refer to?

So the question might refer to a map. This sounds jarringly arid, lacking all the patriotic passions we typically attach to the state: 'We the people living in the following GPS coordinates' doesn't quite stir the soul. Yet there is a perverse virtue in those coordinates: a reminder that what we are deliberating about is not an ethno-nationalist fantasy, but power over a given piece of land and all the people living on it.

forward matter—this party or that, candidate X or candidate Y. The complexity is in political deliberation, not in the formal question.

The question therefore should be narrowly framed. Nothing in the rule would prevent a state from asking other questions in other referenda—about autonomy, federalism, linguistic rights, left-side driving, any issue—but those other referenda wouldn't be an exercise of the new right to secession.

No matter how simple the formulation, there will always need to be a process to determine the wording, and any criteria imply someone to adjudicate disputes. Preferably the state and claimant group could agree. But as we saw in Scotland, it is not necessarily the state that wants ambiguity, and even after the United Kingdom conceded the principle, it fought hard to determine the precise question.

Initiating the Process: Petition for a Plebiscite

We have already considered why letting a people identify itself and vote matters morally and politically. Here, a more technical question: We can leave the formation of a people to the political market, but what mechanisms are needed to initiate a plebiscite, and how would it be recognized?

A plebiscite could be initiated by petition, by which the group could indicate it has sufficient support to raise its claim as a matter of international right. As with the plebiscite itself, the petition threshold should be high, to avoid endless disruptions by small, determined groups. A petition that garnered the requisite share in the proposed area—say 10 or 20 percent—would trigger the right to hold a plebiscite. States could accept lower thresholds or use existing standards for referenda or ballot initiatives. The requirement to submit a petition implies secondary rights to organize and assemble: The focus of advocacy might therefore not be on independence, but on ensuring the right to organize a plebiscite.

We could expect challenges to petitions. Who are the signatories, where do they live, are they citizens, how do we know they add up to 20 percent, were they coerced? Precisely because the community must organize itself, petition and plebiscite will occur in a contestable environment. The practical problems with and tactical objections to such a process are many, but that isn't a reason not to attempt it. These are real concerns, but also eminently solvable ones, especially in a state that *is* cooperative.

Comparison to regular elections is again instructive. Even when elections lead to violence, as in Iraq in 2005—or when, as in Bosnia in 1996, it might have been better to wait—one rarely hears the argument that it would be better *never* to have an election. And so it is with democratic secession: A plebiscite is fraught with difficulties, but they are the same ones any electoral system deals with—sometimes well, sometimes badly—and for all the challenges, we don't think elections can *never* work. The problems are rather just that: problems, which arise in doing this thing which our own values urge us to attempt, problems to be solved or put up with. They are not reasons to eschew the attempt.

Supervision: Recognizing Secession

The heart of the new rule is a *self*-determining community; ideally, groups could hold a plebiscite on their own. But conducting a plebiscite would be complex, and there is no way it would come off without controversies of interpretation and implementation, which someone would have to adjudicate. This would be challenging even in cooperative states.

So secession might need to be supervised, and that means a mechanism. As in Scotland, the best model is internal supervision coordinated between state and claimant. Under Ethiopia's constitution, the federal government organizes secession referenda within three years of a region's request; it must also complete a process to transfer power and negotiate division of assets if the vote is successful. But where external supervision is unavoidable, how might an international body be constituted?

Models include the UN Decolonization Committee (which could itself become the responsible institution, thus giving it an actual job), treaty committees of independent experts, or high commissioners. Following the human rights model, the mandate could consist of reviewing reports and issuing general comments on the law and practice of plebiscites. Reporting is a thin obligation, but it's the standard today. And it can be effective: Decolonization was originally based on states' obligations to report on colonies, rather than actually liberate them. The formal obligation would be reporting, but in practice this would look like an obligation to respect the right itself.

The committee could supervise particular referenda, either when states accepted its involvement or it was imposed (in the way some colonial disputes were internationalized through General Assembly or Security Council action). The committee could remain seized of situations in which a community had met the requirements for initiating a plebiscite until it was completed and, if successful, independence negotiated and achieved. This would involve adjudicating disputes about plebiscite boundaries, and monitoring the process for abuse. The committee could report situations in which states refused to cooperate up a chain of authority, to the Security Council—though that would rarely prove effective.

Such a process would also make it easier to police *secessionists'* commitments to human rights. They could be required to accept specific obligations and international supervision in order to gain recognition. This is common practice now: International transitional administrations have been deployed in Kosovo and East Timor, for example. The greater challenge would be getting the existing state to cooperate. A state that blocked a petition would be violating the right to secession in ways that could be identified with existing human rights, such as speech and assembly. It might be possible to bring complaints before existing human rights bodies or a separately constituted committee.

Subordinating the process to outsiders vitiates the rule's democratic logic, allowing some claims to be favored and others to be sidetracked. But a new state never forms in isolation; it is intimately bound up with recognition by other actors. And, on balance, supervision would actually benefit separatists. They face almost overwhelming legal and political odds; internationalization would increase their bargaining power, turning an overwhelmingly unfair two-way contest into a slightly less unequal three-way dispute. Supervision creates a point of leverage outside the dyad of state and secessionist.

This model has notorious weaknesses, but no one has devised a superior alternative.[64] Adopting it would make the same bet that rights advocates make, when playing their weak hand, to invest in institutions. As we'll see in chapter 7, prospects for a permanent supervisory body are vanishingly small, though states have created mechanisms in individual cases. So supervision would have to be ad hoc and in-country. But even without infrastructure, the new rule could be a norm that advocates and sympathetic states could draw upon, making it marginally more difficult for states to ignore their own populations.

The Plebiscite's Authority

Would a plebiscite be authoritative? We have already considered the arguments for taking a local majority's preferences seriously; here we consider the plebiscite's value as a decisional mechanism. Why should we trust it or credit the outcome? Unlike regular elections, plebiscites are called when there is a particular, even urgent reason—sometimes a violent crisis—and holding a plebiscite can increase tensions. Why should we trust the decisions people take under such circumstances?

A violent crisis is hardly the best time to ask people about their long-term plans. They are concerned with flight or revenge; the blood is up, the urge to compromise vanishes. Asking about fundamental change during or right after a war might not yield the same results as in peacetime. But why is that disqualifying? After all, there *has* been a crisis, and pretending there hasn't seems artificial. Reconstituting the state is a choice, too, so why trust *that* choice? This is especially true when the state has been dismantled—as happened in Bosnia, Somalia, or much of Syria—and it isn't a question of continuing the antebellum order, but recreating it. The crisis is a part of that society's history, so why deny that?

If one truly thought a crisis were reason not to trust the results of a plebiscite, the remedy is simple: delay. It would still be a profound shift in the current rule if we acknowledged a right to secession that could be suspended in times of

crisis—especially if states were forbidden to define the mere desire for secession as a crisis. It's a Catch-22: No secession during a crisis, because it's too
unreliable; and no secession during calm times, because why rock the boat?

The new rule is principally designed to be used *before* a crisis; it provides
a pathway for peaceful change so that crisis need not come. Thinking about
secession during a crisis like those in Ukraine, Syria, or Iraq is to think in the
worst circumstances, when there are no good options left. But that is a general
problem: War destroys good options under any rule. In fact, none of those examples tell us much about how the new rule would work, but they tell us a lot
about how the *current* rule does.

A plebiscite creates data about preferences. That doesn't tell us what we
should do with those preferences, but it does provide a basis for evaluation.
There might be circumstances in which we would question the reasoning behind a decision to secede, or suspect that there is too much instability to trust
the result. But that's true in any election, and we don't conclude from that hard
fact that elections are never worth having. A plebiscite, as an informational and
decisional act, is more valid than the intuition underlying our current system:
that we affirm states' legitimacy by never asking about it.

6

Broader Implications: Features
and Effects of the New Rule

What are the broader implications of the new rule? How does it affect other
policies and values?

WE NOW CONSIDER FEATURES and effects not directly evident in the rule's
formal elements, but that are aspects or likely consequences of its operation: its
radically ahistorical quality; its effects on resource distribution, immigration,
and violence; and its minimalism.

A Radically Democratic, Radically Ahistorical Rule

In 2014, I was on a panel discussing Russia's annexation of Crimea. A colleague gave an impassioned presentation showing that Tatars would constitute
a majority in Crimea today if various, very unjust historical events hadn't occurred, from settlement of Russians to Stalin's expulsion of the Tatars during
the Second World War. So, he concluded, the referendum, in which a majority
had voted for union with Russia, couldn't be valid. When I got up to speak, I
departed from my prepared text to suggest some problems with this ambitious
thesis, which was a plea for historical justice. The referendum was defective
on other grounds, but my colleague was saying that not only *this* referendum
was invalid, but *no* referendum ever could be because of the Tatars' historical
marginalization.

What can one say? Stalin's expulsions were reprehensible and would be criminal today; the other acts may be regrettable but were consequences of complex

processes. And right or not, legal or not, all of them happened and had the effects they did. To take my colleague's charts seriously, one would have to forever deny the possibility for any vote in Crimea on any issue, even within Ukraine, that did not weigh the votes of living Tatars to account for their unborn compatriots—and in so doing, assume we know how those never-existing Tatars would vote if they had come into existence in a world quite different from the one we live in. After all, if Tatars hadn't suffered the history they have, and were the majority in Crimea today, perhaps they'd be as eager to withdraw from Ukraine as its Russians were! The only sensible reply to such speculation is to say: Who knows?

Those speculative trajectories were necessary for a simple reason: Most humans actually living in Crimea in 2014 appeared genuinely to prefer joining Russia. If Russia had organized a free and fair referendum, it likely would have gotten a similar result. There was no plausible way for Tatars and others opposing secession to win a vote of the living. Thus the need for all those nonexistent Tatars: so that history could trump votes. A profoundly moral argument, but also a profoundly problematic one if we take democracy seriously, because almost all forms of democracy give priority to the choices of living humans, not dead or hypothetical ones. The new rule does, too.

Problems with Historical Approaches to Evaluating Democratic Claims

Claims of historical justice—vanished demographic dominance or lawful rights unjustly overturned—have appeared ever since the earliest attempts to make democratic decisions about territory. As long as plebiscites have offered a pathway to statehood, history has offered a counterclaim—contextualizing an unfavorable demography, preempting what democracy might decide.

Contextualization includes not only historical arguments but also claims of legal entitlement, security, economic or geographic rationality, and culture. All these arguments contextualize current borders and demography—explaining why they morally matter or can be ignored—in ways that devalue democratic claims.

For example, whatever one thinks about the Israeli presence in the West Bank, there are few *democratic* arguments to bolster Israeli claims to the whole area: No one plausibly argues the majority actually living there supports it. Israel's presence might be justified on other grounds—Jews' historical presence, the Balfour Declaration, divine donation, security imperatives, and so on. You ei-

History or Democracy in Alsace-Lorraine

At the end of the First World War, France reclaimed Alsace-Lorraine, which it had lost to Germany in 1871. France opposed a plebiscite on the grounds that German policies—introduction of German settlers, emigration of French speakers, suppression of French culture—had improperly altered the demographic balance. This historicizing argument constructed French sovereignty before 1871 as natural, German sovereignty as artificial and illegitimate. The population might have voted to join France anyway (just as in 1871, given a chance, it might have voted to stay French), but France annexed Alsace-Lorraine without asking, based on its historical claim and its victory. Although sincerely felt, its argument was also strategic, ensuring that demographic changes wouldn't override its claim. Historical arguments are strategies: One foregrounds them if one fears losing the vote, whether in Alsace in 1919 or Crimea in 2014.

ther find those reasons persuasive or not, but if you do, you accept that states can govern places whose population doesn't wish it.

Indeed, whatever one thinks about Israel and Palestine, we accept limits on democracy. Human rights and constitutionalism constrain majorities. We require supermajorities to change constitutions and claim that certain principles can't be amended. In international law, *jus cogens* limits states' ability to alter fundamental principles. We routinely constrain democratic impulses and think it right to do so.

Yet one of the fundamental values we cherish is democracy itself—governing ourselves as we see fit, which is also the commitment underlying self-determination. Constraints on democracy ought to be minimal, infringing its exercise only to the extent necessary to achieve other equally important purposes. To the degree secession expresses a valid democratic will, every historical claim opposing it limits the agency of individuals and communities and needs clear, compelling justification.

Contextual claims can be used to justify new states or resist them. A minority might demand independence, explaining away the inconvenient facts of demography as artifacts of past oppression: We were the majority here, but these other people were brought in—both explaining away and acknowledging what is clear to all, that the group is a minority. Tibetan nationalists claim areas that no longer have Tibetan majorities—sometimes due to settlement policies pursued by the Communist government in favor of Han Chinese, but also because of historical shifts. There would be no plausible way for Tibetans to claim the whole area democratically, so some other basis is needed.

But states also use context to argue *against* separatism, to help defeat a local majority's claim. Spain points to its historical continuity and the constitutional order established at the end of the Franco regime to claim priority over separatist Catalans (who haven't yet produced a popular majority). Serb claims to Kosovo stress Serbs' historical presence and the area's cultural importance, downplaying the overwhelming demographic dominance of Albanians. And China's claim to areas that still are majority Tibetan is derived from historical imperium as well as contemporary sovereignty norms.

The classical rule privileges state-level democracy at the expense of more granular demography. A state-level majority can govern the whole whether or not it commands a majority throughout the territory, ignoring internal diversity: The Bamar are a majority in Myanmar, but not in the north and east. And because majorities exist only because of existing borders, the classical rule reads democracy through the lens of territorial integrity. Today's frontiers privilege historically contingent dispensations over present demography. So even the general principle of territorial integrity is a historical claim: Units identified in 1945 enjoy special protection, regardless of what has happened since.

We expect those units to represent—to rule—whatever population is in their territory, whether or not that makes sense to the people themselves. The Albanians in Kosovo were never a particularly comfortable fit with a Belgrade-based Slavic state, and as they became an overwhelming majority, Belgrade's rule made ever less sense. Yet the norms of territorial integrity afforded Yugoslavia every opportunity to maintain its rule and offered no incentives for it to alter course. Demography changes, regions come to be dominated by groups with different languages, religions, or mores, but the current rule assumes that units established in the past can and should dictate governance, that the only democratic calculations we ought to make are within units forged in the fires of the mid-twentieth century.

This would be troubling enough if claims were clear, but historical disputes are intractable and indeterminate. There is no end to contestation about history, and justice is as variable as human experience. Consider Crimea again. Russia's annexation violated Ukraine's territorial integrity. But Crimea was (undemocratically) transferred to Ukraine in the 1950s under the Soviet Union. Before that, it had been a part of Russia since 1783. There are yet more ancient claims of Ottoman and Tatar sovereignty—and the Tatars displaced a previous population. Whose history ought we privilege?

We might try to define acceptable and unacceptable usurpations. But these are always contestable and impose present standards on a very different past. There is no claim that couldn't be supported on historical grounds. Some groups stress legal rights, others immemorial presence; some a history of dominance, others of marginalization. There is no agreement on principles and no method to decide. Outsiders are neither authorized nor competent to judge other peoples' histories, but those peoples are too much inside their own overlapping and clashing perspectives to view the matter objectively—as if an objective position existed. Often there is simply no way to agree on what justice requires.

An Ahistorical Approach

The new rule breaks with the dictates of history. It proposes a radically democratic, ahistorical model for deciding the governance of people on territory. It privileges the preferences of the current population, giving little value to ancient claims; claims based on past facts would not defeat an otherwise valid plebiscite. It does this to resolve one of the core tensions that plagues thinking about self-determination. The new rule cuts through history's thicket of contradictory proofs and contesting principles by identifying a moment of decision: a vote. The past can inform voters' choices but not preclude them. It matters, but as motive: What is decisive is the decision itself, in the present tense.

The rule's radically democratic quality means there is no need to make arguments about borders' artificiality or unjustness. Some secessionists challenge the existing state by claiming it is artificial—one frequently hears this argument about Iraq—but all states are artificial, including the secessionists' state! The new rule helps us get away from problematic interpretations of history. Demanding independence for Kurdistan on the grounds that Iraq was an artificial creation is a contestable historical claim; saying Kurdistan should be free because Kurds desire it is a claim in a radically different register, which can survive scrutiny whether or not one accepts any particular historical or justice narrative. Similarly, under the new rule, borders of African states could be changed, not because they were colonial impositions, but because their populations wished it. They might wish it because they *believe* a story about colonial imposition or unfairness, but that would be their reason, not the rule. And, as we discover every time we hold an election, there is no regulating people's reasons.

Democracy as a Right, Not a Remedy

Under the new rule, communities claim the right to form a new state because it is their desire. So long as a population expresses that desire in a recognizable, democratic form—following the procedural requirements for a plebiscite—they have a valid basis for negotiating exit, without reference to the justice of their claim, historical facts, or any other basis.

This is very different from remedial secession, which allows changes only in response to grave harms. Remedial secession is ameliorative and reactive—doctrine playing defense. This not only limits its effectiveness, it denies the reality that sometimes humans simply do not want to live under the arrangements history has bequeathed them. Remedial secession fails to respond to the *logic* of democracy and self-determination: We don't have democracy solely to achieve particular outcomes; we value autonomous decision-making. This uncontroversial idea is almost entirely absent from even the most expansive efforts to rethink external self-determination within the classical framework. By contrast, the new rule is grounded precisely on secession as a right, not a remedy.

Balancing Democracy and History

We also value justice, and believe the past makes claims on us. If the new rule is to be just and perceived as just, there must be limits to its ahistoricity. Demography does not only change peacefully, but through coercion and violence. When injustices are recent, they feel more compelling. It is not just for a rebel group to expel everyone unsympathetic and then hold a vote. On the other hand, injustice cannot freeze politics forever: It cannot create constituencies of nonexistent humans whose notional votes forever prefigure every decision about a land they never inhabited. A just rule must balance the claims of the past against the demands of democracy, but the balance properly tilts toward the present. A historical claim could only prevail over a plebiscite if a change

- was recent, perhaps one or two generations; and
- was principally violent or violated a fundamental norm of international order;

but *not* if such a change

- resulted from nonviolent population movements (even if part of intentional policy) or the administrative prerogatives of the state;
- results from continuing effects of an ancient act of violence; or
- has been perfected through an international process, like a general peace settlement.

The underlying principle for these limits is clear and liberal: What we value most is the power of people to order their own lives. That power properly belongs to the living.

That's a hard rule, but the current one does no better, and often much worse: Currently, those dispossessed by ancient violence have *no* recourse; under the new rule, they might salvage something. The tension between historical justice and democratic participation is endemic. But at least the new rule confronts that tension, in ways the current rule ignores by ignoring almost all claims for change.[1]

The Problem of Ongoing Violence and Harm

The more difficult problem concerns abuses that take place not in some distant past but today—expulsions, genocides, and abusive policies that alter demography now. What if, after the new rule came into effect, a group cleansed some territory and then held on for fifty years? Should the victims be denied redress? It is a question of the future passage of time.

We can draw a line under ancient events, but for new harms, that won't help. If some act violates a core norm, as genocide or aggression does, then in theory the consequences can't ever be accepted, under the principle *ex iniuria jus non oritur:* "law doesn't come from violation." Yet over time this would create a new class of ancient claims—dispossessed groups with historical grievances, creating a larger and larger gap between the law we claim and the practice we keep. The idea that we can freeze the law is a fantasy—though that is what the classical rule tries to do. The immutability of frontiers has not prevented humans from being uprooted, expelled, and barred from returning—over sixty million refugees today. We decree a global order while administering an ever-expanding archipelago of permanent camps. The new rule could do at least as well, and could hardly do worse.

One solution would be to give expelled populations the right to participate in (or initiate) plebiscites affecting the territory on which they lived. But this doesn't solve the other side of the problem: new populations that tip the electoral balance. Moreover, including the displaced presents complications.

How does one determine which populations have a continuing interest? Does it matter if they have settled elsewhere or have new citizenship? How long would the right extend? We can appreciate the injustice suffered by an expelled person, but his descendants' relationship to the territory is speculative: Who can say what would have happened? At some point—perhaps another generation—there has to be some end to it. The vast majority of Palestinian refugees weren't actually expelled from Palestine. They were born in Jordan, Lebanon, or other places and hold the keys to houses long since plowed under, in places they have never seen.

The new rule favors existing demography. No group should be expelled, but if it has happened—and the international community has acquiesced—it is not clear the descendants should be able to claim an eternal veto that democratic means would not otherwise afford. This is a harsh but pragmatic rule: Harms should be prevented, but harms that have been perfected have effects—not as our normative preference, but as a practical matter. If the global community has failed to prevent a change, at some point the balance of our moral concern must tip to the interests of those now living on the land.

This seems unfair, and it is—but no more so than the current rule, which also does not provide effective remedies for mass dislocation. Our current system concedes the effect of ethnic cleansing on things like voter lists: We do not reserve ballots for the dead, and refugees are in fact disenfranchised or denaturalized. (Efforts to integrate refugees actually enable this process, since states can deprive individuals of citizenship if they acquire a new one.) Indeed, this is an example of the new rule's minimalism: In saying that past injustices don't decide present governance, the rule says nothing that the classical system doesn't already; it merely applies the existing principle to border changes.

The correct ethical, political, and legal response to genocide is action to prevent it, not post hoc remediation that pretends time has stopped. The harsh line described by the new rule gives notice that we must act as a moral community when it matters, not comfort ourselves with promises that we will repair the damage in some distant future. The rule does not require affected groups or

Violence during the Plebiscite

The plebiscite itself creates risks for violence. Attempts to disrupt a plebiscite or skew voter rolls have to be policed, but there is a moral hazard: Opponents might commit anonymous provocations to derail the process. In theory, careful investigation would reveal the authors of violence, but in practice this is often unclear and always disputed.

The real challenge is implementation: Who should adjudicate claims about violence during the plebiscite? If an international supervisory mechanism does, it will need sufficient authority to enforce its decisions. If the government or separatists were in charge, it would be hard to trust them. But this is a problem that plagues elections in general, and there are techniques for monitoring elections, which the proposed rule could simply borrow.

Nor should we let the challenge of violence obscure the new rule's potential. Even if we only accepted plebiscites that were free of violence, that would introduce a radical change in the current system, in which the problem of disruption doesn't arise because the 'problem' of plebiscites doesn't, either. This is a problem of complexity we should willingly undertake to resolve, rather than rest easy in the comforting strictures of an idiot rule.

outsiders to tolerate violence; on the contrary, it strengthens the case for protective intervention in the present.

The new rule's radical ahistoricity will discomfit groups whose members genuinely feel aggrieved. True, it is not enough to simply say, "That is past"—the whole point of raising historical injustices is to assert the relevance of the past. Yet a morally consistent vision must recognize that we already accept the fruits of historical injustice—that our current system is premised on doing precisely that. The territorial system decreed in 1945 drew a line under centuries of violence and dispossession, whose most extraordinary spasm was still making a few last-minute corrections to the demography of Mitteleuropa while the UN Charter was being signed. That system has benefited some and disadvantaged others in lasting ways, marked in frozen frontiers.

No rule can simultaneously respect the will of the living and remedy the suffering of the dead, and the new rule does no worse a job than we do now. In fact, it is more responsive: It does not give any benefit to victims of historical

violence *as such,* but it can provide them and their descendants with a democratic remedy the current rule does not. The historical violence at the heart of
the current rule is also the heart of the problem this book observes and its new
rule addresses.

Effects on Shared Economic Space, Inequality, and Distribution

*In a regime of Free Trade and free economic intercourse it would be of little
consequence that iron lay on one side of a political frontier, and labor,
coal, and blast furnaces on the other. But as it is, men have devised ways to
impoverish themselves and one another; and prefer collective animosities
to individual happiness.*

John Maynard Keynes[2]

Borders define communities and divide them. As Scotland and Brexit showed,
a perennial objection to secession concerns its economic effects. There are two
related claims: Secession redistributes resources unfairly and disrupts settled
expectations in a shared economy. Each is less an empirical claim than a problem of definition—and, as so often, each relies on questionable assumptions that
go far beyond economics to reveal almost metaphysical beliefs about the state.

Unfairness: Unequal Distribution of Wealth and Resources

Secession has real and apparent effects on distribution. Both arise from unequal distribution of resources and wealth. Within any state, there are richer and
poorer areas. If wealthy communities or resource-rich areas secede, they take a
disproportionate share with them, leaving the remainder actually impoverished
because they lose resources and subsidies, or relatively so, because per capita
wealth declines. Micro-states are an extreme version of this, but it occurs whenever an economic space is divided. (The withdrawal of poor areas does this,
too, producing two states, one poorer, one wealthier.) This *seems* to increase
inequality, but that is a failure to define things clearly and to consider what the
current rule does. For when it comes to distribution and inequality, the new rule
changes very little.

The inequality secession seemingly increases is an artifact of redefining internal disparities as international ones. When Pakistan divided, its previously
shared economic space was divided, and what had been internal disparities be-

came international ones. Similarly, removing Slovenia from Yugoslavia made the remainder poorer, while removing Kosovo made it richer, per capita. This was not the result of policy changes or loss of subsidies (which we turn to next); it happened in the instant of independence, and would have even if nothing had changed except borders.

REAL DISTRIBUTION EFFECTS: SECESSION BY THE WEALTHY (OR THE POOR)

In attempting to secede, the better off are shirking their obligations of distributive justice to aid the worse off.
Allen Buchanan[3]

Secession can lead to actual changes in distribution—raising what we can call the unfair enrichment objection. A wealthy region might secede in order to escape the burden of subsidizing poorer regions. This will have a real effect on the remainder state. And perhaps the region got wealthy by exploiting those poorer areas. Should it be able to take their money and run?

People's motivations for seceding are complex. There are many reasons a community might wish to secede, and economic interest is only one, and not necessarily the principal motive. The postwar history of secessionist movements gives us little reason to believe that only the wealthy seek to withdraw. After all, the wealthy can plausibly hope to control the whole state. In any case, objecting to wealthy secession actually strengthens the case for secession by underdeveloped or exploited areas. Although poorer regions sometimes benefit from subsidies, state policy is often extractive. In such cases, we would not only approve secession, but allow the secessionists to present a bill on their way out. Even allowing only poor regions to secede would be a radical expansion of the current rule.

Many scholars assume that enrichment is a suspect category, that "Katanga cannot claim a right to self-determination as a way of securing its exclusive control over uranium mines within its territory."[4] But why is self-interest an objection? Humans organize politics to their economic benefit. America's Founding Fathers were concerned with their well-being, but that doesn't delegitimize their secession. Seceding units often wish to escape economically disadvantageous unions, as Slovenia did and Katanga tried. Resource disparities are one reason why people choose to dissociate (or join together); dismissing that as unfair is paternalistic. "[I]f secession is justifiable on other grounds . . . , then secession by the haves, even where this results in their greatly reducing or even eliminating their contribution to their less fortunate former fellow citizens, need not involve any injustice."[5] Indeed, viewed this way, the very thing that looks like a problem—that secession might redistribute resources and shift investment priorities—shows why the new rule is an improvement. When states divide, each unit's population can adjust economic policies to more accurately reflect their preferences.

Even claims of enrichment are definitional, because calling a new state's wealth or resources disproportionate is a function of borders. There is nothing moral about the fact that there is more oil in one place than another, or that tropical hardwood is in short supply near the poles. Each place has the resources it has; it is only after we put borders around them that they become political facts. Many borders formed before anyone had any inkling what resources were there; it's hard to see why a state's claim to those resources *as that unit* rests on anything other than luck. To speak of the proportional distribution of resources requires us to assume the very units secession challenges.

States have exclusive control over their resources. When a region secedes, it withdraws its wealth and resources too, depriving the rest of the state—whether richer or poorer—of the potential benefits from exploiting them. And this is the very question before us: A state's right to its resources stems from its sovereignty over particular territory—from its right to be present. If, on other grounds, some group can form a new state, then resource rights 'from presence' follow the territory. For all its hostility to secession, the current system already does this. Economic impact might be a reason to oppose division, but not a *legal* bar. The best that can be said about secession's redistributive effects is that they are political concerns, not objections to the principle.

ENTANGLEMENT: DIVISION OF SHARED ECONOMIC AND POLITICAL SPACE

> *The Constitution, in all its provisions, looks to an indestructible Union.*
> *. . . What can be indissoluble if a perpetual Union, made more perfect,*
> *is not?*
>
> Texas v. White, 1869[6]

There is another aspect to unfairness: a history of entanglement. States tax, redistribute, and invest; over time, they develop a common economic space and shared expectations. When an area withdraws, it takes shared investments with it and breaks existing markets, damaging that shared space. This is true even if the departing area is poor—it is still part of a statewide space that its withdrawal disrupts.

Entanglement goes beyond the economic. Secession vindicates the interests of one group but violates the shared rights and expectations of all. Citizens normally have the right to travel, move, work, and invest in any part of their country. After secession, those rights and interactions are circumscribed. Current law doesn't prevent such changes, but perhaps those expectations suggest it should.

We can consider a historical example that appears to confirm this objection: the American Civil War. Along with opposition to slavery, a reason for defending the Union was economic interconnectedness.[7] Northern and Southern economies were closely linked, and secession hurt both. Moreover, the United States had made investments in the South, including improving the Mississippi and building coastal fortifications.[8] When South Carolina withdrew, it took federally funded Fort Sumter with it. Taxpayers from Massachusetts had paid for that fort, too, and post offices, roads, and customhouses—investments predicated on a political union, which secession disrupted.

But in seceding, South Carolina not only seized Fort Sumter, it gave up its stake in Fort Warren, which guards Boston Harbor (and held Confederate prisoners!), and many other facilities South Carolinians helped pay for. The idea of lost investment is only half right, because the remainder state gains a full share of whatever remains: nothing of Fort Sumter, but all of Fort Warren. This is an accounting fiction—the forts belonged to the Union as a whole, not to each part by shares—but ownership by the whole is a fiction, too, and one that does not survive if a division is otherwise valid.

I don't know which side received a bigger share of federal largesse,[9] but we don't need to decide. Sometimes the seceding unit is an economic drag, sometimes a net payer. (Yugoslavia had each.) Sometimes the parties themselves cannot agree who benefits. There is no easy calculus for the costs of union or division, but the math can be done, and is done today when states divide their debts and assets; when people argue about the *impossibility* of doing it, something else is driving their thinking.

That something else is a normative intrusion into this supposedly empirical calculation. The objection has less to do with identifiable costs to the remainder than harm to the *whole as such*. The economic argument is linked to a societal

Bonds of Affection, Bonds of Slavery: Remembering America's Civil War

Americans typically remember the Civil War as a fight to end slavery. But though Southern states seceded to preserve their slave economy, the North fought to preserve the Union. On the eve of war, in his first inaugural address, Abraham Lincoln invoked the perpetual indivisibility of the nation, not the immorality of slavery; in fact, he pledged to preserve slavery. That changed, culminating in the Emancipation Proclamation and the 13th Amendment. But as late as August 1862, Lincoln wrote that he aimed to preserve "the Union as it was. . . . My paramount object in this struggle is to save the Union, and is not either to save or to destroy slavery. . . . What I do about slavery, and the colored race, I do because I believe it helps to save the Union[.]"*

The South's claim of oppression—while defending slavery—was an early signal of how problematic it is to rely on perceptions of injustice, since even those who *are* wrong *feel* wronged. But if the North's war seems to offer an obvious solution—oppose secessions that are immoral—we should remember that that wasn't how it actually began.

Lincoln's second inaugural, fervently condemning slavery, is carved on the wall of the Lincoln Memorial. His first isn't. This elision—conflating abolition and union—has left a confused legacy, for what is the value of union? When what we confront is not evil but simply a community wishing to leave, defending union—using violence to defend it—requires justification. Lincoln's defense of union for its own sake signals our continuing challenge: not to substitute the state for judgment.

*Lincoln, Letter to Horace Greeley.

one: that it's harmful to withdraw from the common polity. It sounds a bit metaphysical—the nation, the indissoluble unit.

A different logic supports the new rule: When people living in a place no longer believe the common state is in their interest, why must they continue to accept it, notwithstanding a history of shared investment? Economic arguments really are about the identity of the *demos,* of a people whose identity matters. If we accept that that is the question—and that the existence of the state cannot preempt it—then the fact that an existing economic space will be broken is *politically* important, but not *legally* determinative. At most, the remainder could negotiate compensation, but not prevent departure.[10]

For what exactly is the harm to other citizens' *legitimate* expectations? Often, these expectations are abstract, expressing only a notional or theoretical harm, such as I might suffer if Alaska were to secede. Deference to settled expectations risks giving cover to marginalization. The majority can veto an underdeveloped area's attempt to withdraw, claiming that shared investment has created a sphere of settled, if unfair, expectations. (There has never been a remedial secession based on economic marginalization.) Defending shared expectations sounds like a concern with individuals' rights, but it's really about an abstraction. It places an absolute priority on the citizenry *as a whole*—which is to say, the state: a curious position to arrive at if one started out defending liberal or cosmopolitan values.

THE NEW RULE IS UNFAIR IN THE SAME WAY THE CURRENT RULE IS   Settled expectations are not some freestanding philosophical concept; they are an artifact of law and can be shaped by law. They can be defeated by a clear signal that historical investment doesn't limit a community's right to determine its political future. If the new rule were entrenched in law, it would no longer be true that people's expectations would be violated. It is a policy choice we can make.

We don't even have such expectations today. States sometimes divide, and when they do, their citizens are compelled to choose—or have no choice. None of us has an indefeasible expectation that our country will continue in its current shape, or that our rights will survive its dissolution; law and practice contradict this. Anyone investing in 1990 in property at both ends of Czechoslovakia, the Soviet Union, or Ethiopia expecting to deal with one country's legal system has been sorely disappointed. Relying on shared expectations as a veto misunderstands the world we currently live in.[11]

Indeed, this points to an even more compelling reason to reject the investment objection, which is how closely the new rule conforms to the existing order. In the present system there is no requirement for redistribution between states.[12] States have no claim to each other's territory and resources no matter how urgent the need. (States may acquire obligations through treaties—overflight, water rights—but no state has to give such things up.) The present distribution is not a question of fairness or even good policy—only borders. Although political philosophy has long perceived the problem of borders' arbitrariness and sometimes argued for global distributive justice,[13] that's not the rule we actually use. It's difficult to see why the new rule must adopt a fairer standard than the present system.

And if one thinks that *local* distribution of resources has value, the new rule may well be better. It makes it likelier that wealth would be distributed among people with a closer physical connection to the sources of that wealth. That sounds intuitively superior to the current system of redistribution within historically received frontiers. Nothing in the new rule ensures that local governance would be any more efficient or less corrupt than the more distant variety the current rule reinforces; the new rule is not a cure for human nature. But why should we register *greater* concern about regional elites' proclivity to skim rents than the efforts of more state distant elites to do the same? One would think that, at worst, it would be a matter of moral indifference whether the wealth of Katanga is stolen locally or in Kinshasa.

The new rule would change incentives. It would not only tempt secessionists to establish new states, it would also give existing states reasons to ameliorate regional differences to avoid secession. Extractive policies increase dissatisfaction, so states would have incentives to ensure equitable investment. The EU, for all its problems, is proof that wealthier communities can embrace transfer policies, and any number of countries within the EU prove this principle in their domestic practice.

If a secession were *otherwise* justified, the fact that it would redistribute resources between the remaining and new state is not objectionable in principle. Objecting simply favors the status quo, which requires its own justification. Perhaps an ideal rule would give all humans an equal share of the world's wealth, but the current rule looks nothing like that. So long as we divide resources by territorial sovereignty, there is no reason to oppose secessions simply because they create new units within that system.

The Drawing of Lines: A Defense of Arbitrary Limits

Many elements of the new rule are arbitrary. Small or dispersed groups would not benefit, while some people would be forced into new states against their will. Perhaps the new rule is unfair simply because it distributes its benefits to some but not others.

Rather than seeing this is a problem, we might recognize it as an exercise in realism. Law is often arbitrary for sound reasons. It doesn't matter which side of the road we drive on, so long as we pick one. Often general policy is not arbitrary, only its precise delineation is: We decide when people are old enough to vote, consent to sex, or make financial decisions, knowing some people could make these choices earlier. We cannot treat every instance entirely on its merits; we place limits because some limit is needed to avoid the logical absurdities *any* system is vulnerable to.

We should prefer the good to the perfect. Some communities would not benefit from the new rule, but under the current rule they have no right to secede anyway; others would be better off, and we should not refuse to benefit some because we cannot benefit all. The new rule is Pareto superior: some better off, none worse off. (It might seem that those who lose in a plebiscite are worse off; but since there is no *right* to preserve the current state as it is, no one is deprived of a right he actually has.) It's true we sometimes choose not to do something at all rather than do it in a way that benefits people disproportionately, but it wouldn't ensure a better distribution of secession to deny any right altogether. That's another example of the reflexive, cosmopolitan preference for not doing this kind of thing ever: Integrative impulses are seen as normal and don't need to be interrogated, but disintegrative impulses are presumed to be fleeting or illegitimate. That's not an accurate depiction of social reality, but rather willful blindness to the way human beings actually live.

Rootlessness: Effects of and on Migration

Oh, the leaky boundaries of man-made states!
How many clouds float past them with impunity;

. . .

Only what is human can truly be foreign.
The rest is mixed vegetation, subversive moles, and wind.
Wisława Szymborska[14]

The new rule is grounded on the political priority of human beings in the places they live. So when should migrants be able to exercise self-determination? If the new rule rests on the social and moral connection between human beings and physical place, shouldn't it matter if that connection is recent, shallow, and—well, let's just say it—rootless?

At one level, the new rule is generous to migrants. It doesn't distinguish between recent and ancient groups, but only asks about the population's presence, legitimacy (not necessarily legality), and preferences, from which it draws a legal consequence. This is more generous than the current system. Control of borders and citizenship are areas over which states retain the most unconstrained sovereignty. Under the new rule, this power would be unaltered: States would continue to have the right to impose limitations on immigration. But they might have additional reasons to, for if they *failed* to control or restrict new populations, in time a sufficiently densely settled immigrant group—Muslims in parts of England or France, Latinos in California—might be able to organize a separate political community.

This creates two incentives for states: to limit immigration and to integrate immigrants. The first of these is not a particularly attractive prospect (to liberals), while the second can be acceptable or awful, depending on how it's done. But neither necessarily violates human rights: States have wide latitude to restrict immigration and set policies for language use, education, social norms, and the like; they aren't under any obligation to treat immigrants like recognized minorities or indigenous peoples.

The new rule might therefore incentivize states to discourage immigration, but this effect is likely to be small, because political actors tend to think about the short term. It could take immigrants generations to form a local majority, while the reasons governments encourage or tolerate migration—labor shortages, refugee crises—are calculations made in the present. Americans did not want to admit eleven million illegal migrants, but they liked getting their vegetables picked and their slaughterhouses and restaurants staffed. If Germans had realized their *Gastarbeiter* were actually going to stay, they might have adopted a different policy. But they did admit them, they did stay, and now they are there.

Besides, the new rule would only give migrants a right to form a new state if they were sufficiently clustered—and actually wanted to secede. The state has some control over this by making immigrants feel part of the society. So while the rule might discourage free movement in one respect, it would also help migrants participate in the places they live. Indeed, to view these effects on immigration as a problem is to ignore the current trends in human rights toward integrating migrants—trends that introduce these same incentives and risks. By emphasizing the importance of the actual link between person and place, the new rule undermines the fixity of borders, but its effects on migration and citizenship, though complex, are not radically different from the incentives states now face.

The rule could also affect internal migration. Since the rule requires meaningful links to territory, should someone be able to vote if he just moved the day before? But why not? In practice, it's simpler to adopt an inclusive rule, letting anyone who is legitimately resident on the day take part. Indeed, the more interesting question concerns those who have left but retain real connections; the logic of the rule could counsel for extending the right to vote to them, though that would require complex calculations. For both categories, there is practice from domestic systems dealing with the right to vote upon which we could draw, such as the limited voting rights given to EU citizens who move within that Union. Each plebiscite could use rules for the state's regular elections or follow a uniform global minimum.

Another problem concerns permanent but irregular populations, like those eleven million illegal immigrants in the United States. Excluding all such populations could be troubling, both on grounds of fairness and because that would create incentives for states not to regularize them. Perhaps the best solution would be pragmatic: Anyone in fact resident should have the right to take part. After all, this is the only right one acquires: Nothing in the rule would require states to regularize illegal immigrants for any other purpose.[15] But it would also be possible to restrict the new right to legal populations.[16]

The new rule's effects on states' migration policies must be balanced by the fact that states already use internal migration in illiberal ways. Chinese policies encouraging Han settlement in Xinjiang are surely as troubling as, say, hypothetical restrictions on Chinese citizens immigrating into an independent Turkestan.

Focusing exclusively on the new rule's effects simply accepts the current rule's parameters, in which fixed borders predetermine which population movements are international and which internal. Strategic control of migration already occurs, and the real question is which strategies we wish to tolerate and which units we want exercising control.

The rule's effects on migration are another proof that secession is not necessarily illiberal. A group might secede to make a country with a more liberal migration policy. This was the logic behind calls after Brexit for the secession of Greater London so that it could remain part of the EU, or California after the election of Trump. There might be reasons to doubt the wisdom of those unlikely moves, but a concern that they are illiberal is not one of them.

Not Perfect, Just Less Terrible: Violence and Instability

This brings us to the harshest question: The new rule would cause war and death; is that a problem? Even if the new rule is more just, it's predictable that

Nothing like Lausanne: The Supposed Problem of Population Transfer

Some states confronted with a restive population adopt rather different methods: genocide, extermination, persecution. These are obviously unacceptable and obviously not what the rule is about. There is one measure, however, that some might think is related to the new rule: population transfers. This is foundationally mistaken.

The principle animating population transfers is quite different. Transfer is typically associated with the Greek-Turkish exchanges agreed in the Lausanne Treaty, and ethnic cleansing in the former Yugoslavia. (Vastly larger expulsions after the Second World War are largely forgotten.) The fatal quality those transfers shared is that they moved people: Borders were determined by war or diplomacy, and populations moved to fit within them. Under the new rule, *borders* are moved to accommodate people where they live. People might have to accept a citizenship (making them no worse off than everyone on the planet), and they might have an option to move—which some would surely do—but no part of the rule supports their expulsion or intimidation.

Only if one believed that forced transfers—the very thing the rule aims to avoid—are an inevitable consequence of changing borders* could one suppose that the Lausanne Option is the same as this rule. Even then, we would have to ask if the new rule would create more transfers than already occur; it is not as if ethnic cleansing in the 1990s happened under the *new* rule! The new rule is the moral opposite of what was done to the peoples of the former Yugoslavia, who, had this rule been applied to them, might have stayed where they were as the frontiers moved about them, instead of fleeing the sound of guns and digging up their dead.

*See Lister, "Self-Determination, Dissent, and the Problem of Population Transfers," 145.

some states—more interested in position than principle—would resist. If majorities fear secession and we make secession more likely, they will fear it more; insecure governments would suppress 'disloyal' populations to ensure they couldn't vote to secede.[17] Under the new rule, millions of people might be caught up in conflicts over borders (also millions liberated from states they don't desire—but accompanied by great suffering). So why isn't the new rule irresponsible—theoretically attractive, morally just, but, given the nature of human societies, likely to make things worse? We want justice, but the heavens *will* fall. How is this all right?

It isn't, but it happens under the current rule, too: Conflicts of that kind are going on today even though the system offers secessionists no support and the odds are stacked against them. Although under the new rule some societies would be caught up in violence that might have remained peaceful, others would be spared violence that, under the present rule, they are predictably going to undergo: Their conflicts would be mitigated by an option to exit, leading either to secession or a better union. The proper question—the only morally relevant question, in the absence of absolute peace—is whether the new rule would lead to *more or less* violence. There are good reasons to think it might produce less.

First, human rights obligations would still be in effect. The compliance pull of human rights is weak—the system demonstrably fails to protect people from their own states now, so we could hardly expect it to suddenly become more robust—but at least rights would include the possibility of exit when other protections prove worse than inadequate. Moreover, while majorities might have more to fear, they would also have counterincentives. The new rule's purpose is to improve minorities' negotiating position—power to bargain and mobilize support. In deciding how to react, majorities would have to be careful not to provoke the very thing they fear: that minorities would react by seceding. There would be voices arguing for repression—there are such voices now, even without exit—but also voices urging accommodation, because the costs of failure would be higher.

It's hard to see why giving more negotiating resources to minority communities makes their circumstances worse; it's implausible that a right to exit makes them, on average, worse off. As always, we mustn't invoke the perfect against the good: Under the present rule, states frequently suppress minorities, even though states' territorial integrity is guaranteed. Evidently majorities do not feel reassured now; indeed, it may be that suspicion of minorities is inelastic, or at least is a condition of globalizing modernity,[18] in which case we would do better to give those minorities more resources to resist the predictable depredations of the state.

The Problem of Postindependence Violence and Instability

But violence is not a one-off calculation. What if the new state itself collapses into civil war? Independence can be destabilizing: Often internal divisions have been kept in check by the need for unity against an external threat; once that threat is lifted, factions begin to contest for power. This happened in

South Sudan: After independence in 2011, two factions that had (usually) been united against Khartoum fell out, and the violence has been horrific.

Independence can also destabilize the remainder state. The catalytic chain of violence in the former Yugoslavia was partly driven by the withdrawal of some republics, which changed the relative power in the remainder in dangerous ways. Slovenia's departure made it dangerous for Croatia to remain in a union dominated by Belgrade; in turn, Croatia's withdrawal made it dangerous for Bosnia's Muslims and Croats to remain—and riskier for Bosnia's Serbs when Bosnia left. A similar dynamic threatened the remainder of Nigeria during the Biafra crisis and disrupted relations among groups in Pakistan after Bangladesh's secession.[19] These are real, cautionary examples. Not all states collapse in this way— we should keep the peaceful episodes in mind, because they are data, too—and we should remember that these examples occurred under the *current* system, with its incentives for states to refuse to negotiate and deploy violence. Still, we should take the objection seriously.

We are choosing among violent alternatives. Secession sometimes destabilizes the relationship between communities—and so does maintaining existing relationships. If we are going to place postindependence violence in a place like South Sudan in the scale against secession, we should add the conflicts in existing states to the balance sheet of suffering under the current rule. Evidently Sudan itself had problems of this kind, otherwise how are we to account for its long civil war? South Sudan was a *more* violent place in the decades before independence, and that is saying a lot.

Thinking about secession only in relation to violent cases—in a world that encourages states to oppose it—is to confuse claim and reaction. When demography encourages predatory impulses against a minority, secession can actually stabilize societies by reducing the source of contestation. Kosovo was a violent place *before* it was liberated from Belgrade; the violence largely ended when Belgrade's rule did (though there were attacks on the smaller Serb and Roma populations by returning Albanians). The answer to the objection that the new rule might destabilize societies is—as so often—to recall what is being elided by the question: the null set of cases we cannot see from inside the current rule.

Part of the answer is a matter of design. Constitutional and political provisions can make postindependence risks greater or smaller. Still, we should not conclude that it is a matter for objective, external expertise, as if some panel of experts could choose candidates for secession. One of the lessons from studies like *Balkan Tragedy* or *When Victims Become Killers,* on Africa's Great Lakes crisis, is humility: The origins of conflicts, in new or existing states, are so dynamic and complex that they are best understood in retrospect; to imagine we could predict them is hubris—never an admirable quality, but most undesirable in policymaking. We do better to tip the unknowable scales toward communities' own preferences about how to govern themselves, and let that choice play out as it will.

Instability and the Moral Value of the Status Quo

Even a separatist is likely to concede (albeit reluctantly) that the status quo is sometimes important.

Lea Brilmayer[20]

I swear that . . . I will . . . bear allegiance to the Hong Kong Special Administrative Region of the People's Re-Fucking of Cheena . . .[21]

That was the altered oath uttered in 2016 by a pro-independence activist elected to the Hong Kong Legislative Council. The activist had inserted an expletive, used a derogatory pronunciation of China associated with the Japanese occupation, and referred to the "Hong Kong Nation," while standing before a banner declaring "Hong Kong is NOT China." She was not seated. Whatever one thinks about her provocative method, China's message is equally clear: Supposing you thought Hong Kong deserved independence or even just that Hong Kongers should have a choice, well, that won't be happening.

International law is about creating predictability, even at the cost of injustice, out of a Hobbesian conviction that the greatest threat to justice is war, and war is born of instability. Even if this new rule is a good one, there may be no good way to get there. The transition might be too destabilizing because *any* transition would be. We have a system around which expectations have developed. It may be a bad system, predicated on mistaken assumptions, but even a bad rule can produce a predictable world. The new rule, modest as it may seem, introduces a foundational change and may be too destabilizing.

Even that would be an important lesson, because it would show us that the current rule is not better, just current. Like the QWERTY typewriter or standard gauge rail, it's not a particularly good design, just too costly to change. That's a very different defense of the current system than a belief that it's doing good work. This matters because matters change. It may be too costly to swap rules today, but possibilities might present themselves, and we should be ready. One of the advantages of the new rule is that, rather than pretending secession never occurs and therefore discouraging preparation, it encourages us to think about the conditions that require secession, and the conditions secession requires.

Meanwhile, the current system isn't cost-free. What *are* the costs of our commitment to territorial integrity in places like the Balkans and Africa? The current system may actually increase suffering by strengthening the hand of elites ruling peoples whom they have no business ruling. If existing states are so fragile that allowing their own peoples to challenge them would destroy them, why do we believe it not only necessary but preferable to defend those states? Why not see fragility as a proof of the need for change, if the state's own population doesn't believe in it? The answer is less clear than our confident commitments would suggest.

What Our Fears Say about Us

We cannot know with certainty. But we can know certain things about the present rule and can speculate about an alternative. If for a moment we place the question of instability to the side, we see that the new rule is, in important ways, more just: It allows more people to live in states of their own choosing and fewer to live as minorities. It does this without forcing anyone to move. So if we nonetheless stick to the present rule, it must be because we believe—without proof—that it is more stabilizing, or that we simply prefer the misery we know. In either case, we will arrive at a clearer understanding of why we organize our world as we do. We will see that our commitment is not to some higher and nobler goal, but to a fear-laden calculus that only stability—however unjust— keeps the wolf from the door. We can dispense with the dubious sentiment that somehow we are committed to the current system because it honors diversity, but because we distrust diversity: because in fact we are—believe ourselves to be—Hobbesian creatures through and through.

In fact, for all our celebration of diverse societies, we are quite afraid that we do not naturally incline that way. When the moment comes and we confront the possibility of division, what is our response? "Oh no, we can't; all hell would break loose!" We believe everyone would run to his identity corner; but what does that say about what we believe of ourselves? If we truly believed in our

Wait—Isn't This What White Supremacists Dream Of?

I suppose it is. But lots of other people dream of it, too, so the real question is, who would use this rule? Racists would have to secure the votes of a supermajority in an area of at least one million people. And even if they succeeded, they would have to accept all the population and respect their human rights: The new rule doesn't require us to tolerate secessions that violate *other* core values.

Just down the road from where I live, in Paoli, Indiana, there is a notorious white supremacist group that advocates creating a whites-only country. They have, at most, five hundred members nationwide, and they can't even win a seat on the town council, let alone secede. That doesn't mean groups like them couldn't become a real threat. But if white supremacists or similar groups could achieve enough strength to make a claim under the new rule, we would already have a serious problem under the current one. If you think the only thing standing between us and racial Armageddon is rigid borders, you have a very dark vision of human nature.

own vision, we would think it strong enough to resist the call of nationalism's sirens. Our response—the reflex to lock everyone in, to prohibit the possibility of change—suggests we don't. So by a curious turn, it is the most committed cosmopolitan who is most convinced of our primordial, tribal inclinations. Perhaps that's right: The tolerant, respectful life doesn't come naturally, but must be schooled, structured, even locked in. Perhaps. But if so, it's a bleak vision, which we should squarely confront: We are such creatures. We fear opening Pandora's box, but there are no monsters—only us: We are inside.

Change is destabilizing. But *not* changing is dangerous, too—only its dangers are put off, compounded, surfacing after periods of drift, making the crisis worse when it comes. Everyone knows the expression "Grab the bull by the horns," but we rarely stop to think what it really means: Grabbing a bull by the horns is extraordinarily dangerous, but you do it because the only thing more dangerous is *not* grabbing the horns; better now than later, because later may be too late.

An international order that commands us to fear and avoid any change, no matter how unjust or cruel the present situation, misunderstands human nature and the nature of politics: Change is inevitable, it is always happening. The most implausible quality of the current rule is its rigidity, its attempt to freeze the map of the world, as if the world were not in continuous tumult. *That* is the sign of our decadence—not that change isn't happening, but that we are incapable of responding to it.

It is not change, but obstacles to change that are dangerous. It is good to remember that the new rule is really about secession *before* a crisis. We lack an international norm to regularize secession, instead leaving it to the whim of hostile authorities who drive advocates of change to desperation and defiance. Secessionists should not feel compelled to choose between submission and the gun; they should have the option for peaceful change, but the current rule does not afford them even that. Any transition presents risks, but those risks can be managed. That is possible, and it's what the new rule tries to do.

Although secession—like any change—might be destabilizing in the short term, the benefits could be significant. The present rule offers no alternative to endless reinvestment in existing states; a new, flexible rule would give us options in precisely those cases for which options are most needed. And really, is relying upon the way things have been done—worse, reinforcing states simply because they already exist—a sensible way to respond to a world everyone knows is changing?

> . . . *for readiness to fight to prevent change is just as unmoral as readiness to fight to enforce it. To establish methods of peaceful change is therefore the fundamental problem of international morality and of international politics.*
>
> E. H. Carr[22]

7

The Hardest Part:
Creating a Right of Secession

How could such a rule become reality?

SO, HOW *DO* WE SOLVE THE PROBLEM of peaceful change? How could a right to secession become a practical reality? Assuming we thought it a good idea, how could we move to legal norm and political principle?

We might proceed the way Thomas Franck did in "The Emerging Right to Democratic Governance," and simply announce the imminent arrival of a new right. In theory, there is scope to interpret existing law. References to self-determination in the UN Charter could be repurposed; the Saving Clause could be given a more expansive interpretation; remedial secession's threshold could be pushed lower. One could argue that recent secessions are evidence of an emerging customary norm.

But changes in formal law are lagging indicators, not leading ones. Secession is a hard sell, and the principal battleground is moral and political. A shift in attitudes must precede the legal project; only then will we see doctrinal arguments lining up and making sense. And, after all, the goal is not a new legal right for its own sake, but a change in how societies and states behave.

So, let's see how that might happen. First, we'll consider why a *formal* right of secession is implausible, and what that implies about the best strategies to adopt—the narrow but real possibilities that exist. The path is indirect: It relies on transnational diffusion of norms, and for this we can draw lessons from once-improbable projects that have become orthodoxies, such as decolonization and human rights; also, recent secession attempts suggest that constitutional projects could serve as models. The path leads through many small changes, rather than a single, quixotic swerve toward a new legal rule. But because the *existing* global norm limits the ability to create change within states, we cannot abandon the idea of a new rule: Advocates of secession need a point of triangulation outside the state to advance their cause, and that point will be found in international law. The prospects for change in individual cases will be strengthened if we keep a global claim, however implausible now, clearly in sight.

The Law and Politics of Implementing a Right to Secession

The Implausibility of a Formal Right

Throughout this book, I've argued that a legal right of secession is necessary to realize the substantive goal of improving communities' ability to negotiate their political destinies. But how plausible is a legal right, today? Let's consider the three main ways a legal right might be identified.

THE IMPOSSIBILITY OF A TREATY   States have ratified treaties recognizing a right to self-determination, so might they agree to a treaty declaring a right to secession? No chance: given the entrenched, reflexive opposition to secession, states would not agree to a general treaty and cannot be compelled to. Nor would they accept interpretations of existing treaties creating a general right. Even a regional treaty is implausible: Although some countries accept the right for their own populations, there is no region in which most states do. For the same reasons, a law-making resolution by the General Assembly (whose resolutions aren't binding, but can identify binding norms) isn't plausible.

THE CHALLENGE OF MAKING A CUSTOMARY CLAIM   Creating treaties isn't the only way international law is made. A few states can embrace a practice and advocate for its spread; in time, this can give rise to a new, binding norm, through the process of customary international law. Successful secessions would be interpreted as a fillip for a new right: inspiration for others, a source for an endless stream of scholarship, evidence for an emerging norm extending beyond the colonial context. Even a failed vote could serve as a precedent for a right to decide.

But while custom is more promising than treaty, it's not easy. Customary international law requires *opinio juris*—a sense of legal obligation compelling states to act. Just because a state accepts a right of secession doesn't mean it

Why Scotland's Vote Doesn't (Easily) Make New Law

Even though Scotland doesn't fall into any existing category for self-determination, it came within a few percentage points of independence despite being peacefully and prosperously integrated into the United Kingdom—and may yet secede. So does the Scottish case help establish a customary right of secession? Ironically, the fact that Britain cooperated in the referendum—and its reasons for doing so—makes the Scottish case less useful.

For the Scottish referendum to constitute evidence of a customary right to secession, the United Kingdom would have had to believe it was under an *international obligation* to hold a referendum. But Britain acted on domestic political considerations and constitutional imperatives; international law played no role in the decision to hold a referendum. The United Kingdom published an extensive report on the international legal *implications* of independence—such as if Scotland could continue as an EU member—but didn't concern itself with international *justifications,* noting, "[i]f Scotland were to become independent . . . , it would be with the UK's agreement rather than by unilateral secession."* The Scottish government also based its arguments on UK law; there was no need for external grounds for legitimacy.† The entire process was what in international law is called an act of comity or grace, and that rarely contributes to new customary rule.

*Crawford and Boyle, "Annex A: Opinion."
†If London refused to negotiate after an independence vote, we could expect to see arguments about the sovereignty of the Scottish people and unilateral secession. See Tierney, "Legal Issues," 9–10, 14–6 ("[P]rovided the United Kingdom does not oppose the independence of Scotland . . . this should in turn avoid the need for any serious debate about the legality of the act of secession under international law.").

believes it is under any international obligation. Canada's support for Quebec's referendum was based on Canadian law. (The Supreme Court found an obligation to negotiate in good faith, but rejected a right to unilateral secession.) The South Sudanese referendum, at the end of a long civil war, resulted from a diplomatic deal to which Khartoum agreed. Even Kosovo's supporters assiduously denied the precedential value of its independence. States may sometimes accept secession, but they are not *obliged* to. So states that willingly allow their own populations to secede—precisely because they *are* willing—don't necessarily provide evidence of a new rule. Only if they acknowledge an obligation does their behavior contribute to a new rule.[1]

Besides, there simply aren't many cases. By contrast, plenty of states adamantly oppose the very idea: Madrid's suppression of Catalonia's 2017 referendum is evidence that Spain believes it is *not* under any obligation to allow secession; China believes it can criminalize separatism. That's data, too: If customary law is made by examining what states' behavior shows they believe the law to be, any rigorous analysis would have to conclude there is no obligation for states to recognize a right to secede.

GENERAL PRINCIPLES There is a third pathway, more indeterminate but therefore more open for strategic development. General principles can be used to derive legal rules, and have proved useful for making rights claims in the face of states' opposition or indifference. States can't be made to sign treaties, and customary law requires evidence that states accept a rule, but general principles can be derived deductively or logically. They draw on states' domestic practice, but don't require the same proofs custom does.

General principles tend not to be a first choice for legal argument—they feel weaker and residual. But they provide a pathway to make claims and shape behavior. Most of all, they provide space: The most important general principle that advocates can exploit is called the Lotus freedom principle (named after a case involving a ship called the *Lotus*), which holds that states are generally free to act when there is no positive rule shaping their behavior. Secession is not prohibited, so nothing prevents individual states from promoting a right of secession in their own practice. Eventually that could provide the basis for a new principle supportive of a right of secession—but in the meantime, it allows states, secessionists, and their advocates to act, regardless of the hostile legal framework.

COMPLIANCE WITHOUT INSTITUTIONS These doctrinal limits have practical effects. Without a treaty, it's hard to create institutional architecture, like a supervisory body. Even using an existing institution would require states' acquiescence. States are maximally resistant to outside compulsion, so a right to secession will have to develop, if at all, in a flexible interpretive context—a zone of compliance, rather than enforcement, and in the practice of individual states, gradually accepted, rather than as a single global rule all at once.

This doesn't mean the right would have no meaning. Its power would be independent of formal architecture, as a norm shaping politics, much as decolonization or human rights did. Decolonization was hardly a foregone conclusion—

the system was actually expanding into the 1920s—and the major colonial powers fiercely resisted new interpretations. Yet decolonization rapidly triumphed. Only minimal infrastructure governed the process, but the norm made it harder for colonial powers to maintain their empires without cost, easier for colonial populations to mobilize, and easier for states to support them without being accused of interfering in other states' internal affairs. Similarly, human rights draw their power from diverse actors committed to the idea of rights, more than from the formal treaty architecture. A right to secession could spread in the same way. The prospects for law are slim, but we should care more about the practical results than what the legal rules say. Fortunately, the more fluid realm of politics is precisely where the most promising way is to be found.

The Path of Opportunity: Constitutionalism, Transnationalism, and Intervention

Law isn't only made through formal processes; nor is law the only vehicle for changing politics. Whatever the legal significance of recent secessions, as social and political facts, they matter. The bare fact that they happened changes arguments about the possibility and rightness of such things. They may not constitute a new rule on their own, but the *experience*—the politics of negotiating secession, the diplomacy surrounding the attempt—serves as models for how these things can and should be done. Moments of exit normalize secession as an option: Even when contested, they demonstrate the possibility, the normalcy, of change. Controversies over Brexit, Catalonia, Kurdistan, and Crimea force the question onto the international agenda, and that makes claims of a changing norm more plausible. They can be the engine for expanding the right, because law is often the result of dynamic processes in which domestic politics, international diplomacy, and transnational transmission of values interact.

CONSTITUTIONAL ENTRENCHMENT AND DIFFUSION OF VALUES The Scottish referendum may not signal a breakthrough in customary law, but it does suggest a more promising pathway in one hundred smaller steps: through the constitutions of sympathetic states. International law is not self-enforcing. Mostly it is realized through the actions of states. So even if a right of secession were acknowledged—even if there were an institution to supervise it—states would need to take steps to make it meaningful. They would have to change their constitutions, amend electoral laws, and do many practical things to support its exercise. An international rule may provide the normative justification for these steps, but they must be done at the state level. Domestic practice matters.

Some states already recognize a right of secession similar to the new rule. Canada requires negotiations after a clear vote on a clear question. Ethiopia allows secession with a supermajority in the regional legislature and a majority in a regional vote. Liechtenstein recognizes a right of secession for its individual communes: A majority must vote, and a second vote approving the result of negotiations is required.[2] Burma's 1947 constitution recognized a right to secede after ten years of independence. Some give asymmetrical rights: Saint Kitts and Nevis' constitution allows Nevis to leave the federation, and Uzbekistan's allows autonomous Karakalpakstan to secede;[3] in the United Kingdom, Scotland's right to secede and Northern Ireland's right to join the Republic of Ireland are very different pathways.

These provisions exist; some have been used. Whatever their value in law, observers can and will treat them as inspiration or threat—a challenge to the existing order. We could ignore the doctrinal awkwardness and make use of that fact: If even a few significant powers adopted similar practices, it would bolster the claim that a practice is emerging. Indeed, customary law is often more flexible than I have described, focusing more on what states do rather than elusive motivations. Customary claims can spread rapidly on a small evidentiary base, especially if influential states support it. Consider marriage equality: Worldwide only one in seven states have actually adopted the practice—one in Africa, only Taiwan in Asia—and over seventy still criminalize same-sex relations, but this hasn't prevented advocates from plausibly claiming same-sex protections as human rights.

Nor is actual secession the only relevant event. Whenever a constitution is amended or a new constitution drafted, the opportunity to introduce language about secession—or just deemphasize references to indivisibility—presents itself. Likewise, each time a state expands autonomy or minority rights, that fact can be mobilized as indirect evidence that a protective norm is emerging—in much the way Franck read various strands of evidence to discover a right to democracy.

A constitutionalizing strategy relies on pluralism. Some states might link the right to specific territories; others might define a domestic right similar to the new rule, but with varying content or procedures. But this is not a problem: As we'll see, a right of secession introduces only minimal changes, compatible with the widest range of state practice. It wouldn't limit the diverse possibilities for ac-commodating difference that constitutionalism offers. It is compatible with pres-idential or parliamentary systems, first-past-the-post or alternative transferable voting, unitary or federal or consociational governance, autonomy or identical rights for all—with all the models we know, except the one that says states' bor-ders never change. There's no need for states to apply a uniform rule to contribute to an emerging norm—indeed, that's how international law normally proceeds.

Moreover, states that adopt a favorable view of secession at home can ac-tively influence the position of others. States incorporate their domestic values into their foreign policy, advocating for their preferred positions in interna-tional fora, conditioning aid and trade on ancillary issues of governance, rights, or the like. The British abolition movement is an example of how one society's moral intuitions powerfully shaped a global rights revolution. More generally, when states support reform abroad or establish an international administration, they often impose systems like their own: When the United States occupied Iraq, it introduced a new traffic code, in English, modeled on Maryland's.[4] (Guess where its author was from.) History is full of examples of states offering their own quirks as universal models. States accepting a right to secession for them-selves could do the same, promoting adoption of similar policies abroad, or pro-testing attempts to suppress secessions.

This isn't a matter of coercion and bribery. International law used to speak of civilized nations, but while the phrasing is archaic, the idea of a shared commu-nity—and unequal power—remains. States are social entities, concerned with prestige and position; they take cues about statelike behavior from each other, mimicking and acculturating to each other.[5] Cultural, political, and legal values travel; states tend to adopt human rights standards in regional clusters. So se-cession can have a demonstration effect: The Scottish referendum doesn't di-rectly constitute a customary rule, but it's a model for how states can, even ought to behave, and like-minded states might align their behavior over time.

IDENTIFYING COALITIONS TO SUPPORT SECESSION

> [L]aws (like people) migrate, and seepage is everywhere.
> Judith Resnik[6]

Progress will be piecemeal, ad hoc, and opportunistic. A global secession movement is implausible, but coalitions to support particular secessions will

> **Secession as Subsidiarity**
>
> Subsidiarity is a concept, much used in the EU, to decide the distribution of governing power to different levels. But missing from discussions of subsidiarity is the idea that secession is also a redistribution of governing power. Secession means escape from a state, but not from the broader international system, whose rules still apply. (New states are subject to human rights treaties their parent states signed, for example.) Seen that way, secession is just a repositioning within the international order—an assertion that some community ought to have whatever rights and powers a state has. There is no secession from our shared world.

predictably form, creating opportunities to make general arguments arising out of specific cases. Each secession, and each change in domestic practice, is a development in its own right, providing evidence of a broadening pattern.

States are the predominant actors, but not the only ones, and they aren't monolithic. During the antiapartheid movement, cities, federal states, universities, corporations, unions, and churches adopted divestment policies even when their governments did not, which had a real economic effect on South Africa. More recently, actors have acted on climate change at trans- and subnational levels; when the Trump administration withdrew from the Paris Accords, California's governor met the Chinese president to affirm shared policy commitments. On secession—whether as a general right or in particular cases—we could expect non- or substate actors to mobilize coalitions based on their own shared values, advocating positions their governments wouldn't.[7] Networks of similarly situated actors can deploy translated, transnational norms; court cases—such as the *Quebec Reference*—can constitute valuable evidence for changing norms in transnational contexts.

The broadest coalition could center on democratic values. The right to secession is grounded in democratic logic, and the rule's democratic credentials could attract allies even if they are uninterested in, or suspicious of, secession as a practical solution. Even actors opposed to particular secessions are more favorable to the right to decide. More Spaniards favor Catalonia's right to vote than its secession, and a similar sentiment governed the politics of the Scottish referendum.

More particularly, critics of the current global system could support secession as a way to advance their own agendas. Advocates of regionalization and decentralization will find the rule's effects on negotiating outcomes useful. Though it is rarely thought of that way, secession is really just another form of subsidiarity—a claim about the right level for governance within a multilayered system extending from the personal through the local, regional, and transnational. Critics of the global economic system will also find much to support. Doctrinally the new rule makes little change—those who wish for a world in which states have redistributive obligations will find the new rule no better than the present one. But it makes the logic of distribution within and across units transparent, and could appeal to actors interested in economic inequality.

Each secessionist movement is a constituent, as are their advocates and allies. Mainstream human rights NGOs (nongovernmental organizations) are unlikely to support a general right, which would seem too political, but they might advocate for individual cases—which in turn can bolster general arguments—and groups focused on minority rights would be more receptive. Tibet, for example, has a global network of committed supporters who would welcome a general legal and political framework supporting their aims. Even those with entirely different agendas may be attracted to the rule's ability to leverage better outcomes: A right of exit alters the negotiating calculus, and this benefits those seeking to get better specific outcomes in a diverse range of policy realms. The rule's pluralistic compatibility with a variety of governance models means it could be useful to many actors when it converges with their agendas.

Cross-cutting coalitions are possible, because the persistence of claims that sound Wilsonian isn't just a mistaken conceptual survivor; it represents the seepage of ideas. Confronted with the classical rule's arbitrary definition of peoples, humans naturally ask why it can't and shouldn't apply to other groups. Rights are naturally expansive, and a right to secession—the dignity to determine one's own political destiny in a democratic process—arises plausibly out of the rights we already recognize.

OBSTACLES TO TRANSNATIONAL DIFFUSION Still, this is no overwhelming trend. Far from a broad movement, only a few states allow secession. Many more states—five times as many—prohibit or criminalize separatism, through references to indivisibility (Luxembourg), the military's obligation to defend territorial integrity (Bolivia, Spain), or specific prohibitions (Ecuador).[8] Even constitutions that are silent have been interpreted to preclude secession (Germany, United States[9]), and international law's own silence enables states to ignore or suppress separatism. Nor do the few constitutions that allow secession contemplate anything like the new rule: None give the right to self-organizing groups—instead, they typically give it to existing subunits. If we rely on the accretion of sympathetic states, we might wait a very long time. A global norm won't be built on cooperative states and generalized advocacy alone. The hard cases of self-determination are precisely those in which the state is resistant to secession. A robust, globalized right would require those states' acquiescence, otherwise, only in those rare, enlightened states that are prepared to accept it would the right exist, and that is no right at all.

A strategy of constitutional entrenchment also faces conceptual obstacles. Far from being open to the virtues of "low-commitment" constitutions, "the opposite mindset—territorial insecurity—is a common preoccupation in national constitutions. Constitution makers are in the business of building, not demolishing, states."[10] The dominant view cautions against constitutionalizing secession—preferring to leave constitutions silent or even explicitly rejecting any right—for reasons that replicate the assumptions underpinning the current global norm.[11] So piecemeal entrenchment is insufficient for the same reasons that relying on minority rights, federalism, autonomy, and indigenous rights is self-limiting: Having developed within the classical system of territorial integrity, constitutional drafting assumes states' territorial integrity. Constitutions are products of domestic negotiation, subject to the logic of a system in which exit is not possible and the majority has limited incentives to accommodate minorities. Almost by definition, separatism's supporters will be outnumbered, and usually outgunned, by supporters of state sovereignty and unity.

And if constitutionalization doesn't work alone, neither will diffusion of values. International socialization can only do so much work—and socialization works both ways: Current global norms not only allow states to ignore secession, they enable its suppression, even with violence. Transnational advocacy coalitions' ability to affect this logic is quite limited. On other issues—climate, gender, and so on—substate actors can have a real impact; they can adopt parts of international treaties in local practice, even if their states don't. Secession and recognition of new states seem harder to disaggregate in this way. The issues that affect secession are not merely linked to the state system—they *constitute* the system. They must at some point resolve themselves at that level, and that means in international law.

In the absence of an overarching norm supporting the right of secession—in the way that human rights exist independently of individual states—domestic and transnational advocacy will produce pro-secession constitutions only in places where such ideas are otherwise already part of domestic politics, like in the United Kingdom, and not in places they aren't, because there already is a global norm shaping those negotiations: territorial integrity. The constitutional politics of each state will be decisive, and without an external point of triangulation, there is no escape from the logic of secession's unconstitutionality. The challenge is to move from a position in which secession is disfavored—and states are free to suppress it—to one in which states are willing, even obliged, to tolerate or facilitate a right to decide.

Recall the purpose of a new right: The right of secession—which is a right to exit—is principally a mechanism to enable better results in negotiations within states. Much of the time, the result will not be secession, but autonomy, federalism, increased rights—but without a credible right of exit, those negotiating outcomes will predictably be less favorable. Strategically this means that in advocating for secession, it is critical to articulate an international legal basis, not merely a domestic one. Without a new norm, we will not see sufficiently improved results. So even though the right is not the goal, it is important as a means; the question is how to advance a credible claim that there is such a right.

THE INTERACTION OF DOMESTIC POLITICS AND INTERNATIONAL LAW These aren't competing initiatives, rather complementary ones. A new global norm makes constitutionalization more possible, and constitutionalization provides evidence to advance the norm. Changing a global rule like territorial integrity requires a new global rule, but that rule will be realized through constitutional enactments long before it is fully recognized at the international level.

The process is dynamic: A rule forms over time, and during its formation, has effects on the very processes that form it. Articulating a global norm facilitates constitutionalization, since, to the degree the norm is recognized as binding, it encourages states to bring their domestic regimes into compliance. Advocates of constitutional entrenchment could then make a case based on international legality as well as domestic preferences, by appealing to domestic institutions to apply global norms or to international institutions to pressure the state to act, in the way Black American civil rights groups appealed to the UN to put pressure on the United States to reform Jim Crow laws—pressure intended to embarrass the US government into action even if the UN could not compel action.[12] Each time constitutional advocates make that case, they strengthen the very norm on which they rely. As more states adopt the practice, the idea that there might be an emerging right becomes more plausible, in turn creating more space for advocacy in other states. In international law—as in so many things—one has to claim the right before it actually exists.

States need not wait until they confront an actual secession crisis, but could instead amend their constitutions to include a right of exit. Doing so can actually reduce the risks of secession:

> It is intuitive to think of . . . the right to secession as centrifugal, in the sense of [its] leading to a further disintegration of the state. However, there is also reason to think that these strategies might lead to a stronger sense of loyalty that comes from an active, voluntary commitment.[13]

A dynamic constitutional-international strategy would include several elements beyond direct advocacy for a right of secession. One would be to remove references to territorial indivisibility or overt prohibition that encourage states to be rigid in negotiating with minorities. Even without authorizing secession, this would help shift the norm from prohibition to neutrality. Whenever a state moved from textual prohibition to constitutional silence, this would signal movement toward a position in which prohibition was disfavored and eventually no longer possible.

Another move would be to adopt procedural models that, without affirmatively supporting secession as a right, anticipate its possibility and provide an orderly pathway if a claim arises. Even without advocating secession, "law has the flexibility to develop constitutionally permissible legal procedures to resolves claims of secession. . . . [I]n the face of mobilized demand, a procedural approach to resolving such claims has obvious benefits over violence."[14] This is what Canada has done, and what Spain has failed to do in responding to Catalan claims, relying instead on constitutional prohibitions to uphold a policy of neglect and resistance, which has predictably enflamed secessionist sentiment:

> [A] constitutional text that explicitly prohibits the possibility, which can be invoked as a reason sounding in authority for not considering the option, is not likely in the long run to be persuasive, and insistence on it may be more likely to discredit the constitution than to discourage secession.[15]

The Scottish case shows the pathways a state could follow. Negotiating the terms of a referendum with a sovereign that opposes the outcome but concedes the principle—and treating the exercise as a sequence of decisions, rather than a single moment—is a model that can be emulated. As Scotland showed, even the most permissive case involves close, hard negotiation, both of the process leading to decision and beyond. Indeed, it is precisely the cooperative cases in which negotiations will be most prominent; in divisive, violent secessions, negotiations will be minimized, though at great cost; even then, as we'll see, there's no escaping the need to deal with the new neighbors.

Scotland suggests an evolutionary process, political in nature but guided by existing institutions. The alternative, like Kosovo or Bangladesh or the US Civil War, is a revolutionary process, in which new institutions make decisions about the organization of society, under enormous, often violent pressure in conditions of considerable uncertainty about legality and legitimacy. Although the UK and Scottish governments disagreed strongly about what would follow a yes vote, both accepted that the postreferendum, preindependence period would be one of negotiation to determine the contours of the new state's authority. By contrast, in a contested secession, many of these are things the new state simply does under its own authority, in the teeth of resistance from the parent state. The Scottish case—more precisely, the British case—is instructive of the attitudes states would need in order to foster an international norm. The world has not yet embraced its model, but a model it nonetheless may be.

EFFECTIVENESS AND RECOGNITION: QUEBEC A further reason not to restrict secession to a domestic constitutional project—and a further pathway—is that states exist in a broader international context. States recognize each other, which means they have to decide when to. Recognition may not formally constitute a state, but it is vital to a new state's prospects in an interdependent global order. We have repeatedly seen how hostile that order is to secession. But it doesn't actually prohibit secession, and in this empty space there is room for maneuver. Secessions happen, and states need to respond. Some cases garner sympathy and diplomatic support. A few succeed in withdrawing by force of arms. Either way, states are practically forced to take positions, often making arguments that have more general application.

In its opinion about Quebec, Canada's Supreme Court noted that beyond a certain point, the question ceases to be one of domestic law; it enters the realm

of international politics. Although Canada's constitution doesn't allow for unilateral secession, the court acknowledged:

> Secession of a province from Canada, if successful in the streets, might well lead
> to the creation of a new state. Although recognition by other states is not, at least
> as a matter of theory, necessary to achieve statehood, the viability of a would-be
> state in the international community depends, as a practical matter, upon recogni-
> tion by other states. That process of recognition is guided by legal norms. . . .
>
> [O]ne of the legal norms which may be recognized by states in granting or with-
> holding recognition of emergent states is the legitimacy of the process by which the
> *de facto* secession is, or was, being pursued.[16]

The court is describing conditions a unilateral secession must meet to gain—
and deserve—recognition. If a seceding entity fails to negotiate in good faith,
other states might refuse to recognize it:

> [A]n emergent state that has disregarded legitimate obligations arising out of its
> previous situation can potentially expect to be hindered by that disregard in achiev-
> ing international recognition. . . . On the other hand, compliance by the seceding
> province with such legitimate obligations would weigh in favour of international
> recognition.[17]

It is a matter of secessionists' good faith. But equally, if the *state* doesn't negotiate in good faith, the case for other states to recognize the secession is stronger—
in the same way that persecution can give rise to remedial secession. There are
consequences to rejecting a good-faith effort to secede.

Even unrecognized, de facto states can conduct themselves in ways that can
bolster the right to secede. Well-ordered, peaceful units that contribute to regional stability will be tolerated; the principle of effectivity suggests that eventually other states need to make their peace with the fact of secession—and when
they do, claims that the law has changed will become more plausible. Still,
eventually can be a long time: some de facto states have existed for decades
unrecognized. Some have garnered recognition, but only from a small number
of states—such as Russia's recognition of South Ossetia or Turkey's of Northern Cyprus—which argue against an expanded right. Yet the mere fact that
these frozen conflicts persist suggests the system of territorial integrity is under
challenge. This is not a pretty process, but it opens space for a more ordered,

principled norm that might challenge the monolithic hostility of the high classical rule.

The role separatist entities themselves play reminds us that international law is not made only by states; many actors' voices matter in the cacophony. Treaties are still the purview of states and international organizations, but broader claims about the rules we live under are voiced by rebel movements, political parties, NGOs, and others; their tactics matter, too.

INTERNATIONAL DIPLOMACY: KOSOVO AND SOUTH SUDAN States do not simply wait passively to evaluate claimants for recognition. They actively involve themselves in secession crises, acting as "friends in high places,"[18] and shape their outcomes in ways that help indicate a pathway toward something like the new rule.

Kosovo: Although principally discussed in debates about remedial secession and humanitarian intervention, Kosovo is also an example of how international administration can open a multistaged pathway to independence. Even Kosovo's liberators did not support immediate independence after it separated from Serbia in 1999, instead establishing an international administration. But when Kosovo declared independence in 2008, some of those states pointed to that nearly decade-long administration as the basis for justifying secession and distinguishing it from other cases.

That administration was not some autonomous fact. Kosovo had long been out of Serbia's control, but unlike the *Quebec Reference*'s "effectivity," Kosovo hadn't really controlled its own affairs, and other states had actively intervened to create its independence. Taken together, intervention, international administration, and broad recognition make Kosovo a clear example of a pathway to recognized secession.

But it's also a rare and contested one: The intense efforts to deny Kosovo's value as a precedent should discourage advocates of secession—in customary law, that denial constitutes depressing data—although the denials are only so vehement because Kosovo so obviously *is* a precedent. The more cases there are, the more difficult it becomes to ignore them. Indeed, the really disruptive precedents were the earlier Yugoslav secessions: Slovenia's and Croatia's departures—and the unusual diplomatic maneuvering that led to their rapid recognition—suggest a considerable relaxation in the previously rigid commitment to territorial integrity, if one so far limited to chaotic and violent circumstances.

International Intervention and Administration

Kosovo was not the sort of territory that was supposed to benefit from self-determination. When Yugoslavia dissolved, it was not considered a latent holder of sovereignty: It was a province inside Serbia rather than a republic like Slovenia. A 1991 independence referendum held by Kosovar Albanians was ignored by all states except Albania. Kosovo only succeeded in breaking away through violent guerrilla warfare and NATO bombing. After the conflict, the Security Council passed Resolution 1244, effectively approving the NATO presence and establishing the United Nations Mission in Kosovo (UNMIK). Resolution 1244 affirmed Belgrade's sovereignty and anticipated a negotiated settlement, but it also created interim governance mechanisms that, over time, entrenched de facto independence. UNMIK established a constitutional framework for Provisional Institutions of Self-Government—including a presidency and a parliament—institutions whose members, in 2008, unilaterally declared independence after the failure of protracted negotiations with Belgrade. Serbia refused to recognize Kosovo, but many states did. By then, Serbs had no effective governing presence in the south, but still controlled the north of Kosovo. The intervention and international administration helped make independence practical and unavoidable.

This pathway doesn't require permanent institutions to work. It is highly unlikely a permanent institution could be created, but existing institutions will have to deal with secessions or other crises in which territorial reorganization plays a role. Sometimes, as in Kosovo or East Timor, an ad hoc administration is established; other times, existing institutions will be drawn into these questions, as the Security Council and the Organization for Security and Cooperation in Europe (OSCE) were in the Balkans. When they are, inevitably their actions and statements will provide traction for arguments about changing norms. Thus, when the Security Council authorizes an intervention, it unavoidably provides evidence that can be mobilized. Even when it condemns a particular secession, or instructs states not to recognize a de facto state formed in violation of international norms—as it has done for Northern Cyprus or Republika Srpska—it indirectly provides a basis for arguing that other secessions are licit. Likewise, claims for remedial secession create an opportunity—a logical pressure to ask, why not for other reasons? This will always be a marginal, contested analysis.

States routinely pay obeisance to sovereignty and territorial integrity, and that will remain the dominant interpretation. But precisely because international law doesn't actually prohibit secession, institutions and courts have to respond to the events that occur; when they do, they create opportunities to argue that new rights are forming in the penumbra of their actions.

South Sudan: In South Sudan's case, it wasn't necessary to argue for the relevance of transitional arrangements, because Khartoum agreed to the division, and other states have always been willing to recognize voluntary secessions. But that voluntariness was the product of sustained diplomatic intervention, which suggests a shift in attitudes toward territorial integrity.

In 2005, after decades of civil war, the Sudanese government and southern rebels agreed to a transitional period leading to a referendum. During the transition the south was autonomous but Khartoum retained some powers; at independence in 2011, those powers devolved to Juba. This arrangement came at the end of protracted negotiations. An essential element was the Sudan People's Liberation Army's (SPLA's) success on the battlefield, which convinced Khartoum that victory was impossible, but even that would not have been enough—many rebels have done well in war, but almost never won independence—if it had not been for unprecedented diplomatic intervention by the United States and many African states. The Bush administration had taken a particular interest in South Sudan and invested considerable resources in facilitating a resolution. African states—previously the most doctrinaire defendants of territorial integrity—were highly supportive of the process. Like Scotland, the South Sudan case formally contributes little to a claim about a legal right, since Khartoum cooperated. But it only did so as the result of sustained international pressure that is difficult to square with the classical system.

There is no reason to think secession crises are a thing of the past. They will continue to force themselves onto the international agenda, and even a hostile system will have to deal with them. Each crisis presents an opportunity to argue that a modified norm might produce better results; and often enough, resolution introduces new evidence of a possible pathway. Intervention, diplomacy, and administration can produce secessions, sometimes even against the interveners' will, and doctrinal moves to isolate these cases as nonprecedents are exercises in denial.[19] Resistance to secession remains strong, but norms prohibiting intervention are decaying, and it is not credible to imagine that interventions, once undertaken, won't ever lead to partition. The current system pretends that crises justifying invasion needn't lead to a new territorial dispensation—but intervention is an inherently dangerous instrument: When we intervene in a country—and when, inevitably, we withdraw—we will find the problem of its governance, and therefore its people and territory, still in front of us.

The obstacles to a recognized right of secession are considerable, and the most promising path is one of slow transformation in values and perspectives. It is a very long game, and every move faces considerable obstacles. A good idea is not enough; it needs favorable material conditions. The moral case for decolonization was available long before it gained traction, and that only happened once the colonial empires were gravely weakened, increasingly irrational as political and economic projects. The same is true for the abolition of slavery, human rights, or democracy. But that simply shows that material conditions precede and shape doctrinal shifts. Perhaps those conditions have changed: The collapse of the Cold War order and the rise of globalized society have reduced the felt necessity of rigid territorial integrity. That is a terrifying prospect, but also an opportunity. Besides, there is no avoiding it: If conditions have changed, we can expect law to follow—slowly, painfully, but inexorably.

These are not necessarily winning strategies, merely plausible ones. Opponents of secession will always be able to make powerful arguments against it and can point to the lack of treaty or custom to deny that the new rule has legal force. But the same structure they rely on does not prohibit secession, and its plural quality precludes them from anathematizing arguments in favor of any particular secession or the right in general. Advocates for a new right are in a position like many guerrilla movements: They cannot win outright, but neither can they be defeated. And that is all that is required.

The goal, after all, is not a new legal rule, but changed practice. The rule is a critical part of the pathway, but not the goal itself, so a sensible strategy should not focus on doctrine for its own sake, but rather encourage practice, and let law follow. Such a strategy only focuses on the rule, as this book has, when that itself would facilitate change. A world in which secession was regularly accepted as part of how we decide on governance, even without a formal rule, would be better than this one. Indeed, if we lived in such a world, we would announce the rule and think it reasonable and just. Someday, someone will publish an article called "The Emerging Right to Secession," because it will already have happened.

Minimalism: The New Rule's Effect on (and in) the Current System

Se vogliamo che tutto rimanga com'è, bisogna che tutto cambi.
Giuseppe Tomasi di Lampedusa[20]

Giving communities the right to withdraw from their existing states is a significant innovation: If the rule became widespread, it would have a radical effect. Yet doctrinally, it only introduces a small change. It preserves almost the entire edifice of international law and the norms of interstate conduct.

The new rule does not alter rules prohibiting aggression. It might be necessary to clarify that recognizing a secession would not violate the remainder state's sovereignty. But the law governing recognition is so fluid that it is difficult to show that recognizing a new state violates territorial integrity anyway. And while the new rule gives communities the right to secede, that doesn't give other states a right to intervene, just as human rights violations don't automatically authorize intervention.[21]

The new rule doesn't require any change to human rights. Today, new states must honor the same rights commitments as their parent states, and the new rule would continue that practice. It could even be used to promote rights: New states need outside support, so states could condition recognition on adherence to rights treaties. This is consistent with recent practice: The EU required Soviet and Yugoslav republics to sign treaties (more than existing members!) in order to secure recognition or start accession talks. Nor would anything in the rule affect law governing minorities or indigenous peoples, except to indirectly bolster them: Minorities and indigenous peoples have no right to external self-determination, but under the new rule, they could pursue independence through a plebiscite, and this would improve their position in bargaining with the state.

The other ways to make new states would still exist: Colonial or alien rule, illegal occupation, or remedial secession could still be grounds for separating, so they could be invoked against states formed under this new rule, too. So the new rule only makes a small shift in the classical system's structure. That shift aims to moderate the bias of the current system, letting communities bargain more effectively, by giving them a right to exit that allows them to extract a better deal. What that deal would be is left up to the claimants and the state: The rule converts discussions about law into politics, negotiated under a rule marginally more favorable to minority communities than the current one.

And this is all the new rule aims to do—this is its heart and purpose. Its goal is not necessarily secession, but an improved environment for negotiating the nature of union. In some cases, a community would use the rule to gain independence—in which case the current rule had been stifling that desire. But in others, communities would use that leverage to extract a better deal, rather than leave. This happened in Quebec, where there have not only been referenda, but negotiations over the distribution of power between federation and provinces. Similarly, before and after the Scottish referendum, London offered generous expansions of autonomy to discourage secession.

Even a small change produces knock-on effects: changes in one part of a system inevitably cause changes in others. This minor but radical revision might necessitate other changes, challenge conventional approaches to political identity, and more. But its initial intervention is discrete, and many of its larger effects are the very kinds of things one would *want* to change, if only one could.

Changes to Domestic Regimes

Domestic legal systems would be affected. In countries from which some group actually seceded, there would be enormous change. Dividing a state brings legal, social, and political transformations; the cases we have—the Soviet Union, Yugoslavia, Ethiopia, British India, Pakistan—show these changes can course through society, sometimes violently, for decades.

Unstitching a political union is complex. The rules governing state succession are notoriously indeterminate: which states inherit which assets and liabilities; which state is the legal continuator of the original state's rights and obligations— its UN seat, membership in organizations—and which has to begin afresh (or is released from obligations); which individuals become citizens; and so on.

The new rule doesn't answer these difficult questions; it presumes they will be answered in the same imperfect way the current system does. When Czechoslovakia split, there were complex legal and political issues to resolve—and they were resolved. There might be more *frequent* disputes about state succession, but they would not be different in nature from those we already deal with.

Changes would also happen in states from which no group tried to secede, and this might be the most productive arena for advocacy. States trying to comply with the new rule would have to bring their laws into conformity. Those that forbid division or criminalize secession would need to amend their constitutions and laws. States would need to create legal and political frameworks in which claims could be brought effectively—electoral machinery, administrative provisions. Implementing the right to conduct a plebiscite would require states' cooperation, as happened in Canada and the United Kingdom. Most states wouldn't do this, but the rule would marginally increase the pressure on them.

Effects Varying by Region

In Europe . . . while one frequently hears and reads about popular criticism of the nation-state as an "obsolete" mode of social organization . . . [I]n Africa, the contemporary states remain firmly grounded in the doctrine and practice of territorial sovereignty. . . . In Community Europe, the emphasis is on decentralization of territorial, administrative, and decision-making processes; in postcolonial Africa, the trend is to the ever-increasing centralization of control.[22]

The new rule is for the entire globe, but like any norm, it would play out differently in different places. In the absence of central authority, international norms are translated by many actors. A right to secession, touching the sovereignty and core interests of the state, would be subject to self-interested interpretations by the very states whose cooperation would be essential to realizing the right.

So we could expect considerable variation. Some states have accepted practices very similar to the new rule, even though secession threatens their territorial integrity—proof that opposition is not absolute, that a culture of acceptance is possible. But different regions would respond in different ways.

In the European heartland of the state, the new rule's effects would be the most manageable and predictable. The rule would be both more likely to be used there, because the liberal culture of many European states make them relatively more amenable to it, and less likely to create disruption, because Europe's history has produced relatively homogeneous units. It is easiest to use and least needed there.

By contrast, the new rule could yield the greatest benefits and produce the greatest stresses in Africa. The heterogeneity of African states is often orders of magnitude greater than in Europe—dozens of languages, radically divergent levels of development, weaker institutions and democratic traditions. The likelihood of conflict would be greatest and its consequences most dangerous there. Yet for the same reasons, the potential benefits would be greatest, too, since nowhere are borders less aligned with the preferences of the humans within them than in Africa. After decolonization, African states were lockstep in asserting the primacy of territorial integrity. That uniform view has become more nuanced: the African Union now acknowledges intervention to protect human rights, and many African states supported the diplomacy leading to South Sudan's secession—a process close to the principles of the new rule. The Africa of the 1960s would not have supported the kind of deal struck in Sudan in the 2000s, and this suggests marginally greater openness to the kinds of changes the new rule would bring.

We might expect effects between these two extremes in other regions. In South America—after Europe, the continent with the oldest frontiers, but with relatively undeveloped regions in its interior—some states have homogeneous populations, but others contain large indigenous communities. Many groups in the Amazon Basin are too small to take advantage of the rule, although regional groupings might. Asian states range from highly diverse to highly homogeneous. Some have large territories populated by diverse communities with developed national identities—including secessionists—or the potential to develop them; those states would see the new rule as a threat. But this also suggests that large populations in Asia could benefit from the negotiating leverage the rule would give them.

This regional variation raises an interesting possibility. The rule might work well in Europe, but not in Africa; why not deploy it on a regional basis? The current system allows regional treaties and custom, so it would be possible to implement the rule regionally. (A treaty like the European Convention on Human Rights could develop an optional protocol recognizing such a right—admittedly unlikely). Even if it were true that the rule would produce more violence in Africa than the current rule does—which would be saying a lot!—that is not a reason to forego its application elsewhere.[23]

This would also provide an aspirational target. To say the rule might work in Europe but not in Africa is a way of saying that, in general, the political culture and institutions of Europe are better positioned to do a thing we think is a good idea. This is why the experience of a country like the United Kingdom is instructive for very different societies: Far from being irrelevant, it reminds us that the rule is not a bad idea but requires certain social, political, and institutional conditions to work well—and that when those conditions exist, other things are better, too. That is not something to object to, but work toward.

A Rule Consistent with Underlying Values

The real, disruptive challenge this rule poses to the global order is nonetheless limited and modest. It does not require one to commit to different values—unless one is attached to the intellectually and ethically dubious proposition that territorial integrity is a value in itself. The new rule is consistent with commitments to stability, peace, and prosperity—indeed, these are its goals, every bit as much as for the current system. It simply differs about the best means to achieve them, because it takes into account the neglected costs of the current model's extreme rigidity.[24]

The new rule in no way challenges the idea of the territorial state—in fact, it will disappoint advocates of global governance or one-worldism eagerly anticipating the end of Westphalia. Secession dismantles *a* state, not *the* state. All the rule does is change the rules for changing states; it does not challenge their relevance. It calls upon each state to justify its existence—to persuade its own population that it is the best, most sensible, most humane option for their governance and their flourishing—and failing that, to negotiate its own peaceful reconstitution. Secession does not mean the overthrow of the global order or escape from it. It is simply the creation of a new unit within that order: another state.

Secession neither requires nor prohibits any particular agenda of revolution, reaction, or reform. Having more states might actually promote the values of cosmopolitan postnational globalism. New states don't mean closed frontiers; they could mean more open ones, because each state's policy is its own to make. The point is to allow as many people as possible to take meaningful part in that deliberation. There is a tendency to view secession as a bad thing, as failure. But dividing a state is not a worst-case scenario; it is change. It can be change for the better, and it is better if the people living inside wish it. Change is consistent with division but also with integration, if that is what we want; if it can be achieved peacefully, there is no reason to oppose it. But it is change, and that's not an objection: We shouldn't defend the states we have simply because we have them. We should subject them to searching scrutiny; we should expect not only the secessionist, but the state, to justify itself in what Ernest Renan rightly called "the daily plebiscite."[25]

Conclusion: The Value of Asking

There are all sorts of objections, but the new rule might actually be better—and what about the value of remembering that we choose the rules we live under?

Imposing Values

Why don't you try your theories out on someone else's country?
A drunken Englishman

THAT WAS THE ANGRY REBUKE I received from a man—an 'international'—who worked in the alphabetic welter of organizations in postwar Sarajevo, when I suggested letting Bosnians decide if they wanted a single state. He considered it an abrogation of morality and duty to let Bosnia's people divide. Along with too much beer, he had imbibed a full dose of the classical system's assumptions.

The new rule is an imposition, a new order. That's true even if I have convinced you it is fairer, more rational, and more just than the rule we have now. But what is to be done? Anyone who has ever advocated the spread of liberal democracy, human rights, the rule of law, or—for those with longer memories—worldwide socialism has been imposing his vision on an unready world. What greater imposition could one imagine than the state itself—the "contagion of sovereignty"[1] devised in the West, for the West's circumstances, now replicated across the dry land of the planet? In places where the model is utterly unfit, we speak of failed states, as if the failure were theirs, not the model's. So when it comes to imposing, this new rule may do little better, but certainly does no worse. In this, its essential modesty appears: It accepts the general state of affairs—the division of the world into states—and seeks only to change the way we change units when we have reason. If anything, the rule is defective for its failure to impose more.

As for that drunken Englishman, his rebuke was as ironic as it was misplaced, because as anyone familiar with Bosnia's recent history knows, we're already trying out our theories there. We have insisted on its unity despite considerable obstacles, including the opposition of much of its population, who frustratingly keep electing the wrong parties. His job, his very presence, was the real imposition. That's true even if it's justified: Whatever one's views about the policies of Western powers in Bosnia, or Iraq, or Afghanistan, who could deny that we have imposed our preferences on their peoples?

A reflexive commitment to existing states is not necessarily the more sensible thing to do. When that commitment is more deeply insisted upon in foreign capitals than in the places themselves, then it may not only make bad policy, but trespass upon other values, such as the autonomy of individuals and societies, living in the wake of their own history, to make and unmake of themselves what they will.

There is no escaping it. We live in a shared world, and we impose on each other in every way: We impose if we divide countries and if we hold them together; we impose when we maintain a legal order that makes secession nearly impossible; and we impose if we change that order to make secession easier. The true measure and the only test is the degree to which our impositions allow human beings to exercise choice and agency and if, on the margins, the result is a better world.

Questioning the Rules We Make

The new rule is a global rule, like the existing one. Each, in its way, offers a global approach that inevitably encourages a single type of solution. This "totalism" can be dangerous

> when the search for identity becomes an insistence on a "category-to-be-made-absolute." . . . [I]nstead of inspecting (and confronting) the social and economic

conditions and history that form and deform individual lives, identity could dangle the dangerous panacea of a single global fix. Could a nation succumb to the same temptation? What happens when a government champions a unitary image as a substitute for reckoning with its country's real historical baggage and grappling with its citizens' real problems?[2]

It is possible the new rule would make things worse: destabilizing more societies than it would help; making it harder for groups to get along; producing more illiberal societies and violence. If it did—if we thought it would—we should stay far away from this dreadful, dangerous idea.

But these are empirical questions: They may or may not be true. Is it true that more homogeneous states tend to be less liberal? Would more people die in Central Africa if secession were possible than have died in the charnel decades since independence, in internal slaughters carried out in the shadow of the current rule? Is it true that relaxing territorial integrity would lead to endless fracturing? Our beliefs about the answers to questions like these underpin support for the classical rule, but as we have seen, our answers may not be right. And there are normative assumptions buried in this unfinished calculus. Even if fracturing resulted, why is this bad? How many states are too many? Then there is the messy business of all those human communities that continue to demand a state of their own: Evidently they do not see the obvious benefits of the current system; evidently they do not agree.

So even if what I've proposed is wrong, it's good to think about *why* it is, and what that tells us about the rule we have now. If, by imagining an alternative, we can better see that the current rule really is the best possible one—or the best we can manage—then we will have put our assumptions on a firmer footing. And imagine if we discovered the new rule was better! Either way, questioning our commitments is useful. Because the one thing we do know, with empirical clarity and moral certainty, is that this world isn't perfect, often not even very good. The fixity of our commitment to rigid borders isn't matched with outcomes we ought to find acceptable, whether measured in morality, lives lost, prosperity, or human happiness. It is only because of the impossibility of knowing what a different world might look like that we can retain our unshakable confidence in the rule we happen to have.

The fact of millions dying, of wars not avoided, of poverty actually endured, of oppression actually suffered is so appalling as to make us ask: Is there not some other way? Of course there is, if we have eyes to see it. It is only the blinding fixity of our commitment that makes us call Biafra the problem instead of Nigeria, Katanga instead of the Congo, Darfur instead of Sudan. And what, exactly, is Nigeria, or the Congo, or Sudan? Not natural units, economic or geographic necessities; not repositories of moral meaning. Their populations don't form a cohesive cultural, ethnic, religious, linguistic, or social group. They don't necessarily even represent those populations' preferences, certainly not of their minorities. They represent nothing other than what they are: states—the means to govern the places we live, in our diversity and mutability. Precisely because our world is changing, we should ask ourselves, not once but often, always: What is the proper shape to contain our lives?

Idealism and 'Real' Realism

But perhaps this whole idea is not simply dangerous, but worse than that: it is idealistic. That charge has been leveled since Wilson's day; we saw his own secretary of state, Robert Lansing, express his skepticism, and it's worth returning to his view:

> The more I think about "self-determination" the more convinced I am of the danger of putting such an idea into the minds of certain races. It is bound to be the basis of impossible demands. This phrase is simply loaded with dynamite. . . . [It is] the dream of an idealist.[3]

We have already seen why the assumptions underpinning Lansing's doubts may not be true. The "certain races" Lansing worried about—the Irish, Indians, Egyptians, Boers, "Mohammedans" of Syria and Palestine and "possibly" of Morocco and Tripoli, Zionists—are almost all independent countries today, and we tend to think it better that way, for all the trouble 'they' might give 'us.' One is a member of the EU—in two parts! The one exception, Palestine, represents one of the most intractable problems in the world precisely because it has *not* been resolved in the way Lansing feared.

Wilson's dangerous idealism looks like the order of things now; it's Lansing who's holding onto a fading, impossible ideal, and an imperial one at that—an ideal about things always staying as they are. Isn't that, in its way, the same ideal the opponents of secession expound today? They invoke the same con-

cerns about a new order that Lansing found so distressingly, dangerously idealistic. Who here is fetishizing the state, and the state of things? Which vision
now informs our understanding, or should?

Lansing's concerns, while they sound like principled objections to the very
idea of self-determination, are those of the status quo politician—and one with
very limited creative horizons. There is no necessary, no morally compelling
reason to shape our law and our policy around such concerns. His very trepida-
tions, as outmoded as his language, show that fear of change is the only bar to
what people can achieve and to what states will accept. The real curse of Pandora's box is not the evils it contains, but our fear, locking us within boxes of
our own making.

If you have read this far, perhaps you, unlike Lansing or our drunken Englishman, can see that this idea might be a good one. But perhaps only in theory:
Like the resort to war, we can imagine something better but can't see how to get
there. How lovely if every soldier laid down his gun—"You go first"! Whatever
its theoretical merits, the likelihood of a right to secession being accepted is
vanishingly low. So why is this whole book not just politico-legal fantasy?

I'll give three answers. First, there's real value in imagining an ideal. An un-
realized, even unrealizable political project can be meaningful: The implausibility of Kant's *Perpetual Peace* has in no way diminished its influence. Practicality
is not the only point of thinking about the world and how it might be. Second,
we should not let *present* implausibility deter us, because just considering the
question may increase the possibility for change. Many shifts in modern society
have sprung from ideas even less likely when first proposed: democracy's challenge to monarchy, nationalism's challenge to multinational empires, human
rights. Even decolonization hardly seemed plausible shortly before it succeeded:
The mandates created after the Great War were supposed to run until 1989, and
there wasn't even a notional independence date for colonies, whose numbers
were increasing into the 1920s. Yet within decades the winds of change were
blowing and the writing was on the wall: Less than a lifetime separates colonialism's peak from its repudiation. When my father was a child, white people
in tropical places wore pith helmets; today, it's a tricky fashion statement. Third,
for all the radical feel of the new rule, it makes only a small change. It tweaks
the bias of the current system, a limited transfer of diplomatic resources. And
its purpose is equally modest: to shift relative bargaining strength.

What makes the rule seem implausible is not the radical nature of the change, but deeply embedded, reflexive assumptions about the necessity and rightness of the rule we have—the radical inflexibility of the classical system's norms. So, finally, consider the idealizing project underpinning our *current* commitment: a liberalism that insists questions of deepest identity are to be celebrated but never allowed to shape or challenge the existing order. A worthy goal, perhaps, but how realistic? Wouldn't it be better to respond to the human desire to organize our shared lives around our identities, allowing for their waxing and waning, rather than pretending we can banish them from law?

Perhaps this new rule is impractical—I admit it is—and if you're still asking "What's the point?" I don't have any more answers. Except that we are already engaged in an impossibly unrealistic project, based on a belief that borders can and should last forever, that whatever problems arise, however unimaginable the community and however difficult its disputes, it's always better to lock people in, and expect, with glowing, fervent belief in our higher humanity, that it will all work out. Which is to say, a belief in our present, untested rule.

If you remember Pandora's story, you'll know that all the evils inside have already escaped. They are already here, among us: They *are* us. There's only one thing left inside, but that thing is also part of who we are. And if you remember what it is, you'll know why we should say: Open the box.

APPENDIX: SCHOLARLY FERMENT ON A DECADENT TOPIC

Over the past one hundred years, a flood of material has been written on self-determination. But as it happens—in part because of the decadent trends I have outlined—that flood is curiously manageable. Themes repeat, and one doesn't wade far into the mainstreams of scholarship without recognizing the pull of the current. Nothing's ever the same, of course, and there's more than one path across; anyway, the passage is always rewarding. It does mean one can profitably summarize scholarship's main lines.

I am uncertain to what degree scholarly arguments make a real difference. *Ideas* matter: I would hardly have written this book if I didn't believe that. But ideas matter most when addressed to the world. Even so, it is helpful to orient oneself, to get a sense of which authors and works have influenced my argument. Some readers will simply find it useful to consider what else they might read, because many of the works mentioned below, while mostly not taking the position I do—often because they don't—say valuable things about this important question.

This appendix discusses the main lines of scholarship regarding secession and self-determination, both historically and in law, philosophy, and the social sciences. It focuses on literature engaged with secession, including pro-secession arguments, and notes works I've found especially useful. But this should not deceive you into thinking that secession is the main thing going. The weight of thinking rests on a spectrum from animus, to hostility, to reasoned opposition, to indifference or inattention.

Historical Patterns

John Locke developed a theory of the state based on an analogy to property. The implications for secession did not impress themselves on him, and for centuries, political philosophers hardly engaged the question, focusing instead on the state's relationship to individuals in a way that effectively took the state's existence (and shape) as given. This tendency was general: "Neither Plato, Hobbes, Locke, Rousseau, Hegel, Marx, nor Mill devoted any serious attention to secession."[1]

This inattention is curious, given the creation of new states throughout this period; the American Declaration of Independence's obvious debt to—and implications for—political theory seems not to have been fully reciprocated. But individual incidents have produced their own literatures. Thus American scholars have debated secession because of the American Civil War, though often with partisan purpose. (One wonders if Americans' suspicion of secession, even in other people's countries, is a result of working out their own national trauma.) The aftermath of the Great War led to discussion of self-determination, the mechanics of plebiscites, and minority rights. The postwar era drew attention to self-determination as decolonization.

Law

Secession is just one element in legal treatises' review of the classical system's treatment of territory, along with conditions for creating and recognizing states, membership in organizations, and so on. James Crawford's *The Creation of States in International Law* (1979, 2nd ed. 2007) is a standard reference; R. Y. Jennings' *The Acquisition of Territory in International Law* (1963) has been reissued with a new introduction by Marcelo Kohen (2017); and Malcolm Shaw's *Title to Territory in Africa* (1986) focuses on one continent with particular importance for the classical system. A recent work of note is Jure Vidmar's *Democratic Statehood in International Law* (2013).

The latter stages of the Cold War saw increased attention to human rights, democratization, and minority and indigenous rights, part of the turn to internal self-determination. We can see the two sides of this tendency: in Thomas Franck's "The Emerging Right to Democratic Governance" (1992)—working out that internal logic—but also Cass Sunstein's "Constitutionalism and Secession" (1991), drawing the dominant conclusion from that turn, a classical status quo prudentialism, developed, ironically, against the resurgence of independent states in Eastern Europe. (The Soviet and Yugoslav dissolutions also led to lively debate about whether federalism implied secession.) So there is an extensive legal literature on democratization, rights, and federalism, but that literature long had little to say about or was even implicitly hostile to secession from existing states.

Significant works focused on self-determination and secession include Karl Doehring's *Das Selbstbestimmungsrecht der Völker* (1974), informed by the late stages of decolonization; Hurst Hannum's comprehensive *Autonomy, Sovereignty, and Self-Determination: The Accommodation of Conflicting Rights* (1990)—a book that greatly influenced my thinking (Hannum was one of my teachers); and Antonio Cassese's *Self-Determination of Peoples: A Legal Reappraisal* (1995).

None of the major works could be characterized as favoring a broad right of secession. They interpret the existing system—Cassese calls his text "unashamedly doctrinal" (p. 2)—and it would be an almost objective error to see a right of secession in the law we currently have. So rare were (and are) major theoretical, doctrinal, or practical defenses of a general right that scholars who offer even limited support for secession, in very narrow circumstances, are seen as advocates. Lea Brilmayer's influential "Secession and Self-Determination: A Territorial Interpretation" (1991) is a good example (and one I found important to my thinking): its careful argument identifies very narrow grounds for secession, much like Allen

Buchanan's work, but like his, is sometimes pointed to as pro-secessionist (when at most they support a remedial approach). I have even heard people refer to Cassese as favoring secession—a dramatic misreading of the limited remedial support he offers for "exceptional cases" (p. 350). Cassese's work is a magisterial description of the prevailing system—and an example of its malaise: It observes that the current system "is blind to the demands of ethnic groups, and national, religious, cultural or linguistic minorities" (p. 328), but his solution: distrust of the "new tribalism" (p. 339), more internal self-determination, and civic politics.

Still, with the press of events, secession is again actively discussed, though often in patterned ways that reveal the limits of the classical system's paradigm. Countervailing voices have critiqued this system's assumptions. Steven Ratner's 1996 "Drawing a Better Line" criticizes the repurposing of internal boundaries as international frontiers—there are few better introductions to the problematic assumptions of the contemporary system. Diane Orentlicher's 1998 "Separation Anxiety" challenges the inattention of law and philosophy to the interplay of democratic rights and borders. And as noted, secession crises produce extensive literatures—Quebec, Scotland, Catalonia—addressing the particulars of each crisis and locating each in more general debate. Scholars like Montserrat Guibernau, writing on Catalonia, have advocated for a general 'right to decide,' while Kosovo—indeed the whole Yugoslav dissolution crisis—generated robust arguments about dissolution and state formation.

Two further strands of scholarship are worth noting. The constitutionalization of secession—the position Sunstein argued against—has been revisited. Following the example of the Canadian Supreme Court, if not its logic, scholars have sometimes taken a more sympathetic view, including Wayne Norman's *Negotiating Nationalism* (2006); Zachary Elkins' "Logic and Design of a Low-Commitment Constitution" and Vicki Jackson's "Secession, Transnational Precedents, and Constitutional Silences," both in Sanford Levinson's 2016 *Nullification and Secession;* Stephen Tierney's *Constitutional Referendums* (2012) is a strong example. The other strand is internal self-determination. In addition to Hannum, early examples include Otto Kimminich's "A 'Federal' Right of Self-Determination?" and Patrick Thornberry's "The Democratic or Internal Aspect of Self-Determination," both in Christian Tomuschat's 1993 *Modern Law of Self-Determination* and Susanna Mancini's excellent "Rethinking the Boundaries of Democratic Secession" (2008), addressing minority rights. This literature is vast—the main field of discourse today.

Other works I have found of great interest, especially from historical and critical perspectives, include Antony Anghie's *Imperialism, Sovereignty and the Making of International Law* (2004), Karen Knop's *Diversity and Self-Determination in International Law* (2002), and Nathaniel Berman's "Sovereignty in Abeyance" (1988–1989) and "But the Alternative Is Despair" (1993).

But the overwhelming weight of scholarly opinion finds no general right and doesn't see that as a problem. Marc Weller's writing, including *Escaping the Self-Determination Trap* (2008), is among the best explications of the view this book challenges. A recent survey, John Dugard's *The Secession of States* (2013), looking through the lens of recognition, is an indication of how much secession has returned to the center of attention, if also of how the main lines remain firmly fixed. This can even be seen in the one area of robust discussion about external self-determination: remedial secession. A lively debate has developed about the legality of secession to remedy injustice, and the threshold of harm required, but this debate elides the idea that there might be reasons to secede not founded on desperate circumstances but instead on the very idea of what it means to belong to a community living in a place.

Political Philosophy

Recently there has been greater openness to that idea among political philosophers. But before, there was that curious absence from centuries of theory—how little it engaged, until recently, with territory. Even philosophers like John Rawls advanced theories in which both the political community and the state are assumed and were concerned with the state's just operation, not its existence. One thing that makes Allen Buchanan's work important is that so little came before it. This striking absence is noted in even recent works, such as Margaret Moore's *A Political Theory of Territory* (2015).

Buchanan draws on the discourses of property and justice, and his work—regularly cited by legal scholars—indicates the traditional limits he pushes against. His *Secession: The Morality of Political Divorce* (1991) is highly qualified, admitting a right to secede in extremely narrow circumstances. Other approaches—including democratic choice and liberal nationalism—imagine a larger space for secession, and recent work on territorial rights has expanded this field.

Theories grounded on democratic choice are closest to those in *Boxing Pandora*. In the 1980s and 1990s, Harry Beran produced several significant works advocating a democratic basis for secession, including *The Consent Theory of Political Obligation* (1987); Daniel Weinstock has made similar proceduralist arguments. Christopher Wellman's *A Theory of Secession* (2005) develops "a thorough and unapologetic defense of the right to secede" (p. 1), one of the most significant expositions of a democratic right. With his argument distinguishing political self-determination from claims of past injustice, supporting secession as a primary right (even if it causes other harms), and showing that self-determination needn't have an ethnic or cultural basis but can be based on preference, Wellman's is the work to which my argument's logic mostly closely compares. And that's a rare thing; as Wellman notes, "To call this thesis a minority position is an understatement" (p. 1). Instead, the dominant position in philosophy, like law, had been that there is no right to secede absent injustice, and thus secession, like revolution, is a derivative right to secure the primary right to just treatment— not a right in itself, which is precisely what this book proposes.

Along with democratic theories, a recent line of scholarship takes seriously the question of state formation and territorial rights—"one of the most undertheorized elements in political theory[.]"[2] It's still a small discourse: "[E]xceptions notwithstanding, territory remains a major blind spot of contemporary political philosophy, as marginal as ever."[3] But these scholars have arrived at positions far more sympathetic to secession. Some look at property rights: Locke's theory of the state relies on an analogy to private property, and although Locke himself didn't derive from this a right to secession, it can be seen as a logical extension of his premises. More often, though, analogizing from property has actually discouraged attention to a right of secession, and even pro-secession property theories tend to founder on the irrealism of individuals' seceding. Cara Nine's *Global Justice and Territory* (2012) develops a collectivist account of territorial rights to counter the individualist tendencies of most property-based theories; her argument partly rests on the value added to property by state activity, shading into justice theories that try to objectively evaluate states' behavior.

Justice theories look for indications that the sovereign is governing in a just way, and therefore anticipate a space—often small and hypothetical—for secession as a response to manifest injustice. Buchanan was an early advocate of attention to the justification of territorial authority in this way; Brilmayer can similarly be read as a mix of property and justice arguments yielding a very limited right when there are no preexisting valid claims. Remedial secession is also a justice-based discourse, showing the narrow constraints within which secession is typically contemplated.

Nationalist justifications have predominated among secessionists but were long distrusted in academia. Yet "[i]n the last two decades, nationalist thought has enjoyed a remarkable revival within liberal political philosophy."[4] Influential work includes Yael Tamir's *Liberal Nationalism* (1993) and, more recently, Chaim Gans' *The Limits of Nationalism* (2003) and Tamar Meisels' *Territorial Rights* (2009). Another strand, including David Miller's *Citizenship and National Identity* (2000) and Avery Kolers' *Land, Conflict, and Justice* (2009), emphasizes identification with place or the cultural coherence of communities—lines tracing back to Will Kymlicka's *Multicultural Citizenship* (1995).

These approaches overlap. Liberal nationalists often acknowledge the importance of a present-day majority—thereby adverting to democratic principles.[5] Miller's account is thickly democratic yet still focuses on an empirical evaluation, much like justice accounts. And while many property and justice theories focus on the individual or group, others, such as Jeremy Waldron, Buchanan, Nine, and Anna Stilz, focus on those communities' state-formative qualities—as many national theorists do, too.

One place where I depart from these approaches is in abandoning the quest for objective, verifiable evaluation of a group's claim—the kind of approach Avishai Margalit and Joseph Raz develop in their 1990 article "National Self-Determination" when they describe the six features self-determining groups share. My approach is as thin and procedural as victory in an election. *Boxing Pandora* also aims to be practically applicable (notwithstanding the political challenges), and in this differs from more theoretical approaches in the philosophical literature. Thus Kolers' concept of "plenitude" as an indication of when an area can be claimed is close to my thinking but seems incapable of practical application, especially in determining where that area runs out. Moore admits her occupancy principle and concept of a heartland are blurriest precisely at the border: Her approach "does not decisively determine boundaries" (p. 118)—the very place my project engages. But their theoretical approaches are very much in concord with the rationale for the legal-political project I outline.

Finally, a small number of scholars' work arrives at quite similar conclusions to mine, even if approaching the question quite differently. Zoran Oklopcic (*Beyond the People*, 2018) addresses territorial rights in a rich, idiosyncratic idiom, while Uriel Abulof writes in political theory in ways I have often found strikingly close to my own conclusions, like a fortuitous discovery.

Social Sciences

There is a vast literature in the social sciences focused on the conditions under which secession (or negotiations about governance more broadly) occurs, as well as the operations of related strategies like autonomy and federalism. The social sciences describe the ways states affect identity, construct the nation, and integrate populations (or alienate them)—what Harris Mylonas calls strategies of "assimilation, accommodation or exclusion."[6] Mylonas' *The Politics of Nation-Building* (2012) is a good example of examining how states construct political communities; Viva Ona Bartkus' *The Dynamics of Secession* (1999) is an example of how they undergo the reverse process. Philip Roeder's *Where Nation-States Come From* emphasizes how already having a sub-national unit can be critical to a secession movement's success, while Jason Sorens's *Secessionism* adopts a regional focus that looks at secession as a negotiation.

Much of my argument takes issue with common assumptions about how states function, and the social sciences provide a valuable frame evaluating those assumptions. Alberto Alesina and Enrico Spolaore's *The Size of Nations* (2003) is an excellent example: Discussing the optimal size of nations, they offer both normative and positive arguments—a systematic analysis of country size, which in many respects supports my argument, as well as why states should be a certain size. Important work on the logic and conditions of violence, and its relationship to territory and governance, has been done by Stathis Kalyvas (*The Logic of Violence in Civil War,* 2006) and Monica Duffy Toft (*The Geography of Ethnic Conflict,* 2003), reframing ethnic violence as complex continua, while Bridget Coggins's article "Friends in High Places" develops a model of violent conflict in states with active secessions. Donald Horowitz's *Ethnic Groups in Conflict* (1985, updated 2000), though reaching different conclusions, was a great influence.

More broadly, my thinking has been shaped by studies of ethnicity and nationalism—Alfred Cobban's *The Nation-State and National Self-Determination* (1969), Elie Kedourie's eminently readable *Nationalism* (1960, updated 1993, Eric Hobsbawn's misguided *Nations and Nationalism since 1780,* Ernest Gellner's *Nations and Nationalism* (1983), Benedict Anderson's *Imagined Communities* (1991), Rogers Brubaker's *Nationalism Reframed* (1996)—which, while ancillary to this book's approach, are important to questions of collective identity. I have also been influenced (as anyone thinking about international law should be) by international relations, including E. H. Carr's *The Twenty Years' Crisis.* Anyone who thinks my book is idealistic would do well to read Carr and remember that ideals are not incompatible with realism, and that any sensible approach to legal change has to think about power.

I have relied on legal and philosophical approaches because the thrust of my argument is normative; but social science is important for empirical questions about process and outcome, and for questions of design. When will a grievance trigger a movement, and under what conditions will the state negotiate, capitulate, or resist? How will different plebiscitary processes incentivize voting behavior? These are important questions, though less concerned with normative justification, at least directly.

Other Resources

Plebiscites: These cover many subjects besides state-making that inform their application to secession. The post–World War I era was examined by Sarah Wambaugh in *Plebiscites since the World War* (1933), still an important resource. I also found Lawrence Farley's *Plebiscites and Sovereignty* (1986) helpful. Recently, two thorough discussions of plebiscites and their mechanics have appeared: Matt Qvortrup's *Referendums and Ethnic Conflict* (2014) and Ilker Gökhan Şen's *Sovereignty Referendums in International and Constitutional Law* (2015). Each deals extensively with important technical and procedural questions my book only notes. For example, Qvortrup develops a typology of ethno-national referenda (analyzing over two hundred) and conditions under which they occur, while also discussing procedural design, including ballot questions and majority size. If my general argument persuades you, the details are to be worked out from texts like these.

Neither study is normative. Both are about the positive conditions for and even mathematical logic of holding a referendum. They aren't justifications for a right of secession; indeed, they would have far less to describe if they had limited themselves to that. Closer to my approach is Tierney's *Constitutional Referendums* (2012), a thorough review, which, while critical of referenda's shortcomings, defends their democratic value and sees shortcomings as questions of design. Still, as Qvortrup points out, despite other works—Cronin, Bogdanor, Laponce—the field is understudied.

Edited volumes: Finally, many edited volumes cross disciplinary boundaries or aggregate varied perspectives. Aleksandar Pavković and Peter Radan's *The Ashgate Research Companion to Secession* (2011) is a valuable resource for theories and particular conflicts. Other useful volumes include Christian Tomuschat's *Modern Law of Self-Determination* (1993); Margaret Moore's *National Self-Determination and Secession* (1998); Wolfgang Danspeckgruber's *The Self-Determination of Peoples* (2002); Christian Walter, Antje von Ungern-Sternberg, and Kavus Abushov's *Self-Determination and Secession in International Law* (2014); Uriel Abulof and Karl Cordell's *Self-Determination in the Early Twenty-First Century* (2016); Sanford Levinson's *Nullification and Secession in Modern Constitutional Thought* (2016); and Peter Hilpold's *Autonomy and Self-Determination* (2017).

NOTES

Preface

1. Cf. Scott, *Art of Not Being Governed* (describing Zomia, a region of Southeast Asia whose communities have defied or escaped state control).

Introduction

1. Shany, "Redrawing Maps, Manipulating Demographics," 286.
2. Cf. Ignatieff, *Human Rights as Politics and Idolatry,* 14–15.
3. See Beary, "Separatist Movements."
4. See Koh, "Why Do Nations Obey International Law?"
5. Franck, "Postmodern Tribalism," 13–14.

Chapter 1. The Failure of a Flourishing Idea

1. See Musgrave, *Self-Determination and National Minorities,* 2–14. On the philosophical development of nationalism and self-determination, see Kedourie, *Nationalism.*
2. See Locke, *Two Treatises of Government,* ¶ 119.
3. Declaration of Independence (noting also that the people ought to explain their reasons). On antecedents in the Declaration, see Brownlie, "Rights of Peoples," 4.
4. Cited in Farley, *Plebiscites and Sovereignty,* 31 (citing Mattern, *Employment of the Plebiscite,* 65).
5. Lalonde, *Determining Boundaries.*
6. Hyde, *International Law,* 506, cited in Surya Sharma, *Territorial Acquisition,* 123.
7. Ghebrewebet, *Identifying Units,* 21–41 (surveying disputes in Latin America), 44 ("[S]trict adherence [to colonial boundaries there] appears to be the exception.").
8. Mill, *Considerations on Representative Government,* chap. 16, cited in Waldron, "Principle of Proximity," 4.

9. Buchanan, *Secession: Morality of Political Divorce,* vii.
10. "James Madison to Daniel Webster, March 15, 1833."
11. Plebiscites weren't always carried out. The treaty ending the Austro-Prussian War ensured the population of Schleswig's northern district a free choice to join Denmark. See Wambaugh, *Plebiscites,* 39–40. Prussia never held a vote. This influenced the decision for a plebiscite there after the First World War. Similarly, Germany's failure to consult the population of Alsace-Lorraine before annexing it was widely condemned. *See* Farley, *Plebiscites and Sovereignty,* 3–6.
12. Jennings, *Approach to Self-Government,* 55–56.
13. Decree on Peace, in Lenin, "Report on Peace."
14. Resolution on the National Question, April 24–29, 1917. See also Lenin, "Socialist Revolution."
15. Letter from Georgi Chicherin to Lenin, March 10, 1922, in "Vladimir Lenin to Soviet Foreign Minister Gregory Chicherin."
16. Cassese, *Self-Determination of Peoples,* 19–26; Whelan, "Wilsonian Self-Determination," 99.
17. Whether the Kingdom of Serbs, Croats, and Slovenes represented or was even consistent with self-determination is a contested question, the more so given the country's subsequent history. But at the time, it was commonly thought of as an act of self-determination by diverse but similar South Slavs.
18. "Lansing Emphasizes Pledge to Slavs," (quoting the secretary's statement).
19. Schuker, "Rhineland Question," 291. See also Seymour, *Intimate Papers of Colonel House,* 356.
20. Temperley, *History of the Peace Conference of Paris,* vol. 2, 176, 177, 182–83.
21. Wilson, "President Wilson's Fourteen Points."
22. Carr, *Conditions of Peace,* 39.
23. Six major plebiscites were held as part of the postwar settlement: Schleswig, 1920—revised border between Denmark and Germany; East Prussia (Allenstein and Marienwerder), 1920—revised border between Germany and new Polish state; Klagenfurt, 1920—revised border between Austria and new South Slavic kingdom (later Yugoslavia); Upper Silesia, 1921—revised border between Germany and new Polish state; Sopron, 1921—revised border between Austria and Hungary; and Saar, 1935—reversion of Saar to Germany. Others were held or mooted for Finland, Iceland, Kars (eastern Turkey), and Tyrol. See Qvortrup, *Referendums and Ethnic Conflict,* 27–30.
24. See Kolb, *Frieden von Versailles,* 94–95 (describing the emotional effect of propaganda campaigns).
25. Farley, *Plebiscites and Sovereignty,* 34.
26. Brubaker, *Nationalism Reframed,* 6–7.
27. See Hilpold, "League of Nations," 8–15.
28. Hemingway, *Complete Short Stories,* 64.
29. Certain populations, such as Greek Orthodox in Constantinople and Muslims in Thrace, were exempted; Constantinople's Greeks held on until the pogroms of the 1950s; there is still a Turkish Muslim population in Thrace.
30. See "Lausanne Principle."

31. Keynes, *Economic Consequences of the Peace,* 33.
32. Whelan, "Wilsonian Self-Determination," 102–3.
33. See Kolb, *Frieden von Versailles,* 54.
34. *Aaland Islands Question,* 27.
35. Atlantic Charter (Roosevelt–Churchill).
36. See Waters, "Remembering Sudetenland"; de Zayas, *Nemesis at Potsdam.*
37. See Horowitz, "Cracked Foundations," 6–7.
38. Moyn, *Last Utopia,* 93.
39. Macklem, "Self-Determination in Three Movements," 99.
40. UN Charter, art. 1(2). Self-determination is also mentioned in art. 55.
41. Higgins, *Problems and Process,* 111.
42. UN Charter, art. 73.
43. UN Charter, art 76(b).
44. UN Charter, art. 73(b).
45. UN Charter, art. 73(e).
46. UN Charter, art. 73 (emphasis added).
47. UN Charter, art. 74.
48. Higgins, "Postmodern Tribalism," 29, n. 7, cited in Marauhn, "Anspruch auf Sezession?," 109.
49. G.A. Res. 1514, art. 2.
50. Ibid., art. 1, 4, 5.
51. Ibid., art. 6 (also mentioned in arts. 4, 7).
52. G.A. Res. 1541, princ. VIIa.
53. Ibid., princ. VIII.
54. To make the point, the next resolution, 1542, names colonies ruled by Portugal—which had refused to list any—that the General Assembly considered non-self-governing.
55. G.A. Res. 1541, princ. IV, and continuing: "[A]dditional elements may be, inter alia, of an administrative, political, juridical, economic or historical nature. If they affect the relationship between the metropolitan State and the territory concerned in a manner which arbitrarily places the latter in a position or status of subordination, they support the presumption. . . ." (princ. V).
56. Buchanan, *Secession: Morality of Political Divorce,* 20.
57. "[W]estern powers, in particular, argued at first that the right [in the covenants] was only a political principle, that it was a vague and undefined concept, that it was a collective rather than an individual right and therefore unsuited to a treaty enumerating individual, as opposed to collective, rights[.]" Ghebrewebet, *Identifying Units,* 107. An argument they lost.
58. ICCPR, art. 1.1; ICESCR, art. 1.1. The ICCPR addresses minority rights separately and does *not* grant them a right to self-determination. ICCPR, art. 27.
59. Ghebrewebet, *Identifying Units,* 108, citing McGoldrick, *Human Rights Committee.*
60. *South West Africa,* Advisory Opinion, p. 31, ¶¶ 52–53.
61. *East Timor (Portugal v. Australia),* Judgment, p. 102, ¶ 29.
62. Declaration on Friendly Relations, G.A. Res. 2625, Annex, ¶ 1, princ. V (emphasis added).
63. G.A. Res. 3070, ¶ 2 (reaffirming "the legitimacy of the people's struggle for liberation from colonial and foreign domination and alien subjugation by all available means including

armed struggle"). This does not necessarily mean *other* states may *militarily* aid colonial peoples.

64. See Brownlie, *African Boundaries,* 6.

65. Griffiths, *Atlas of African Affairs,* 51.

66. The Sixth Pan-African Congress, in 1945, adopted a resolution declaring "the artificial divisions and territorial boundaries created by the Imperialist Powers are deliberate steps to obstruct the political unity of the West Africa peoples." Padmore, *History of the Pan-African Congress,* 11. The All-African Peoples Conference in Accra in 1958 passed a resolution "denounc[ing] artificial frontiers drawn by imperialist powers to divide the peoples of Africa, particularly those which cut across ethnic groups and divide people of the same stock," and "call[ing] for the abolition or adjustment of such frontiers[.]" Cited in Emerson, "Pan-Africanism," 278. See McEwen, *International Boundaries of East Africa,* 23–24.

67. Ghebrewebet, *Identifying Units,* 49 (and noting, at 50–52, that triggers for this revised view were continuing involvement by European powers in the Congo crisis and Algerian war, and the Moroccan-Mauritanian dispute).

68. Rudolph Grimes, Liberian secretary of state, at the Conference of Independent African States, Addis Ababa, June 1960, cited in Touval, *Boundary Politics,* 65.

69. Organization of African Unity, "Resolutions Adopted by the First Ordinary Session."

70. Tsiranana, Speech at the Organization of African Unity's 50th Jubilee.

71. Connor, "Self-Determination," 32.

72. The 1933 Montevideo Convention on the Rights and Duties of States established four criteria for recognizing a state: a permanent population, a defined territory, a government, and the capacity to enter into relations with other states. The dominant view, called the declarative theory, is that statehood is independent of recognition, although a countervailing theory holds that recognition constitutes a new state. The convention is a treaty among sixteen states, but is considered a codification of customary law.

73. *Frontier Dispute (Burkina Faso v. Mali),* p. 554. Six years later, the Badinter Commission applied this same principle to recognize the independence of Yugoslavia's republics, even though they were not colonial territories. Badinter Commission, Opinion no. 3.

74. Technically, *uti possidetis* applies to *internal* boundaries, not frontiers between territories ruled by different sovereigns, for whom the general rule preserving boundary treaties applies. See Ghebrewebet, *Identifying Units,* 68–70.

75. Ibid., 56.

76. Franck, *Power of Legitimacy,* 75.

77. See Deng, *Self-Determination.*

78. Joint Declaration of Emperor Haile Selassie and the President of India, October 13, 1964, cited in Touval, *Boundary Politics,* 304, n. 24; see *also* Fisch, *Right of Self-Determination,* 200.

Chapter 2. The Map of Our World

1. "International legal thinking on the idea of self-determination has arguably been marked by a constant decay since the principle was first mooted in international law after the First World War." Mégret, "Right to Self-Determination," 45.

2. Cf. Barzun, *From Dawn to Decadence.*

3. Compare these to those framing a prominent study of secession: "1. Who are the people? 2. What is the relevant territorial unit in which they should exercise self-determination? 3. Does secession have a demonstration effect?" Moore, "Self-Determination Principle," p. 2. My answers have a lot to do with peoples and units, and we'll consider the third question later.

4. Crawford, "Right of Self-Determination," 10.

5. "Peoplehood must be seen as contingent on two separate elements, one objective and the other subjective. The objective element is that there has to exist an ethnic group linked by common history. . . . It is not enough to have an ethnic link in the sense of past geneal-ogy and history. It is essential to have a present ethos or state of mind. A people is both entitled and required to identify itself as such." Dinstein, "Collective Human Rights," 104.

6. "[A]ny territorial community, the members of which are conscious of themselves as mem-bers of a community, and wish to maintain the identity of their community, is a nation." Cobban, *The Nation-State and National Self-Determination,* 107, cited in Tamir, *Liberal Nationalism,* 65. "A nation is a historically constituted, stable community of people, formed on the basis of a common language, territory, economic life, and psychological make-up manifested in a common culture." Stalin, *Marxism and the National Question,* 9. "Apart from the entire people of a state, a group of people can hold the right of self-determination, if the following criteria exist: homogenous cultural structure (in the broadest sense); con-viction of homogeneity and intention to preserve it; common historical destiny; common identifiable area of living." Doehring, *Das Selbstbestimmungsrecht der Völker,* 53.

7. UN Charter, art. 2.

8. ICCPR, art. 1; ICESCR, art. 1.

9. Kelsen, *Law of the United Nations,* 52–53.

10. See Dugard, *Secession of States.*

11. The Vatican may be a state, but it's unlikely its transient, recruited population is a self-determining people. See Morss, "International Legal Status of the Vatican."

12. G.A. Res. 1541, princ. IV.

13. A colony should not be integrated with unfavorably asymmetrical rights. G.A. Res. 742, 3rd pt., C.2 (listing as a factor "an identical degree of self-government for the inhabitants and local bodies of all parts of the federation"). It is not clear this applies to territories that were not colonies, however.

14. See, e.g., Summers, *Peoples and International Law,* 350 (discussing several states' ob-jections to the terms).

15. See *Legal Consequences of the Construction of a Wall,* 136; *Report of the Independent International Fact-Finding Mission on Israeli Settlements,* 9 ("[T]he right to self-deter-mination of the Palestinian people . . . is clearly being violated by Israel through the ex-istence and ongoing expansion of the settlements.").

16. See, e.g., Benvenisti, "Sovereigns as Trustees of Humanity," 295: "In past decades the predominant conception of sovereignty was akin to owning a large estate separated from other properties by rivers or deserts. . . . [T]oday's reality is more analogous to owning a small apartment in one densely packed high-rise that is home to two hundred separate families."

17. "The Issues," *Cultural Survival.* On indigeneity in general, see Anaya, *Indigenous Peoples.*
18. *Reference re Secession of Quebec,* ¶ 125: "While much of the Quebec population certainly shares many of the characteristics (such as a common language and culture) that would be considered in determining whether a specific group is a 'people,' as do other groups within Quebec and/or Canada, it is not necessary to explore this legal characterization. . . . Similarly, it is not necessary for the Court to determine whether, should a Quebec people exist within the definition of public international law, such a people encompasses the entirety of the provincial population or just a portion thereof. Nor is it necessary to examine the position of the aboriginal population within Quebec. . . ."
19. Hobsbawm, *Nations and Nationalism since 1780,* 36.
20. One common definition is a "group numerically inferior to the rest of the population, in a nondominant position, consisting of nationals of the State, possessing distinct ethnic, religious or linguistic characteristics and showing a sense of solidarity aimed at preserving those characteristics." Capotorti, *Study on the Rights of Persons,* 97.
21. Higgins, *Problems and Process,* 124.
22. Thornberry, "Self-Determination, Minorities, Human Rights," 874–75. See also G.A. Res. 1514, 66; Mancini, "Rethinking the Boundaries," 554–61 (reviewing the unstable distinction between minorities and peoples).
23. Musgrave, *Self-Determination,* 152–53.
24. Rigo Sureda, *Evolution of the Right of Self-Determination,* 215: "In practice, all peoples are considered to have exercised self-determination except those falling within the category of colonial peoples."
25. Weller, "Legal Rules on Self-Determination," 20.
26. See, e.g., del Mar, "Myth of Remedial Secession," 85: "The 'right of self-determination' refers to two very different notions that differ both in terms of the content of the right, and in relation to the holder of the right."
27. Declaration on Friendly Relations, G.A. Res. 2625.
28. See G.A. Res. 1541, princ. VI: "A Non-Self-Governing Territory can be said to have reached a full measure of self-government by: (a) Emergence as a sovereign independent State; (b) Free association with an independent State; or (c) Integration with an independent State." The Declaration on Friendly Relations adds "emergence into any other political status freely determined by a people constitute modes of implementing the right to self-determination[.]" Territories that choose association can usually opt for independence later.
29. Sudan, Uzbekistan, Ethiopia, Saint Kitts and Nevis, Yugoslavia, France, the Soviet Union, and Liechtenstein. Four have been invoked, but the causality is unclear: Perhaps "secession clauses simply legitimated a process that would have occurred under more factitious methods?" Elkins, "Logic and Design of a Low-Commitment Constitution," 301–4. We might add the United Kingdom and Canada.
30. Constitution of the Socialist Federal Republic of Yugoslavia (1974), Preamble (princ. I) and art. 5(3). See Bagwell, "Yugoslavian Constitutional Questions," 516–17.
31. Constitution (Fundamental Law) of the Union of Soviet Socialist Republics (1977), art. 70, 72.
32. A former British colony, Somaliland was independent for five days before its previously

agreed union with the Trust Territory of Somaliland, the former Italian Somalia, in the Somali Republic. In this sense, Somaliland arguably has a better claim to latent self-determining statehood than, say, Slovenia or Kyrgyzstan: It really was a colony, the kind of territory that was supposed to become a state.

33. Hannum, "Self-Determination, Yugoslavia, and Europe," 64–65: "Such a rule would no doubt astonish the government of the United States, Canada, Germany and other federal states[.]"

34. See Kohen, *Secession;* Burri, "Kosovo Opinion," 884–89; Shelton, "Self-Determination Regional Human Rights Law."

35. See Hannum, *Autonomy, Sovereignty, and Self-Determination,* 498: "[T]he term 'secession' was never used by the United Nations or individual states. Rather, the international community claimed to be simply responding to the fact of the dissolution . . . and purported to recognize the new states only after that dissolution had occurred." Slovenia's departure may have been agreed by Slobodan Milošević, the president of Serbia and strongest figure in Yugoslavia. Yugoslav forces fought a desultory ten-day war before withdrawing, conceding Slovenia's independence.

36. See generally Hannum, *Self-Determination, Yugoslavia, and Europe.* See Hanauer, "Irrelevance of Self-Determination Law," 175 (discussing the "Wilsonian" nature of claims in the Soviet and Yugoslav collapses).

37. Lister, "Self-Determination, Dissent, and the Problem of Population Transfers," 150.

38. Weller, *Escaping the Self-Determination Trap,* 59.

39. Thornberry, "Self-Determination, Minorities, Human Rights," 881. See *also* Cassese, *Self-Determination of Peoples,* 61–62.

40. Declaration on Friendly Relations, G.A. Res. 2625, 124.

41. Thornberry, "Self-Determination, Minorities, Human Rights," 876.

42. See, e.g., Kosovo Advisory Opinion, Written Statement of Albania, ¶¶ 75–79. Other states supporting remedial secession included Estonia, Finland, Germany, Ireland, Poland, and Switzerland, which relied on the Saving Clause of the Declaration on Friendly Relations. Kosovo Advisory Opinion, Written Statement of Switzerland, ¶¶ 62–63.

43. Kosovo Advisory Opinion, Written Statement of Finland, ¶ 9.

44. Its advocates point to the *Aaland Islands* case, whose arbitral Commission of Rapporteurs noted, "The separation of a minority from the State of which it forms a part and its incorporation in another State can only be considered as an altogether exceptional solution, a last resort when the State lacks the will or the power to enact and apply just and effective guarantees." *Aaland Islands Question,* 28. Finland, the islands' sovereign, argued in favor of this interpretation in the Kosovo Advisory Opinion. See Kosovo Advisory Opinion, Verbatim Record, December 8, 2009, p. 62, ¶ 23 (Koskenniemi): "[I]nstead of us, here, imagining a new rule, it is better to think of this as part of the traditional law of self-determination that was always to be balanced against territorial integrity and contained the possibility of its application, as the Aaland Islands case demonstrates, through an external solution."

45. Kosovo Advisory Opinion, Separate Opinion of Judge Trindade, ¶ 175.

46. See, e.g., Kosovo Advisory Opinion, Verbatim Record, December 7, 2009, p. 35, ¶ 23 (Xue). See discussion in del Mar, "Myth of Remedial Secession," 82–83.

47. Kosovo Advisory Opinion, Verbatim Record, December 10, 2009, p. 33, ¶ 23 (Dinsecu).
48. Arguably, the Saving Clause's purpose was to limit rather than expand challenges to states' territorial integrity; it refers to previous clauses discussing the classical categories for external self-determination—colonies, alien occupation, and racist regimes—and wouldn't apply to metropolitan states, regardless of how they behave. See, e.g., del Mar, "Myth of Remedial Secession," 93–95; Summers, *Peoples and International Law,* 335 ("The drafting [of the Friendly Relations Declaration], in fact, reveals virtually no positive intention to establish any rights for minorities to secede under any circumstances."). But logically or not, the Savings Clause has been widely interpreted as applying to all states.
49. Kosovo Advisory Opinion (I.C.J., 2010), ¶ 82. Two judges accepted the claim in separate opinions. Kosovo Advisory Opinion, Separate Opinion of Judge Trindade, ¶ 175; Kosovo Advisory Opinion, Separate Opinion of Judge Yusuf, ¶ 11.
50. Tancredi, "A Normative 'Due Process,'" in Kohen, *Secession,* 175–76 (citing eighteen prominent scholars).
51. From the Kosovo Advisory Proceedings, see the following Written Statements: Albania, 49, ¶ 95; Denmark, 6, ¶ 2.4; Estonia, 11, ¶ 2.2; France, 41; Germany, 26; Ireland, 12, ¶ 34; Japan, 5; Latvia, 2, ¶ 8; Luxembourg, 3, ¶ 5; Maldives, 1; Poland, 22, ¶ 5.1; Slovenia, 2.
52. See generally Hannum, *Autonomy, Sovereignty, and Self-Determination.*
53. ICCPR, art. 27.
54. Thornberry, "Self-Determination, Minorities, Human Rights," 878, 880.
55. G.A. Res. 61/295, art. 46.
56. Sovereignty has been defined as "final and absolute political authority in the political community . . . and no final and absolute authority exists elsewhere[.]" Hinsley, *Sovereignty,* 26. See Krasner, *Sovereignty: Organized Hypocrisy* (identifying four distinct subcategories: mutual state recognition; noninterference; formal political organization and control over territory; and control of cross-border movement). Sovereignty is not "natural, inevitable or immutable . . . [but] a juridical idea and institution. . . . [A]s seen from inside a state, sovereignty is paramount authority, and as seen from outside it is self-governing authority." Jackson, "Sovereignty in World Politics," 432–33. See also Henkin, "That 'S' Word: Sovereignty"; Taylor, "A Modest Proposal" (calling for decoupling sovereignty and statehood).
57. Buchanan, *Secession: Morality of Political Divorce,* 108.
58. Vienna Convention on Succession, art. 16. Humanitarian treaties do continue.
59. See Vienna Convention on the Law of Treaties, art. 62.2(a). (The right to terminate treaties because of changed circumstances does not apply "if the treaty establishes a boundary.") Several states entered reservations to this provision, arguing that unequal boundary treaties violated the right to self-determination. Ibid., pp. 496 (Afghanistan), 500 (Morocco), 505–6 (Syria).
60. See Higgins, *Problems and Process,* 121: "The evolving norms on self-determination contained—undeniably and consistently—an anxious refrain whereby self-determination is to be harnessed to, and not the enemy of, territorial integrity."
61. Until aggression was prohibited, "it made little sense to talk about the right to become a state. Thus the reason that self-determination (despite its salience as a political value after 1789) did not fit into classical international law was that it aspired to something which

classical international law precisely did not try to achieve, that is to constitute or reconstitute states." Crawford, "Right of Self-Determination," 12. Crawford uses "classical" in a different sense than I do, but otherwise we are in agreement here.

Chapter 3. The Measure of Nations

1. Musil, *Man without Qualities,* vol. 1, 569.
2. The UN Charter system was "intended to allow states to avoid unilateral reliance on the military instrument to guarantee their own security." Higgins, *Problems and Process,* 238. On norms of aggression and conquest, see Korman, *Right of Conquest,* 179ff.
3. Mearsheimer and Walt, "Leaving Theory Behind," 429 (noting the "inherent complexity and diversity of the international system and the problematic nature of much of the available data").
4. See Concept Stew, "Statistics for the Terrified."
5. The Nurses' Health Studies surveyed 121,000 participants—all female, married, aged thirty to fifty-five, and living in eleven U.S. states. "Nurses' Health Study."
6. Mearsheimer and Walt, "Leaving Theory Behind," 446 ("this literature may be a poor model for the field as a whole, because relationships as robust as the democratic peace are rare"); Simmons, *Mobilizing for Human Rights,* chaps. 3–4.
7. Lansing, *Peace Negotiations,* 96–97 (partly quoting his own notes).
8. Gellner, *Nations and Nationalism,* 2.
9. Schaffer, *Amadeus.*
10. See, e.g., Kumar, "Troubled History of Partition."
11. See *Ethnologue.*
12. Plischke, "Self-Determination."
13. See Dietrich, *Sezession und Demokratie,* 372.
14. Southern Sudan Referendum 2011 (just under 99 percent in favor of secession).
15. See *Reference re Secession of Quebec;* Argitis and Tomesco, "Quebec Separatists Trounced."
16. On Austria, 1938, quoted in Cobban, *Nation-State and National Self-Determination,* 20 (first ellipsis original to Cobban).
17. See, e.g., Bookman, "Economics of Secession," 85ff.
18. *World Atlas,* "Countries of the World"; Rosenberg, "Average Country."
19. Alesina, "Size of Countries," 308.
20. Alesina, Spolaore, and Wacziarg, "Trade, Growth and the Size of Countries," 1499 (noting both advantages of size and costs of managing heterogeneity). Larger countries more frequently suffer violent conflicts, although the reasons for this are complex. See Raleigh and Hegre, "Population Size, Concentration, and Civil War."
21. See Alesina, Spolaore, and Wacziarg, "Trade, Growth and the Size of Countries," 1499 (arguing small states and trade liberalization are correlated).
22. A common objection to secession (to which we will return) concerns *wealthy* regions withdrawing, which hardly suggests that new units aren't viable. If anything, the challenge is that the *remainder* might not be viable. Cf. Wellman, *Theory of Secession,* 1 ("Any group has a moral right to secede as long as its political divorce will leave it and the remainder state in a position to perform the requisite political functions.").

23. See, e.g., Chu, "Under EU, Independence Feels Viable."

24. Butler, *Lost Peace,* 130.

25. *UN Monthly Chronicle,* 65, *quoted in* Farley, *Plebiscites and Sovereignty,* 135 (referring to Trust Territories).

26. We are less skeptical about existing states: "The outstanding assumption about the developing world since World War II has been that countries can develop within their existing boundaries. . . . Yet the view that development can occur without changes in boundaries is relatively recent. Before World War II . . . it was certainly not assumed that all countries, irrespective of their internal capacities, would inevitably prosper." Herbst, "Is Nigeria a Viable State?"

27. Thoreau, *Civil Disobedience,* 18.

28. See Peace Research Institute Oslo, "UPCD/PRIO Armed Conflict Dataset" (listing, as of 2013, twenty-four intrastate conflicts, no interstate conflicts, and nine internationalized intrastate conflicts.) It can be difficult to decide if a conflict is international or internal. See International Committee of the Red Cross, "Opinion Paper: How Is the Term 'Armed Conflict' Defined . . . ?"

29. See International Committee of the Red Cross, *Violence and the Use of Force,* at 6.

30. Many definitions of secession commit a logical error "by assuming that violence must be an element of it." Armitage, "Secession and Civil War," 39.

31. Ignatieff, *Human Rights as Politics and Idolatry,* 22.

32. Carr, *Twenty Years' Crisis,* 209, 222.

33. Horowitz, "Cracked Foundations," 6.

34. de Tocqueville, *Old Regime and the Revolution,* 214.

35. Sunstein, "Constitutionalism and Secession," 634. See also Buchanan, *Secession: Morality of Political Divorce,* 100; Jenne, *Ethnic Bargaining.*

36. Cassese, *Self-Determination of Peoples.*

37. See Glendon, *Rights Talk.*

38. Cf. Toft, "Indivisible Territory and Ethnic War"; Ignatieff, *Human Rights as Politics and Idolatry,* 22 ("Even when secessionist challenges are not explicit, repressive regimes raise the specter of their threat to justify authoritarian rule.").

39. See "Bargaining 101 (#7): Ultimatum Game."

40. It is certainly not the only reason: Generational shifts and economic fears also played a role. But "it is quite possible that the exit options themselves . . . can lead to a stronger set of commitments and attachments by disaffected groups than one would otherwise see." Elkins, "Logic and Design of a Low-Commitment Constitution," 304.

41. Garrison, "A Covenant with Death."

42. Allen Buchanan's groundbreaking treatment is more sympathetic to secession than most commentators, but it is shot through with assumptions that secessions are normally carried out by illiberal communities seeking to escape a liberal state.

43. Weiler, "Catalonian Independence."

44. Fisher, "A Revealing Map" (greatest preponderance of ethnic homogeneity in Europe and highest heterogeneity in sub-Saharan Africa). See also Alesina et al., "Fractionalization" (analyzing mapping of states' diversity).

45. See Alesina et al., "Fractionalization."

46. Ibid.
47. See Tomuschat, "Secession and Self-Determination," 42.
48. "Bangladesh Islamist Leader Ghulam Azam Charged."
49. Tancredi, "Normative 'Due Process,'" 175.
50. See Ratner, "Drawing a Better Line," 624 (warning against "formalized self-determination that enables a new state to form along the administrative lines of the old territorial unit but neglects the underlying territorial issues").
51. Walzer, "Comment," 99–100.
52. Donnelly, *Universal Human Rights,* 207.
53. "[M]inorities *as such* do not have a right of self-determination. . . . [S]elf-determination is interlocked with the proper protection of minority rights—but that they are discrete rights[.]" Higgins, *Problems and Process,* 124–25 (emphasis original).
54. The domestic and international peace benefits of consolidated democracy have been widely analyzed, but transition can increase the likelihood of war, particularly when democratizing states begin with weak institutions. See Mansfield and Snyder, *Electing to Fight.* Rapid democratization can open space for extremist politics and ethnic conflict. See Chua, *World on Fire.*
55. See Sunstein, "Constitutionalism and Secession," 635, 670.

Chapter 4. A New Right to Secession

1. Farley, *Plebiscites and Sovereignty,* 140.
2. Ibid., 81. See Beran, "Border Disputes," 485.
3. Dietrich, *Sezession und Demokratie,* 354, citing Beran, "Liberal Theory of Secession," 29ff. Beran's "recursive" principle calls for groups to determine the territory along lines similar to my model. See Beran, *Consent Theory of Political Obligation,* 39–41; Beran, "Who Should Be Entitled to Vote in Self-Determination Referenda?," 154ff. See also Aleksandar Pavković, "Recursive Secessions."
4. Qvortrup, *Referendums and Ethnic Conflict,* 138.
5. The EU proposed 55 percent as a condition for recognizing Montenegro's independence. Canada's Supreme Court spoke only about a "clear majority" and a "clear question. *Reference re Secession of Quebec,* ¶¶ 92–93, 100, 104, 148, 150–51, 153 ("it will be for the political actors to determine what constitutes 'a clear majority on a clear question' in the circumstances under which a future referendum vote may be taken"). See Qvortrup, *Referendums and Ethnic Conflict,* and Şen, *Sovereignty Referendums,* on both issues; Margalit and Raz, "National Self-Determination," 458 (arguing for a supermajority "[g]iven the long-term and irreversible nature of the decision").
6. See Tushnet, "Secession as a Problem in Negotiation," 343.

Chapter 5. People, Territory, Plebiscite

1. Geertz, "Integrative Revolution," 120. See also El Ouali, *Territorial Integrity in a Globalizing World,* xv.
2. Waldron, "Principle of Proximity," 1, 4.

3. Rawls, *Political Liberalism,* xxv.

4. Rawls, *Theory of Justice,* 11.

5. Rawls, *Law of Peoples.*

6. See "Europeans and Their Languages," 386; Bokamba, "Multilingualism as a Sociolinguistic Phenomenon," 33.

7. "[D]emocratic procedures themselves cannot define who counts as part of the 'people' among whom democratic decisions are to be taken." Stilz, "On Colonialism and Self-Determination," 12. See Saunders, "Defining the Demos."

8. Sharma, "Sushil Koirala, Ex-Premier of Nepal" (but noting leaders of Madhesi minority ended a strike after parliament amended the constitution to address their concerns).

9. South Asia Collective, *South Asia State of Minorities Report 2016,* 29 ("Ahmadis are "turned into a de-facto minority and refused identification within the larger and dominant Muslim identity. They suffer a double jeopardy when they are neither officially declared a minority—thus accepting them as citizens entitled to basic rights—nor being able to access those rights without denouncing their religious beliefs.").

10. Rawls, *Political Liberalism,* 137.

11. Rawls, "Kantian Constructivism in Moral Theory," 517.

12. Habermas, *Structural Transformation of the Public Sphere;* Habermas, *Theory of Communicative Action,* vol. 1.

13. Fraser, *"Rethinking the Public Sphere,* 123.

14. Finnis, N*atural Law and Natural Rights,* 231–59, discussed in Waldron, "Principle of Proximity," 17.

15. Waldron, "Principle of Proximity," 5 (emphasis original). See Moore, *Political Theory of Territory,* 4 ("little attention was drawn to the fact that Rawls also assumed that justice operated within a *territorially* delimited political community (a state) and that the territorial dimension of the state was not addressed in anything like adequate terms [emphasis original]"); see also Kolers, *Land, Conflict, and Justice,* 2.

16. Žižek, *Welcome to the Desert of the Real!,* 122–23 (critiquing Habermas' *Verfassungspatriotismus*).

17. See Stilz, "Why Do States Have Territorial Rights?," 205–6: "[O]ur Kantian theory additionally ties a state's right over its territory to its authorization, in a representative process, by the people who inhabit that territory. It is thus the state's special relation to that territory's population that confers territorial rights upon it: it represents this *particular people*" (emphasis original).

18. We should be careful about reading ethnicity backward. Names like Deutschland and Germania have existed longer than any German nation in the modern sense; early usages such as Imperium Romanum Sacrum Nationis Germanicæ or Luther's 1520 address *An den christlichen Adel deutscher Nation* carry a very different connotation.

19. See Vidmar, *Democratic Statehood in International Law,* 78ff.

20. Weiler, "Catalonian Independence."

21. See Roeder, *Where Do Nation-States Come From?* (preexisting "segment-states" are more likely to achieve independence).

22. Anderson, *Imagined Communities.*

23. *Quoted in* James and O'Rourke, "Italy and the First Age of Globalization," 39.

24. *Reference re Secession of Quebec*, ¶ 59: "The social and demographic reality of Quebec explains the existence of the province of Quebec as a political unit and indeed, was one of the essential reasons for establishing a federal structure for the Canadian union in 1867."

25. See Krisch, "Catalonia's Independence."

26. Examples include Southeast Asian mandala models and pre-colonial African polities. Even in the heartland of the territorial state, the Holy Roman Empire was based less on fixed territory than allegiances. Stollberg-Rilinger, *Das Heilige Römische Reich,* 10.

27. Meyrowitz, *No Sense of Place,* 315.

28. Habermas, *Further Reflections on the Public Sphere,* 456.

29. Horowitz, "Cracked Foundations," 14.

30. The answer is 3 percent. There were 244 million migrants in 2015, but the world's population is 7.3 billion. United Nations Department of Economic and Social Affairs, *International Migration Report 2015.* More people live abroad at some point, and many more move within their own state. But even there we find surprising levels of sedentariness.

31. Corey Lau, quoted in Ramzy and Wong, "Young People Have Their Say."

32. Smith, *Theory of Moral Sentiments,* 90.

33. Waldron, "Principle of Proximity," 14.

34. *Nottebohm* Case (*Liechtenstein v. Guatemala*), at 23.

35. Locke, *Two Treatises of Government,* ¶ 122.

36. See de Groot, Vink, and Honohan, "Loss of Citizenship": Thirteen European states terminate citizenship for permanent residence abroad.

37. Convention on the Reduction of Statelessness, art. 10 (1–2).

38. UNHCR, "Nationality Laws of the Former Soviet Republics."

39. Arieli and Schwartz, "Injustice and Folly," 75.

40. Declaration on the Consequences of State Succession, art. 13a.

41. Kattan, "Nationality of Denationalized Palestinians," 91 n. 115 (listing scholars, including Oppenheim and Brownlie, who assert this rule).

42. International Law Commission, Draft Articles on Nationality.

43. "The successor States may make the exercise of the right of option conditional on the existence of effective links, in particular ethnic, linguistic or religious, with the predecessor State"—meaning states have power to shape any option. Declaration on the Consequences of State Succession, art. 14.

44. Brownlie, *Principles of Public International Law,* 646, cited in UNHCR, "Nationality Laws of the Former Soviet Republics." I'm not making a property-based argument; I'm talking about the political logic of place. I've never found social contract theory or 'first to labor the land' justifications helpful in thinking practically about the relationship between states and the people in them. We are not dealing with property but governance— "meta-jurisdictional powers [that] confer authority . . . to decide who has powers to make primary rules over which pieces of territory." Stilz, "Why Do States Have Territorial Rights?," 196 (calling the right to secede "an example of such a metajurisdictional power").

45. Stilz, "Why Do States Have Territorial Rights?," 210, 205.

46. A philosopher might call this a question of *association*. See, e.g., Stilz, "On Colonialism and Self-Determination" (distinguishing democratic and associative accounts of self-determination, and using the latter term in ways similar to how I talk about democracy.) I'd happily use that term to describe people's decisions about what political institutions to affirm.

47. Cf. Naticchia, *Law of Peoples,* 186: "Is it worse to be a secessionist with no right to secede, or an antisecessionist living in a society in which others may exercise their right to secede?"

48. Cf. Hirschl, "Nullification," 254–55 (calling nullification "a somewhat different impulse within the broad class of separatist political voices"); Wellman, *Theory of Secession,* 77 ("The Confederates were not trying to unfairly pick and choose which democratically enacted laws to follow. . . . [T]hey merely sought to exit the cooperative.").

49. Buchanan, "Secession," *Stanford Encyclopedia.*

50. Smith, "Fences," 24.

51. Renan, "Qu'est-ce qu'une nation?"

52. Farley, *Plebiscites and Sovereignty,* 81.

53. Rushdie, *Shalimar the Clown,* 102, cited in Sterio, *Right to Self-Determination under International Law,* 1.

54. See Dietrich, "Secession of the Rich."

55. Act on Greenland Self-Government Arrangement (Denmark).

56. GovTrack, "Illinois's 4th Congressional District."

57. India and Bangladesh—whose enclaves are the world's most complex—recently swapped some to simplify their border.

58. See Farley, *Plebiscites and Sovereignty,* 55, 82.

59. See Friese, "Marooned by History" (discussing transfers of enclaves).

60. See Şen, *Sovereignty Referendums,* 255–66, and Qvortup, *Referendums and Ethnic Conflict,* on this question.

61. *Reference re Secession* of *Quebec,* ¶ 100.

62. Donolo, "Clarity Act."

63. Rüegger and Oleschak-Pillai, "State Secession in International Law," 61, citing Venice Commission Referendum Guidelines 1.3.1(c). See also Laponce, "National Self-Determination and Referendums," 53.

64. See Şen, *Sovereignty Referendums,* 91–98.

Chapter 6. Broader Implications

1. See Waldron, "Superseding Historical Injustice."

2. Keynes, *Economic Consequences of the Peace,* 99.

3. Buchanan, *Secession: Morality of Political Divorce,* 115.

4. Margalit and Raz, "National Self-Determination," 459.

5. Buchanan, *Secession: Morality of Political Divorce,* 119, continuing: "*How* it came to be the better-off group may be highly relevant. If its greater prosperity is a result of unjust government preferment—if, for example, it has been the beneficiary rather than the victim

of discriminatory redistribution—then its secession may be unjust, unless it pays appropriate compensation[.]" (Ibid., 120). This rarely happens: Groups that can harness state power don't need to secede. Buchanan, writing in 1991, used the example of English secession, since England profited from 'internal colonial' exploitation of Scotland. A few decades later, it was the Scots who considered seceding. Still, a group might see its hold weakening and exit before the bill comes due.

6. *Texas v. White,* 725.
7. See Wellman, *Theory of Secession,* 70–71, 81–83 (critiquing Lincoln's economic arguments against secession).
8. Buchanan, *Secession: Morality of Political Divorce,* 104.
9. Ibid., 104–5 (suggesting federal tariffs affecting the poorer South may have exceeded federal investments).
10. See Wellman, *Theory of Secession,* 90: Even if Britain deserved compensation for its American colonies, "this does not justify denying the colonists' political liberty; at most it can set limiting conditions upon the political divorce."
11. See Nine, *Global Justice and Territory* (describing the current model and advancing a general theory justifying exclusive territorial allocation).
12. See Buchanan, *Secession: Morality of Political Divorce,* 115–6: "[I]t is often said that our positive obligations to our fellow citizens are much more substantial than those we have towards 'strangers.' . . . [At most,] the better off do . . . owe *some* positive assistance to the worse off who are not their fellow citizens; but these obligations are *much less substantial,*"
13. See, e.g., Pogge, "Egalitarian Law of Peoples," 195–224. Rousseau noted the arbitrariness of borders: "How can a man or a people seize an immense territory and keep it from the rest of the world except by a punishable usurpation[?]" Rousseau, *Social Contract,* 20.
14. "Psalm," in Szymborska, *View with a Grain of Sand,* 99–100.
15. It might be necessary to prohibit acts of retaliation against aliens for exercising their right; this would likely be a *de minimis* problem, however: in states willing to retaliate, aliens would already be keeping a low profile.
16. See Şen, *Sovereignty Referendums,* 236–52, especially 245–51) on the status of non-native residents.
17. See Kumar, "Troubled History of Partition," 22; Kaufmann, "When All Else Fails," 120 (rebutting Kumar). See also Horowitz, "Cracked Foundations," 6: "Since most secessionist movements will be resisted by central governments and most secessionists receive insufficient foreign military assistance to succeed, propounding a right to secede, without the means to success, is likely to increase ultimately fruitless secessionist warfare, at the expense of internal efforts at political accommodation and at the cost of increased human suffering."
18. Appadurai, *Fear of Small Numbers,* 49, 84–85.
19. Horowitz, "Cracked Foundations," 11.
20. Brilmayer, "Secession and Self-Determination," 199.
21. Yau Wai Ching, quoted in Wong, "At Hong Kong Swearing-In."
22. Carr, *Twenty Years' Crisis,* 222.

Chapter 7. The Hardest Part

1. Although the United Kingdom recognizes a right for parts of its own population to secede, it doesn't for others. In 2008, it abandoned its long-standing recognition of Tibetan autonomy and accepted China's sovereignty. Barnett, "Tibet," 489.
2. Verfassung des Fürstentums Liechtenstein, art. 4(2), in Elkins, "Logic and Design of a Low-Commitment Constitution," 302.
3. Federación de San Kitts y Nevis Constitución de 1983, art. 113; Constitution of the Republic of Uzbekistan, art. 74, both in Elkins, "Logic and Design of a Low-Commitment Constitution," 302.
4. Langewiesche, "Welcome to the Green Zone."
5. See Goodman and Jinks, *Socializing States.*
6. Resnik, "Law's Migration," 1576.
7. See Keck and Sikkink, *Activists beyond Borders.*
8. Elkins, "Logic and Design of a Low-Commitment Constitution," 306. "Under no circumstances shall the exercise of autonomy allow for secession from the national territory." Constitucion de la Republica del Ecuador, art. 238.
9. See *Kohlhaas v. Alaska* (drawing on *Texas v. White* to refuse to certify a petition proposing a referendum on secession or instructing the state to work for its constitutionalization); Taylor, "German Court Shuts Down Hopes."
10. Elkins, "Logic and Design of a Low-Commitment Constitution," 312–13.
11. See Sunstein, "Constitutionalism and Secession," 670 (arguing that substate units should waive any right to secede). Vicki Jackson, "Secession, Transnational Precedents, and Constitutional Silences," 336 ("[S]ecession should not be encouraged through law; but in the face of mobilized demand, a procedural approach to resolving such claims has obvious benefits over violence."); see also Haljan, *Constitutionalizing Secession,* 26 (Secession is subject to constitutional law but "secession provisions are not and should not be incorporated expressly into a constitution."). But see Ginsburg and Versteeg, "From Catalonia to California," 58 ("constitutional drafters ought to be as explicit as possible about their intentions regarding secession. Either a prohibition or an explicit clause allowing secession may be superior to . . . ambiguity.")
12. Resnik, "Law's Migration," 1591–93, 1598–1606 (discussing attempts to invoke the UN Charter in US courts).
13. Elkins, "Logic and Design of a Low-Commitment Constitution," 312. See also Norman, *Negotiating Nationalism.* (arguing that secession clauses can "reduce incentives for secessionist politics while enhancing . . . political stability for the national majority").
14. Vicki Jackson, "Secession, Transnational Precedents, and Constitutional Silences," 335–36. But see Ginsburg and Versteeg, "From Catalonia to California" (arguing that explicit clauses regarding secession lower the risk of violence).
15. Ibid., 336. See Sorens, *Secessionism,* arguing that providing legal pathways for secession rather than prohibiting it leads to less violent outcomes.
16. Reference re Secession of Quebec, ¶¶ 142–43.
17. Ibid., ¶ 143.
18. Coggins, "Friends in High Places."
19. East Timor's transitional administration offers similar lessons; but Timor was considered

a colony, so its belated liberation is pigeonholed, the precedential effects dismissed. Montenegro's 2006 referendum was consistent with the State Union of Serbia and Montenegro's constitution, but the process—like the State Union agreement—was influenced by EU diplomacy.

20. di Lampedusa, *Il Gattopardo;* di Lampedusa, *The Leopard,* 26 ("If we want things to stay as they are, things will have to change.").

21. See Margalit and Raz, "National Self-Determination," 442 (noting that a claim to territory and the right to use force to vindicate that claim aren't identical).

22. Asiwaju, "Transfrontier Regionalism," 133.

23. See Nelson, "Power and Proximity," on regional effects on secession.

24. Even that model's defenders acknowledge this: "International legal rules are too rigid and rudimentary to prove alert to the new wave of tribalism and secessionism. In particular, they are unmitigatedly geared to self-determination as a form of acquisition (or recovery) of independent statehood by colonial or militarily occupied peoples, and at the same time exceedingly unresponsive to the needs of ethnic or racial groups[.]" Cassese, *Self-Determination of Peoples,* 340–41.

25. *[U]n plébiscite de tous les jours.* Renan, "Qu'est-ce qu'une nation?"

Conclusion

1. Armitage, "Secession and Civil War," 49.

2. Faludi, *In the Darkroom,* 326.

3. Cassese, *Self-Determination of Peoples,* 316, citing Lansing, *The Peace Negotiations,* 96.

Appendix

1. Buchanan, *Secession: Morality of Political Divorce,* vii.

2. Moore, *Political Theory of Territory,* 3.

3. Kolers, *Land, Conflict, and Justice,* 2.

4. Dietrich, "Changing Borders by Secession," 87.

5. Ibid., 89.

6. Harris Mylonas, "Assimilation and Its Alternatives: Caveats in the Study of Nation-Building Policies," in Chenoweth and Lawrence, *Rethinking Violence,* 85.

WORKS CITED AND CONSULTED

Aaland Islands Question—Report Submitted to the Council of the League of Nations by the Commission of Rapporteurs. League of Nations Doc. B7. 21/68/106 (April 16, 1921).

Abulof, Uriel, and Karl Cordell, eds. *Self-Determination in the Early Twenty-First Century.* New York: Routledge, 2016.

Act on Greenland Self-Government Arrangement (Greenland–Denmark) (Amalienborg, June 12, 2009). Act. No. 473, entered into force June 21, 2009. http://www.stm.dk/_p_13090 .html.

Alesina, Alberto. "The Size of Countries: Does It Matter?" *Journal of the European Economic Association* 1 (2003).

Alesina, Alberto F., William Easterly, Arnaud Devleeschauwer, Sergio Kurlat, and Romain T. Wacziarg. "Fractionalization." Harvard Institute Research Working Paper, No. 1959 (June 2002).

Alesina, Alberto, and Enrico Spolaore, *The Size of Nations.* Cambridge, MA: MIT Press, 2003.

Alesina, Alberto, Enrico Spolaore, and Romain Wacziarg. "Trade, Growth and the Size of Countries." In *Handbook of Economic Growth.* Vol. 1B, edited by Philip Aghion and Steven N. Durlauf. Boston: Elsevier, 2005.

Allansson, Marie, Erik Melander, and Lotta Themnér. "Organized Violence, 1989–2017." *Journal of Peace Research* 55 (2018).

Alston, Philip, ed. *People's Rights.* Oxford: Oxford University Press, 2001.

Anaya, James S. *Indigenous Peoples in International Law.* New York: Oxford, 2004.

Anderson, Benedict. *Imagined Communities.* London: Verso, 1991.

Anghie, Antony. *Imperialism, Sovereignty and the Making of International Law.* Cambridge: Cambridge University Press, 2004.

Appadurai, Arjun. *Fear of Small Numbers: An Essay on the Geography of Anger.* Durham, NC: Duke University Press, 2006.

Argitis, Theophilos, and Frederic Tomesco. "Quebec Separatists Trounced as Secession Support Wanes." *Bloomberg Business,* April 8, 2014. https://www.bloomberg.com/news/articles /2014-04-08/quebec-separatists-trounced-as-secession-support-wanes.

Arieli, Shaul, and Doubi Schwartz (with Hadas Tagari). "Injustice and Folly: On the Proposals to Cede Arab Localities from Israel to Palestine." *Floersheimer Institute for Policy Studies,* no. 3/48e (July 2006).

Armitage, David. "Secession and Civil War." In *Secession as an International Phenomenon: From America's Civil War to Contemporary Separatist Movements,* edited by Don Harrison Doyle. Athens: University of Georgia Press, 2010.

Asiwaju, Anthony I. "Transfrontier Regionalism: The European Union Perspective on Postcolonial Africa, with Special Reference to Borgu." In *Holding the Line: Borders in a Global World,* edited by Heather N. Nicol and Ian Townsend-Gault. Vancouver: UBC Press, 2005.

Atlantic Charter, agreement between the United States and the United Kingdom. August 14, 1941. 55 Stat. 1603; E.A.S. 236.

Badinter Commission: Peace Conference on Yugoslavia Arbitration Commission. Opinion no. 3. (January 11, 1992).

Bagwell, Ben. "Yugoslavian Constitutional Questions: Self-Determination and Secession of Member Republics." *Georgia Journal of International and Comparative Law* 21 (1991).

"Bangladesh Islamist Leader Ghulam Azam Charged." *BBC News,* May 13, 2012. http://www.bbc.com/news/world-asia-18049515.

"Bargaining 101 (#7): The Ultimatum Game (Continuous)." *Game Theory 101.* Accessed February 9, 2019. http://gametheory101.com/courses/bargaining-101/the-ultimatum-game-continuous/.

"Bargaining 101 (#9): The Power of Counteroffers." *Game Theory 101.* Accessed February 9, 2019. http://gametheory101.com/Outside_Options.html.

Barnett, Robert. "Tibet: Secession Based on the Collapse of an Imperial Overlord." In *The Ashgate Research Companion to Secession,* edited by Aleksandar Pavković and Peter Radan. Burlington, VT: Ashgate, 2011.

Bartkus, Viva Ona. *The Dynamics of Secession.* Cambridge: Cambridge University Press, 1999.

Barzun, Jacques. *From Dawn to Decadence: 1500 to the Present: 500 Years of Western Cultural Life.* New York: HarperCollins, 2000.

Beary, Brian. "Separatist Movements," *CQ Researcher* 2 (2008).

Benvenisti, Eyal. "Sovereigns as Trustees of Humanity: On the Accountability of States to Foreign Stakeholders." *American Journal of International Law* 107, no. 2 (2013).

Beran, Harry. "Border Disputes and the Right of National Self-Determination." *History of European Ideas* 16 (1993): 479.

———. *The Consent Theory of Political Obligation.* New York: Croom Helm, 1987.

———. "A Liberal Theory of Secession." *Political Studies* 32 (1984): 21.

———. "Who Should Be Entitled to Vote in Self-Determination Referenda?" In *Terrorism, Protest and Power,* edited by Martin Warner and Roger Crisp. London: Edward Elgar, 1990.

Berman, Nathaniel. "But the Alternative Is Despair: European Nationalism and the Modernist Renewal of International Law." *Harvard Law Review* 106 (1993): 1792.

———. "Sovereignty in Abeyance: Self-Determination and International Law." *Wisconsin International Law Journal* 7 (1988–1989): 51.

Bieber, Florian. "The Challenge of Institutionalizing Ethnicity in the Western Balkans: Managing Change in Deeply Divided Societies." *European Yearbook of Minority Issues* 3 (2003).

Black, Andrew. "Scottish Independence: SNP Accepts Call to Change Referendum Question." *BBC News,* January 20, 2013.

Bokamba, Eyamba G. "Multilingualism as a Sociolinguistic Phenomenon: Evidence from Africa." In *Languages in Africa: Multilingualism, Language Policy, and Education,* edited by Elizabeth C. Zsiga, One Tlale Boyer, and Ruther Kramer. Washington, DC: Georgetown University Press, 2014.

Bookman, Milica C. "The Economics of Secession." In *Separatism: Democracy and Disintegration,* edited by Metta Spencer. Lanham, MD: Rowan & Littlefield, 1998.

Brilmayer, Lea. "Secession and Self-Determination: A Territorial Interpretation." *Yale Journal of International Law* 16 (1991).

Broelmann, Catherine, R. Lefeber, and Marjoleine Zieck, eds. *Peoples and Minorities in International Law.* Boston: Martinus Nijhoff Publishers, 1993.

Brooks, Thom. *Current Controversies in Political Philosophy.* New York: Routledge, 2015.

Brownlie, Ian. *African Boundaries: A Legal and Diplomatic Encyclopedia.* London: C. Hurst, 1979.

———. *Principles of Public International Law.* Oxford: Oxford University Press, 1990.

———. "The Rights of Peoples in Modern International Law." In *The Rights of Peoples,* edited by James Crawford. Oxford: Clarendon Press, 1988.

Brubaker, Rogers. *Nationalism Reframed: Nationhood and the National Question in the New Europe.* Cambridge: Cambridge University Press, 1996.

Buchanan, Allen. *Justice, Legitimacy, and Self-Determination: Moral Foundations for International Law.* Oxford: Oxford University Press, 2004.

———. "Secession." *Stanford Encyclopedia of Philosophy,* 2003, rev. June 22, 2017. https://plato.stanford.edu/entries/secession/index.html#ref-6.

———. *Secession: The Morality of Political Divorce from Fort Sumter to Lithuania and Quebec.* Boulder, CO: Westview Press, 1991.

———. "Uncoupling Secession from Nationalism and Intrastate Autonomy." In *Negotiating Self-Determination,* edited by Hurst Hannum and Eileen F. Babbitt. Lanham, MD: Lexington Books, 2006.

Buchanan, Allen, and Stephen Macedo, eds. *Secession and Self-Determination: NOMOS XLV.* New York: NYU Press, 2003.

Buchheit, Lee C. *Secession: The Legitimacy of Self-Determination.* New Haven, CT: Yale University Press, 1978.

Buckley, Chris. "27 Die in Rioting in Western China." *New York Times,* June 27, 2013.

Burri, Thomas. "The Kosovo Opinion and Secession: The Sounds of Silence and Missing Links." *German Law Journal* 11 (2010).

Butler, Harold. *The Lost Peace: A Personal Impression.* New York: Harcourt Brace, 1942.

Cameron, David R., Gustav Ranis, and Annalisa Zinn. *Globalization and Self-Determination: Is the Nation-State Under Siege?* London: Routledge, 2006.

Capotorti, Francesco. *Study on the Rights of Persons Belonging to Ethnic, Religious and Linguistic Minorities.* New York: United Nations, 1991.

Carr, Edward Hallett. *Conditions of Peace*. New York: Macmillan, 1942.

————. *The Twenty Years' Crisis, 1919–1939*. 2nd ed. New York: Harper & Row, 1964.

Cassese, Antonio. *Self-Determination of Peoples: A Legal Reappraisal*. Cambridge: Cambridge University Press, 1995.

Chagos Islands Advisory Opinion: *Legal Consequences of the Separation of the Chagos Archipelago from Mauritius in 1965,* Advisory Opinion, International Court of Justice Rep. 2019 (February 25).

Chenoweth, Erica, and Adria Lawrence, eds. *Rethinking Violence: States and Non-State Actors in Conflict*. Cambridge MA: MIT Press, 2010.

"China Jails Prominent Uighur Academic Ilham Tohti for Life." *BBC News,* September 23, 2014. http://www.bbc.com/news/world-asia-29321701.

Chu, Henry. "Under EU, Independence Feels Viable to Europe's Secessionists." *Los Angeles Times,* December 24, 2012.

Chua, Amy. *World on Fire: How Exporting Free Market Democracy Breeds Ethnic Hatred and Global Instability*. New York: Free Press, 2003.

Cobban, Alfred. *The Nation-State and National Self-Determination*. New York: Thomas Y. Crowell, 1969.

Coggins, Bridget. "Friends in High Places: International Politics and the Emergence of States from Secessionism." *International Organization*. 65 (2011): 433.

Concept Stew. Statistics for the Terrified. "The Importance of n (sample size) in Statistics." https://conceptstew.co.uk/resources/the-importance-of-n-sample-size-in-statistics/.

Conference on Security and Co-operation in Europe: Final Act (Helsinki, August 1, 1975) 92 Stat. 3875 (July 12, 1978), principle VIII.

Connor, Walker. "Self-Determination: The New Phase." *World Politics* 20 (1967).

Constitucion de la Republica del Ecuador [Constitution of the Republic of Ecuador] (2008). Amended December 3, 2015. In *World Constitutions Illustrated,* edited by Jefri Jay Ruchti, translated by Maria del Carmen Gress and J. J. Ruchti. Buffalo, NY: William S. Hein, 2016.

Constitution (Fundamental Law) of the Union of Soviet Socialist Republics (1977). Translated by F. J. M. Feldbrugge and William B. Simons. Alphen aan den Rijn, Netherlands: Sijthoff & Noordhoff, 1979.

Constitution of the Republic of Uzbekistan (1992). In *World Constitutions Illustrated*. Getzville, NY: William S. Hein, 2014.

Constitution of the Socialist Federal Republic of Yugoslavia (SFRY) (1974). Translated by Marko Pavicic. Ljubljana, Parmova: Dopisna Delavska Univerza, 1974.

Convention on the Reduction of Statelessness (New York, August 30, 1961). 989 United Nations Treaty Series 175, entered into force December 13, 1975.

Crawford, James. *The Creation of States in International Law*. New York: Oxford University Press, 2007.

————. "The Right of Self-Determination in International Law: Its Development and Future." In *People's Rights,* edited by Philip Alston. Oxford: Oxford University Press, 2001.

Crawford, James, and Alan Boyle. "Annex A: Opinion: Referendum on the Independence of Scotland—International Law Aspects." *Scotland Analysis: Devolution and the Implications of Scottish Independence,* December 10, 2012.

"Crimea Referendum: What Does the Ballot Paper Say?" *BBC News,* March 10, 2014. http://www.bbc.com/news/world-europe-26514797.

Cronin, T. E. *Direct Democracy: The Politics of Initiative Referendum and Recall.* Cambridge, MA: Harvard University Press, 1999.

Danspeckgruber, Wolfgang F., ed. *The Self-Determination of Peoples: Community, Nation, and State in an Interdependent World.* Boulder, CO: Lynne Rienner Publishers, 2002.

Declaration of Independence (United States, 1776) National Archives. https://www.archives.gov/founding-docs/declaration.

Declaration on the Consequences of State Succession for the Nationality of Natural Persons (CDL-NAT(1996)007e-rev-restr). Venice Commission 28th Plenary Meeting. September 14, 1996.

Declaration on Friendly Relations. G.A. Res. 2625 (XXV). "Declaration on Principles of International Law Concerning Friendly Relations and Co-Operation Among States in Accordance with the Charter of the United Nations," UN GAOR, 25th Sess., annex, U.N. Doc. A/RES/25/2625 (October 24, 1970).

de Groot, Gerard René, Maarten Vink, and Iseult Honohan. "Loss of Citizenship." EUDO Citizenship Policy Brief no. 3. http://eudo-citizenship.eu/docs/policy_brief_loss.pdf.

del Mar, Katherine. "Myth of Remedial Secession." In *Statehood and Self-Determination: Reconciling Traditional and Modernity in International Law,* edited by Duncan French. Cambridge: Cambridge University Press, 2013.

Demissie, Derege. "Self-Determination Including Secession vs. the Territorial Integrity of Nation-States: A Prima Facie Case for Secession." *Suffolk Transnational Law Review* 20, no. 1. (1996).

Deng, Francis Mading, ed. *Self-Determination and National Unity: A Challenge for Africa.* Trenton, NJ: Africa World Press, 2009.

de Tocqueville, Alexis. *The Old Regime and the Revolution.* Translated by John Bonner. New York: Harper & Brothers, 1856.

de Zayas, Alfred. *Nemesis at Potsdam.* Lincoln, NE: University of Nebraska Press, 1988.

Dietrich, Frank. "Changing Borders by Secession: Normative Assessment of Territorial Claims." In *The Ashgate Research Companion to Secession,* edited by Aleksandar Pavković and Peter Radan. Burlington, VT: Ashgate, 2011.

———. "Secession of the Rich: A Qualified Defence." *Politics, Philosophy & Economics* 13 (2013): 62.

———. *Sezession und Demokratie: Eine philosophische Untersuchung* [Secession and democracy: A philosophical investigation]. Berlin: De Gruyter, 2010.

Dinstein, Yoram. "Collective Human Rights of Peoples and Minorities." *International and Comparative Law Quarterly* 25 (1976).

Doehring, Karl. *Das Selbstbestimmungsrecht der Völker als Grundsatz des Völkerrechts* [The right of self-determination of peoples as a principle of international law]. Heidelberg, Germany: Verlag C. F. Müller, 1974.

Donnelly, Jack. *Universal Human Rights in Theory and Practice.* Ithaca, NY: Cornell University Press, 2003.

Donolo, Peter, ed. "Clarity Act." In *Parli—The Dictionary of Canadian Politics.* Campbell Strategies, 2017. http://www.parli.ca/clarity-act/.

Dugard, John. *The Secession of States and Their Recognition in the Wake of Kosovo.* Maubeuge, France: AIL Pocket, 2013.

Duursma, Jorri. *Fragmentation and the International Relations of Micro-States: Self-Determination and Statehood.* Cambridge: Cambridge University Press, 1996.

East Timor (Portugal v. Australia), Judgment, International Court of Justice Rep. 1995 (June 30).

Elkins, Zachary. "The Logic and Design of a Low-Commitment Constitution (Or, How to Stop Worrying about the Right to Secede)." In *Nullification and Secession in Modern Constitutional Thought,* edited by Sanford Levinson. Lawrence: University Press of Kansas, 2016.

El Ouali, Abdelhamid. *Territorial Integrity in a Globalizing World: International Law and States' Quest for Survival.* Heidelberg, Germany: Springer, 2012.

Emerson, Rupert. "Pan-Africanism." *International Organization* 16, no. 2 (1962).

Engle, Karen. *The Elusive Promise of Indigenous Development: Rights, Culture, Strategy.* Durham, NC: Duke University Press, 2010.

Ethnologue: Languages of the World. 20th ed. (2017). https://www.ethnologue.com/.

"Europeans and Their Languages." *Special Eurobarometer 386,* June 2012. http://ec.europa.eu/public_opinion/archives/ebs/ebs_386_en.pdf.

Faludi, Susan. *In the Darkroom.* New York: Henry Holt, 2015.

Farley, Lawrence. *Plebiscites and Sovereignty: The Crisis of Political Illegitimacy.* Boulder, CO: Westview Press, 1986.

Federación de San Kitts y Nevis Constitución de 1983. [Federation of Saint Kitts and Nevis 1983 Constitution]. Washington, DC: Georgetown University 2005. English translation provided by Political Database of the Americas. http://pdba.georgetown.edu/Constitutions/Kitts/kitts83.html#Chapter10.

Finnis, John. N*atural Law and Natural Rights.* Oxford: Clarendon Press, 1980.

Fisch, Jörg. *The Right of Self-Determination of Peoples: The Domestication of an Illusion.* Cambridge: Cambridge University Press, 2015.

Fisher, Max. "A Revealing Map of the World's Most and Least Ethnically Diverse Countries." *Washington Post,* May 16, 2013.

Franck, Thomas. "The Emerging Right to Democratic Governance." *American Journal of International Law* 86 (1992).

———. "Postmodern Tribalism and the Right to Secession." In *Peoples and Minorities in International Law,* edited by Catherine Broelmann, R. Lefeber, and Marjoleine Zieck. Boston: Martinus Nijhoff Publishers, 1993.

———. *The Power of Legitimacy among Nations.* New York: Oxford University Press, 1990.

Fraser, Nancy. "*Rethinking the Public Sphere: A Contribution to the Critique of Actually Existing Democracy.*" In *Habermas and the Public Sphere,* edited by Craig J. Calhoun. Cambridge: MIT Press, 1992.

Friese, Kai. "Marooned by History in India and Bangladesh." *New York Times,* July 3, 2015.

Frontier Dispute (Burkina Faso v. Mali), Judgment, International Court of Justice Rep. 1986 (December 22).

Gans, Chaim, *The Limits of Nationalism.* Cambridge: Cambridge University Press, 2003.

G.A. Res. (United Nations General Assembly Resolution) 47/9, "Question of the Comorian Island of Mayotte." U.N. Doc. A/RES/47/9 (October 27, 1992).

G.A. Res. 60/1,"2005 World Summit Outcome." U.N. GAOR, 60th Sess., U.N. Doc. A/RES/60/1 (October 24, 2005).

G.A. Res. 61/295, "Declaration on the Rights of Indigenous Peoples." U.N. GAOR, 61st Sess., Annex, U.N. Doc. A/RES/61/295 (September, 13 2007).

G.A. Res. 742 (VIII), "Factors Which Should Be Taken into Account in Deciding Whether a Territory Is or Is Not a Territory Whose People Not Yet Attained a Full Measure of Self-Government." U.N. GAOR, 8th Sess., Annex U.N. Doc. A/RES/742 (November 27, 1953).

G.A. Res. 1514 (XV), "Declaration on the Granting of Independence to Colonial Countries and Peoples." U.N. GAOR, 15th Sess., U.N. Doc. A/RES/1514 (SV) (December 14, 1960).

G.A. Res. 1541 (XV), "Principles Which Should Guide Members in Determining whether or Not an Obligation Exists to Transmit the Information Called for under Article 73e of the Charter," UN GAOR, 15th Sess., U.N. Doc. A/RES/1541(XV) (December 15, 1960).

G.A. Res. 3070 (XXXVIII), U.N. GAOR, 28th Sess., U.N. Doc. A/3070 (November 30, 1973).

Garrison, William Lloyd. "A Covenant with Death and an Agreement with Hell." Speech before Massachusetts Anti-Slavery Society, Framingham, MA, July 4, 1854. Massachusetts Historical Society.

Geertz, Clifford. "The Integrative Revolution: Primordial Sentiments and Civil Politics in the New States." In *Old Societies and New States: The Quest for Modernity in Asia and Africa,* edited by Clifford Geertz. New York: Free Press, 1963.

Gellner, Ernest. *Nations and Nationalism.* Ithaca, NY: Cornell University Press, 1983.

Ghebrewebet, Helen. *Identifying Units of Statehood and Determining International Boundaries: A Revised Look at the Doctrine of Uti Possidetis and the Principle of Self-Determination.* Bern: Peter Lang Publishing, 2006.

Ginsburg, Tom, and Mila Versteeg. "From Catalonia to California: Secession in Constitutional Law." *Alabama Law Review* 70 (2019).

Gleditsch, Nils Peter, Peter Wallensteen, Mikael Eriksson, Margareta Sollenberg, and Havard Strand. "Armed Conflict 1946–2001: A New Dataset." *Journal of Peace Research* 39, no. 5 (2002). http://www.pcr.uu.se/research/ucdp/datasets/ucdp_prio_armed_conflict_dataset/.

Glendon, Mary Ann. *Rights Talk: The Impoverishment of Political Discourse.* New York: Free Press, 1993.

Goldston, James A. "Holes in the Rights Framework: Racial Discrimination, Citizenship, and the Rights of Noncitizens." *Ethics and International Affairs* 20 (2006).

Goodman, Ryan, and Derek Jinks. *Socializing States: Promoting Human Rights through International Law.* Oxford: Oxford University Press, 2013.

GovTrack, "Illinois's 4th Congressional District." https://www.govtrack.us/congress/members/IL/4.

Griffiths, Ieuan L. *The Atlas of African Affairs.* New York: Routledge, 1994.

Gros Espiell, Héctor. "The Right to Self-Determination: Implementation of United Nations Resolutions." U.N. Doc. E/CN.4/Sub.2/405/Rev.1. (1980).

Habermas, Jürgen. *"Further Reflections on the Public Sphere."* In *Habermas and the Public*

Sphere, edited by Craig Calhoun, translated by Thomas Burger. Cambridge, MA: MIT Press, 1989.

———. *The Structural Transformation of the Public Sphere.* Translated by T. Burger and F. Lawrence. Cambridge, MA: MIT Press, 1989 (German, 1962).

———. *The Theory of Communicative Action.* Vol. 1: *Reason and the Rationalization of Society.* Translated by T. McCarthy. Boston: Beacon, 1984 (German, 1981).

Haljan, David. *Constitutionalizing Secession.* Portland, OR: Hart Publishing, 2014.

Hanauer, Laurence S. "The Irrelevance of Self-Determination Law to Ethno-National Conflict: A New Look at the Western Sahara Case." *Emory International Law Review* 9 (1995).

Hannum, Hurst. *Autonomy, Sovereignty, and Self-Determination: The Accommodation of Conflicting Rights.* Philadelphia: University of Pennsylvania Press, 1990.

———. "Self-Determination, Yugoslavia, and Europe: Old Wine in New Bottles?" *Transnational Law and Contemporary Problems* 3, no. 1 (1993).

Hemingway, Ernest. *The Complete Short Stories of Ernest Hemingway.* New York: Simon & Schuster, 1987.

Henkin, Louis. "That 'S' Word: Sovereignty, and Globalization, and Human Rights, Et Cetera." *Fordham Law Review* 68, no. 1 (1999).

Herbst, Jeffrey. "Is Nigeria a Viable State?" *Washington Quarterly* 19 (1996).

Higgins, Rosalyn. "Postmodern Tribalism and the Right to Secession, Comments." In *Peoples and Minorities in International Law,* edited by Catherine Broelmann, R. Lefeber, and Marjoleine Zieck. Boston: Martinus Nijhoff Publishers, 1993.

———. *Problems and Process: International Law and How We Use It.* Oxford: Oxford University Press, 1994.

Hilpold, Peter, ed. *Autonomy and Self-Determination.* Cheltenham, UK: Edward Elgar, 2017.

———. "The League of Nations and the Protection of Minorities—Rediscovering a Great Experiment." *Max Planck Yearbook of United Nations Law* 17 (August 5, 2013).

Hinsley, F. H. *Sovereignty.* London: Watts, 1966.

Hirschl, Ran. "Nullification: Three Comparative Notes." In *Nullification and Secession in Modern Constitutional Thought,* edited by Sanford Levinson. Lawrence: University Press of Kansas, 2016.

Hobsbawm, E. J. *Nations and Nationalism since 1780.* Cambridge: Cambridge University Press, 1990.

Horowitz, Donald L. "The Cracked Foundations of the Right to Secede." *Journal of Democracy* 14 (2003).

———. *Ethnic Groups in Conflict.* Updated Ed. Berkeley: University of California Press, 2000.

Human Rights Watch. *They Say We Should Be Grateful: Mass Rehousing and Relocation Programs in Tibetan Areas of China.* New York: HRW, 2013.

Hyde, Charles C. *International Law Chiefly as Interpreted and Applied by the United States.* Boston: Little Brown, 1947.

ICCPR (International Covenant on Civil and Political Rights). New York, December 16, 1966. 999 United Nations Treaty Series 171, entered into force March 23, 1976.

ICESCR (International Covenant on Economic, Social and Cultural Rights). New York, December 16, 1966. 993 United Nations Treaty Series 3, entered into force January 3, 1976.

Ignatieff, Michael. *Human Rights as Politics and Idolatry.* Princeton, NJ: Princeton University Press, 2001.

International Committee of the Red Cross. "How Is the Term 'Armed Conflict' Defined in International Humanitarian Law?" Opinion paper, March 2008. https://www.icrc.org/en /doc/resources/documents/article/other/armed-conflict-article-170308.htm.

———. *Violence and the Use of Force.* Geneva: ICRC, July 2011. https://www.icrc.org/eng /assets/files/other/icrc_002_0943.pdf.

International Law Commission. Draft Articles on Nationality of Natural Persons in Relation to the Succession of States with commentaries. 51st Session, U.N. Doc. A/54/10, *Yearbook of the International Law Commission* (1999), vol. 2, pt. 2, p. 23.

"Issues, The." *Cultural Survival.* https://www.culturalsurvival.org/issues.

Jackson, Robert. "Sovereignty in World Politics: A Glance at the Conceptual and Historical Landscape." *Political Studies* 47, no. 3 (1999).

Jackson, Vicki C. "Secession, Transnational Precedents, and Constitutional Silences." In *Nullification and Secession in Modern Constitutional Thought,* edited by Sanford Levinson. Lawrence: University Press of Kansas, 2016.

James, Harold, and Kevin H. O'Rourke. "Italy and the First Age of Globalization, 1861–1940." In *The Oxford Handbook of the Italian Economy since Unification,* edited by Gianni Toniolo. Oxford: Oxford University Press, 2013.

"James Madison to Daniel Webster, March 15, 1833." *National Archives,* "Founders Online," June 29, 2017. https://founders.archives.gov/documents/Madison/99-02-02-2705.

Jenne, Erin K. *Ethnic Bargaining: The Paradox of Minority Empowerment.* Ithaca, NY: Cornell University Press, 2007.

Jennings, Ivor. *The Approach to Self-Government.* Cambridge: Cambridge University Press, 1956.

Jennings, R. Y. *The Acquisition of Territory in International Law.* Manchester, NH: Manchester University Press, 1963. (Reissued 2017, with introduction by Marcelo Kohen).

Jovanović, Miodrag. *Constitutionalizing Secession in Federalized States: A Procedural Approach.* Utrecht, Netherlands: Eleven International, 2007.

Kalyvas, Stathis. *The Logic of Violence in Civil War.* Cambridge: Cambridge University Press, 2006.

Kattan, Victor Matthew. "The Nationality of Denationalized Palestinians." *Nordic Journal of International Law* 74 (2005).

Kaufmann, Chaim D. "When All Else Fails: Ethnic Population Transfers and Partitions in the Twentieth Century." *International Security* 23, no. 2 (1998).

Keck, Margaret E., and Kathryn Sikkink. *Activists beyond Borders: Advocacy Networks in International Politics.* London: Cornell University Press, 1998.

Kedourie, Elie. *Nationalism.* Malden, MA: Blackwell Publishers, 1993.

Kelsen, Hans. *The Law of the United Nations: A Critical Analysis of its Fundamental Problems.* New York: Frederick A. Praeger, 1950.

Keynes, John Maynard. *The Economic Consequences of the Peace.* New York: Harper & Row, 1920; repr. 1971.

Kimminich, Otto. "A 'Federal' Right of Self-Determination?" In *Modern Law of Self-Determination,* edited by Christian Tomuschat. Boston: Martinus Nijhoff Publishers, 1993.

Kingsbury, Damien. "West Papua: Secessionism and/or Failed Decolonization?" In *The Ashgate Research Companion to Secession,* edited by Aleksandar Pavković and Peter Radan. Burlington, VT: Ashgate, 2011.

Knop, Karen. *Diversity and Self-Determination in International Law.* New York: Cambridge University Press, 2002.

Koh, Harold. "Why Do Nations Obey International Law?" *Yale Law Journal* 106 (1997).

Kohen, Marcelo G., ed. *Secession: International Law Perspectives.* Cambridge: Cambridge University Press, 2006.

Kohlhaas v. Alaska, 147 P. 3d 714 (Alaska 2006).

Kolb, Eberhard. *Frieden von Versailles.* Munich: C. H. Beck, 2005.

Kolers, Avery. *Land, Conflict, and Justice: A Political Theory of Territory.* Cambridge: Cambridge University Press, 2009.

Korman, Sharon. *The Right of Conquest: The Acquisition of Territory by Force in International Law and Practice.* Oxford: Clarendon Press, 1996.

Kosovo Advisory Opinion: *Accordance with International Law of the Unilateral Declaration of Independence in Respect of Kosovo,* Advisory Opinion, International Court of Justice Rep. 2010 (July 22).

* Separate Opinion of Judge Trindade, July, 22, 2010.
* Separate Opinion of Judge Yusuf, July 22, 2010.
* Verbatim Record: December 7, 2009.
* Verbatim Record: December 8, 2009.
* Verbatim Record: December 10, 2009.
* Written Statement: April 14, 2009, Albania.
* Written Statement: April 3, 2009, Cyprus.
* Written Statement: April 17, 2009, Denmark.
* Written Statement: April 13, 2009, Estonia.
* Written Statement: April 16, 2009, Finland.
* Written Statement: April 7, 2009, France.
* Written Statement: April 15, 2009, Germany.
* Written Statement: April 17, 2009, Ireland.
* Written Statement: April 17, 2009, Japan.
* Written Statement: April 17, 2009, Latvia.
* Written Statement: April 17, 2009, Luxembourg.
* Written Statement: April 15, 2009, Maldives.
* Written Statement: April 15, 2009, Poland.
* Written Statement: April 17, 2009, Slovenia.
* Written Statement: April 15, 2009, Switzerland.

Krasner, Stephen. *Sovereignty: Organized Hypocrisy.* Princeton, NJ: Princeton University Press, 1999.

Krisch, Nico. "Catalonia's Independence: A Reply to Joseph Weiler," *EJIL: Talk!* January 18, 2013. https://www.ejiltalk.org/catalonias-indepence-a-reply-to-joseph-weiler/.

Kumar, Radha. "The Troubled History of Partition." *Foreign Affairs* (January–February 1997).

Kymlicka, Will. *Multicultural Citizenship.* Oxford: Oxford University Press, 1995.

Lalonde, Suzanne. *Determining Boundaries in a Conflicted World: The Role of Uti Possidetis.* Montreal: McGill-Queen's University Press, 2002.

Langewiesche, William. "Welcome to the Green Zone." *The Atlantic,* November 2004.

"Lansing Emphasizes Pledge to Slavs." *New York Times,* June 29, 1918. https://timesmachine .nytimes.com/timesmachine/1918/06/29/issue.html?action=click&contentCollection =Archives&module=LedeAsset&region=ArchiveBody&pgtype=article.

Lansing, Robert. *The Peace Negotiations: A Personal Narrative.* Boston: Houghton Mifflin, 1921.

Laponce, J. A. "National Self-Determination and Referendums: The Case for Territorial Revisionism." *Nationalism and Ethnic Politics* 7, no. 2. (2001).

László, Sebok. "Nationality Map of East Central and Southeast Europe, 1989–1992." Süd-Ost Institut München/Teleki László Foundation, 1998.

"Lausanne Principle, The: Multiethnicity, Territory, and the Future of Kosovo's Serbs." *European Stability Initiative,* June 7, 2004.

Legal Consequences of the Construction of a Wall in the Occupied Palestinian Territory, Advisory Opinion, International Court of Justice Rep. 2004 (July 9).

Lenin, Vladimir. "Report on Peace: Decree on Peace." *Second All-Russian Congress of Soviets of Workers' and Soldiers' Deputies,* November 8, 1917. Marxists Internet Archive. https://www.marxists.org/archive/lenin/works/1917/oct/25-26/26b.htm.

———. "The Socialist Revolution and the Right of Nations to Self-Determination." Theses written in 1916. Marxists Internet Archive. https://www.marxists.org/archive/lenin/works /1916/jan/x01.htm.

Levinson, Sanford, ed. *Nullification and Secession in Modern Constitutional Thought.* Lawrence: University Press of Kansas, 2016.

Lincoln, Abraham. "First Inaugural Address." Washington, DC, March 4, 1861. http://www .abrahamlincolnonline.org/lincoln/speeches/1inaug.htm.

———. Letter to Horace Greeley, August 22, 1862. http://www.abrahamlincolnonline.org /lincoln/speeches/greeley.htm.

Lister, Matthew. "Self-Determination, Dissent, and the Problem of Population Transfers." In *The Theory of Secession,* edited by Fernando R. Tesón. Cambridge: Cambridge University Press, 2016.

Locke, John. *Two Treatises of Government* (1690). London: Thomas Tegg, 1823.

Macklem, Patrick. "Self-Determination in Three Movements." In *The Theory of Secession,* edited by Fernando R. Tesón. Cambridge: Cambridge University Press, 2016.

"Magyarország Hegy- és Vízrajzi Térképe" [Mountain and hydographic map of Hungary]. Magyar Királyi Honvéd Térképészeti Intézet [Royal Hungarian Army Cartographic Institute], 1943. B XV b 132.

Mancini, Susanna. "Rethinking the Boundaries of Democratic Secession: Liberalism, Nationalism, and the Right of Minorities to Self-Determination." *International Journal of Constitutional Law* 6 (2008).

Mansfield, Edward, and Jack Snyder. *Electing to Fight: Why Emerging Democracies Go to War.* Cambridge, MA MIT Press, 2005.

Marauhn, Thilo. "Anspruch auf Sezession?" [Claim to secession?] In *Selbstbestimmungsrecht der Völker—Herausforderung der Staatenwelt: Zerfällt die internationale Gemeinschaft in Hunderte von Staaten?*, edited by Hans-Joachim Heintze. Bonn, Germany: J. H. W. Dietz, 1997.

Margalit, Avishai, and Joseph Raz. "National Self-Determination." *Journal of Philosophy* 87 (1990).

Mattern, Johannes. *The Employment of the Plebiscite in the Determination of Sovereignty.* Baltimore: Johns Hopkins Press, 1920.

McCorquodale, Robert. "Self-Determination: A Human Rights Approach." *International and Comparative Law Quarterly* 43 (1994).

McEwen, A. C. *International Boundaries of East Africa.* Oxford: Clarendon Press, 1971.

McGoldrick, Dominic. *The Human Rights Committee: Its Role in the Development of the International Covenant on Civil and Political Rights.* Oxford: Oxford University Press, 1991.

Mearsheimer, John J., and Stephen M. Walt. "Leaving Theory Behind: Why Simplistic Hypothesis Testing Is Bad for International Relations." *European Journal of International Relations* 19 (2013).

Mégret, Frédéric. "The Right to Self-Determination: Earned, Not Inherent." In *The Theory of Secession,* edited by Fernando R. Tesón. Cambridge: Cambridge University Press, 2016.

Meisels, Tamar. *Territorial Rights.* Dordrecht, Netherlands: Springer, 2009.

Memorandum of Agreement, United Kingdom–Scotland, October 15, 2012, Sec. 30(2) of the Scotland Act 1998.

Meyrowitz, Joshua. *No Sense of Place: The Impact of Electronic Media on Social Behavior.* Oxford: Oxford University Press, 1986.

Mill, John Stuart. *Considerations on Representative Government.* London: Parker, Son, and Baum, 1861; repr., London: Elecbook, 2000.

Miller, David, *Citizenship and National Identity.* Cambridge: Cambridge University Press, 2000.

Montevideo Convention on the Rights and Duties of States (Montevideo, December 26, 1933) 165 League of Nations Treaty Series 19, 49 Stat. 3097 (1933), entered into force December 26, 1934.

Montville, Joseph V. *Conflict and Peacemaking in Multiethnic Societies.* New York: Lexington Books, 1991.

Moore, Margaret. *A Political Theory of Territory.* Oxford: Oxford University Press. 2015.

———. "The Self-Determination Principle and the Ethics of Secession." In *National Self-Determination and Secession,* edited by Margaret Moore. Oxford: Oxford University Press, 1998.

Morss, John R. "The International Legal Status of the Vatican/Holy See Complex." *European Journal of International Law* 26, no. 4 (2015): 927.

Moyn, Samuel. *The Last Utopia: Human Rights in History.* Cambridge, MA: Harvard University Press, 2012.

Musgrave, Thomas D. *Self-Determination and National Minorities.* Oxford: Oxford University Press, 1997.

Musil, Robert. *The Man without Qualities.* Vol. 1. New York: Alfred A. Knopf 1995.

Mylonas, Harris. *The Politics of Nation-Building: Making Co-Nationals, Refugees, and Minorities.* Cambridge: Cambridge University Press, 2012.

Naticchia, Chris. *A Law of Peoples for Recognizing States.* New York: Lexington Books, 2017.

Nelson, Elizabeth A. "Power and Proximity: The Politics of State Secession." PhD diss., City University of New York, 2016.

Nine, Cara. *Global Justice and Territory.* Oxford: Oxford University Press, 2012.

———. "Territorial Rights: An Undisclosed Premise in Theories of Global Justice." In *Current Controversies in Political Philosophy,* edited by Thom Brooks. New York: Routledge, 2015.

Norman, Wayne. *Negotiating Nationalism: Nation-Building, Federalism, and Secession in the Multinational State.* Oxford: Oxford University Press, 2006.

Nottebohm Case (*Liechtenstein v. Guatemala*), International Court of Justice Rep. 1955 (April 6).

Nurses' Health Study, The. "History—Nurses' Health Study: Original Cohort." http://www.nurseshealthstudy.org/about-nhs/history.

Oklopcic, Zoran. *Beyond the People: Social Imaginary and Constituent Imagination.* Oxford: Oxford University Press, 2018.

Orentlicher, Diane F. "Separation Anxiety: International Responses to Separatist Claims." *Yale Journal of International Law* 23, no. 1 (1998).

Organization of African Unity. "Resolutions Adopted by the First Ordinary Session of the Assembly of Heads of State and Government Held in Cairo, U.A.R.," AHG/Res. 16(I), July 17–21, 1964.

Padmore, George, ed. *History of the Pan-African Congress.* Washington, DC: Frederick A. Praeger 1965.

Pavković, Aleksandar. "Recursive Secessions in Former Yugoslavia: Too Hard a Case for Theories of Secession?" *Political Studies* 48 (2000): 485.

Pavković, Aleksandar, and Peter Radan, eds. *The Ashgate Research Companion to Secession.* London: Ashgate, 2011.

Pavković, Aleksandar, and Peter Radan. *Creating New States: Theory and Practice of Secession.* Aldershot, UK: Ashgate, 2007.

Peace Research Institute Oslo, "UPCD/PRIO Armed Conflict Dataset." http://www.pcr.uu.se/research/ucdp/datasets/ucdp_prio_armed_conflict_dataset/.

Pentassuglia, Gaetano. "State Sovereignty, Minorities and Self-Determination: A Comprehensive Legal View." *International Journal of Minority and Group Rights* 9 (2002).

Pettersson, Therese, and Kristine Eck. "Organized Violence, 1989–2017." *Journal of Peace Research* 55, no. 4 (2018): 535–47.

Platon, Arnold. "Ethnic Map of WW2 Hungary," CC BY-SA 3.0, https://commons.wikimedia.org/w/index.php?curid=33528109.

Plischke, Elmer. "Self-Determination: Reflections on a Legacy." *World Affairs* 140 (1977–1978).

Pogge, Thomas. "An Egalitarian Law of Peoples." *Philosophy and Public* Affairs 23, no. 3 (1994).

Pomerance, Michla. *Self-Determination in Law and Practice: The New Doctrine in the United Nations.* The Hague: M. Nijhoff Publishers, 1982.

Quebec Reference. See *Reference re Secession of Quebec.*

Qvortrup, Matt. *Referendums and Ethnic Conflict.* Philadelphia: University of Pennsylvania Press, 2014.

Raleigh, Clionadh, and Havard Hegre. "Population Size, Concentration, and Civil War: A Geographically Disaggregated Analysis." Policy Research Working Papers (2007). World Bank Group ELibrary. https://doi.org/10.1596/1813-9450-4243.

Ramzy, Austin, and Alan Wong. "Young People Have Their Say about the Future of Hong Kong." *New York Times,* June 30, 2007.

Ratner, Steven. "Drawing a Better Line: Uti Possidetis and the Borders of New States." *American Journal of International Law* 90, no. 4 (1996).

Rawls, John. "Kantian Constructivism in Moral Theory." *Journal of Philosophy* 77 (1980): 515.

———. *The Law of Peoples.* Cambridge: Harvard University Press, 1999.

———. *Political Liberalism.* New York: Columbia University Press, 2005.

———. *A Theory of Justice.* Rev. ed. Cambridge: Belknap Press of Harvard University Press, 1999.

Reference re Secession of Quebec (1998), Canada, 2 S.C.R. 217.

"Religious Peace of Augsburg [Holy Roman Empire—Schmalkaldic League], September 25, 1555, The," 24. German History in Documents and Images. http://germanhistorydocs .ghi-dc.org/sub_document.cfm?document_id=4386.

Renan, Ernest. "Qu'est-ce qu'une nation?" [What is a nation?]. Lecture, Sorbonne, March 11, 1882. English translation: http://web.archive.org/web/20110827065548/http://www .cooper.edu/humanities/core/hss3/e_renan.html.

Report of the Independent International Fact-Finding Mission on Israeli Settlements in the Occupied Palestinian Territory, G.A. Human Rights Council, 22nd Sess., U.N. Doc. A/ HRC/22/63 (2013).

Resnik, Judith. "Law's Migration: American Exceptionalism, Silent Dialogues, and Federalism's Multiple Ports of Entry." *Yale Law Journal* 115 (2005–2006): 1564ff.

"Resolution on the National Question." Seventh (April) All-Russian Conference of the Russian Social Democratic Labor Party Bolshevik, April 29, 1917.

Rigo Sureda, A. *The Evolution of the Right of Self-Determination.* Leiden, Netherlands: Sijthoff, 1973.

Roeder, Philip. *Where Do Nation-States Come From: Institutional Change in an Age of Nationalism.* Princeton, NJ: Princeton University Press, 2007.

Rosenberg, Matt. "The Average Country." *ThoughtCo.,* November 5, 2007.

Rousseau, Jean-Jacques. *The Social Contract* (1762). London: J. M. Dent & Sons, 1920.

Rüegger, Vanessa, and Oleschak-Pillai, Rekha. "State Secession in International Law and the 2011 Referendum in the Sudan." In *Peters Dreiblatt: Föderalismus, Grundrechte, Verwaltung, Festschrift für Peter Hänni zum 60. Geburtstag* [Peter's trefoil: Federalism, fundamental rights, administration—Festschrift for Peter Hänni on his 60th birthday], edited by M. Gredig, et al. Bern: Stämpfli, 2010.

Rushdie, Salman. *Shalimar the Clown.* New York: Random House, 2005.

Saunders, Ben. "Defining the Demos." *Philosophy, Politics, and Economics* 11 (2012): 280.

Schachar, Ayalet. *The Birthright Lottery: Citizenship and Global Inequality.* Cambridge, MA: Harvard University Press, 2009.

Schaffer, Peter. *Amadeus*. Film, directed by Milos Forman, 1984. Los Angeles, CA: Orion Pictures, 1997 (DVD).

Schmitt, Carl. *The Concept of the Political*. Expanded ed. Chicago: University of Chicago Press, 2007.

Schuker, Stephen A. "The Rhineland Question: West European Security at the Paris Peace Conference 1919." In *The Treaty of Versailles: A Reassessment after 75 Years,* edited by Manfred F. Boemeke, Gerald D. Feldman, and Elisabeth Glaser, 275, 291. Cambridge University Press, 1998.

Scott, James. *The Art of Not Being Governed: An Anarchist History of Upland Southeast Asia*. New Haven, CT: Yale University Press, 2009.

Searcey, Dionne. "As Cameroon English Speakers Fight to Break Away, Violence Mounts." *New York Times,* June 28, 2018.

Security Council Res. 1674, U.N. Security Council Official Records, 5430th Meeting, Protection of Civilians in Armed Conflict, U.N. Doc. S/Res/1674 (2006).

Security Council. "Security Council Press Statement on Iraq" (press release), SC 13002, September 21, 2017. http://www.un.org/press/en/2017/sc13002.doc.htm.

Şen, İlker Gökhan. *Sovereignty Referendums in International and Constitutional Law*. Heidelberg, Germany: Springer, 2015.

Seton-Watson, Hugh. *Nations and States*. London: Methuen, 1977.

Seymour, Charles, ed. *The Intimate Papers of Colonel House*. Vol. 4. Boston: Houghton Mifflin, 1928.

Shany, Yuval. "Redrawing Maps, Manipulating Demographics: On Exchange of Populated Territories and Self-Determination." *Law and Ethics of Human Rights* 2 (2008).

Sharma, Bhadra. "Sushil Koirala, Ex-Premier of Nepal Who Fought for Democracy, Dies at 77." *New York Times,* February 11, 2016.

Sharma, Surya P. *Territorial Acquisition, Disputes and International Law*. The Hague: Martinus Nijhoff Publishers, 1997.

Shaw, Malcolm N. *Title to Territory in Africa: International Legal Issues*. Oxford: Clarendon Press, 1986.

Shelton, Dinah. "Self-Determination in Regional Human Rights Law: From Kosovo to Cameroon." *American Journal of International Law* 105 (2011).

Simmons, Beth. *Mobilizing for Human Rights: International Law in Domestic Politics*. Cambridge: Cambridge University Press, 2009.

Smith, Adam. *Theory of Moral Sentiments* (1759). In *Adam Smith, Selected Philosophical Writings,* edited by James R. Otteson. Luton, UK: Imprint Academic, 2004.

Smith, Anthony D. *State and Nation in the Third World*. New York: St. Martin's Press, 1983.

Smith, Zadie. "Fences: A Brexit Diary." *New York Review of Books,* August 18, 2016.

Sorens, Jason. *Secessionism: Identity, Interest, and Strategy*. Montreal: McGill-Queens University Press, 2012.

South Asia Collective. *South Asia State of Minorities Report 2016: Mapping the Terrain*. Karnataka, India: Books for Change, 2016.

Southern Sudan Referendum 2011. "Results for the Referendum of Southern Sudan," 2011. http://southernsudan2011.com/.

South West Africa, Advisory Opinion: *Legal Consequences for States of the Continued Pres-*

ence of South Africa in Namibia (South West Africa) notwithstanding Security Council Resolution 276, Advisory Opinion, International Court of Justice Rep. 1971 (June 21).

Stalin, Joseph. *Marxism and the National Question.* The first publication in Prosvescheniye, Nos. 3–5, 1913 ed. Translator not indicated; transcribed by Carl Kavanagh. Marxists Internet Archive. https://www.marxists.org/reference/archive/stalin/works/1913/03a.htm#s1.

Sterio, Milena. *The Right to Self-Determination under International Law: "Selfistans," Secession, and the Rule of the Great Powers.* New York: Routledge, 2013.

Stilz, Anna. "On Colonialism and Self-Determination." Talk at Princeton University, posted February 15, 2013. https://law.yale.edu/system/files/documents/pdf/Intellectual_Life/LTW -Stilz.pdf.

———. "Why Do States Have Territorial Rights?" *International Theory* 1, no. 2 (2009).

Stollberg-Rilinger, Barbara. *Das Heilige Römische Reich Deutscher Nation* [The Holy Roman Empire of the German nation]. Munich: C. H. Beck Wissen, 2009.

Summers, James. *Peoples and International Law: How Nationalism and Self-Determination Shape a Contemporary Law of Nations.* Leiden, Netherlands: Martinus Nijhoff Publishers, 2007.

Sunstein, Cass R. "Constitutionalism and Secession." University of Chicago Law Review 58 (1991): 633.

Szymborska, Wisława. "Psalm," in Wisława Szymborska, *View with a Grain of Sand: Selected Poems,* translated by Stanislaw Baranczak and Claire Cavanagh. Boston: Houghton Mifflin Harcourt, 1995.

Tamir, Yael. *Liberal Nationalism.* Princeton, NJ: Princeton University Press, 1993.

Tancredi, Antonello. "A Normative 'Due Process' in the Creation of States Through Secession." In *Secession: International Law Perspectives,* edited by Marcelo G. Kohen. Cambridge: Cambridge University Press, 2006.

Taylor, Adam. "German Court Shuts Down Hopes for a Breakaway Bavaria." *Washington Post,* January 4, 2017.

Taylor, Celia R. "A Modest Proposal: Statehood and Sovereignty in a Global Age." *University of Pennsylvania Journal of International Law* 18, no. 3 (2014).

Temperley, H. W. V., ed. *A History of the Peace Conference of Paris.* Vol. 2. London: Oxford University Press, 1920.

Tesón, Fernando R., ed., *The Theory of Self-Determination.* Cambridge: Cambridge University Press, 2016.

Texas v. White. 74 U.S. 725 (1869).

Thoreau, Henry David. *On the Duty of Civil Disobedience* (1849). London: Simple Life Press, 1903.

Thornberry, Patrick. "The Democratic or Internal Aspect of Self-Determination with Some Remarks on Federalism." In *Modern Law of Self-Determination,* edited by Christian Tomuschat. Boston: Martinus Nijhoff Publishers, 1993.

———. "Self-Determination, Minorities, Human Rights: A Review of International Instruments." *International and Comparative Law Quarterly* 38, no. 4 (1989).

Tierney, Stephen. *Constitutional Referendums: The Theory and Practice of Republican Deliberation.* Oxford: Oxford University Press, 2012.

————. "Legal Issues Surrounding the Referendum on Independence for Scotland." *European Constitutional Law Review* 9, no. 3 (2013): 359.

Toft, Monica Duffy. *The Geography of Ethnic Conflict.* Princeton, NJ: Princeton University Press, 2003.

————. "Indivisible Territory and Ethnic War." *Security Studies* 12 (2002).

Tomasi di Lampedusa, Giuseppe. *Il Gattopardo.* Milan: Feltrinelli, 1958.

————. *The Leopard.* Translated by Archibald Colquhoun. New York: Pantheon, 2007.

Tomuschat, Christian, ed. *Modern Law of Self-Determination.* Boston: Martinus Nijhoff Publishers, 1993.

————. "Secession and Self-Determination." In *Secession: International Law Perspectives,* edited by Marcelo G. Kohen. Cambridge: Cambridge University Press, 2006.

Touval, Saadia. *The Boundary Politics of Independent Africa.* Cambridge, MA: Harvard University Press, 1972.

Treaty of Versailles (Versailles, June 28, 1919). 225 Consolidated Treaty Series 18, 11 Martens (3rd) 323, entered into force January 10, 1920.

Tsiranana, Philibert. Speech at the Organization of African Unity's 50th Jubilee. Addis Ababa, Ethiopia: 1963. Reprinted in *Celebrating Success: Africa's Voice over 50 Years, 1963–2013.* www.iri.edu.ar/publicaciones_iri/anuario/cd_anuario_2014/Africa/16.pdf.

Tushnet, Mark. "Secession as a Problem in Negotiation." In *Nullification and Secession in Modern Constitutional Thought,* edited by Sanford Levinson. Lawrence: University Press of Kansas, 2016.

Umozurike, U.O. *Self-Determination in International Law.* Hamden, CT: Archon, 1972.

UN Charter: United Nations, Charter of the United Nations, October 24, 1945, I UNTX XVI.

United Nations Department of Economic and Social Affairs. *International Migration Report 2015: Highlights.* ST/ESA/SER.A/375 (2016).

United Nations High Commissioner for Refugees (UNHCR). "Nationality Laws of the Former Soviet Republics." July 1, 1993. https://www.refworld.org/docid/3ae6b31db3.html.

UN Monthly Chronicle, April 1973.

Verfassung des Fürstentums Liechtenstein [Constitution of the Principality of Liechtenstein] (1921). In *World Constitutions Illustrated.* English translation, British and Foreign State Papers 127 (1932). London: Cassidy Cataloguing Services, 2014.

Vidmar, Jure. *Democratic Statehood in International Law: The Emergence of New States in International Practice.* Portland, OR: Hart Publishing, 2013.

Vienna Convention on the Law of Treaties (Vienna, May 23, 1969). 1155 United Nations Treaty Series 331, entered into force January 27, 1980.

Vienna Convention on Succession of States in Respect of Treaties (Vienna, August 23, 1978). 1946 United Nations Treaty Series 3, entered into force November 6, 1996.

"Vladimir Lenin to Soviet Foreign Minister Gregory Chicherin, March 10, 1922." Marxists Internet Archive. https://www.marxists.org/archive/lenin/works/1922/mar/14.htm.

Waldron, Jeremy. "The Principle of Proximity." New York University Public Law and Legal Theory Working Papers, No. 255 (2011).

————. "Superseding Historical Injustice." *Ethics* 103 (1992).

Wallerstein, Immanuel. "Ethnicity and National Integration in West Africa." In *Africa: So-*

cial Problems of Change and Conflict, edited by Pierre L. Van der Berghe. San Francisco: Chandler, 1965.

Walter, Christian, Antje von Ungern-Sternberg, and Kavus Abushov, eds. *Self-Determination and Secession in International Law.* London: Oxford University Press, 2014.

Walzer, Michael. "Comment." In *Multiculturalism: Examining the Politics of Recognition,* edited by Amy Gutman. Princeton, NJ: Princeton University Press, 1994.

Wambaugh, Sarah. *Plebiscites since the World War.* Washington, DC: Carnegie Endowment for International Peace, 1933.

Waters, Timothy William. "The Blessing of Departure: Acceptable and Unacceptable State Support for Demographic Transformation—The Lieberman Plan to Exchange Populated Territories in Cisjordan." *Law and Ethics of Human Rights* 2 (2008).

———. "Remembering Sudetenland: On the Legal Construction of Ethnic Cleansing." *Virginia Journal of International Law* 47 (2006).

Weiler, Joseph. "Catalonian Independence and the European Union." EJIL Talk! December 20, 2012. http://www.ejiltalk.org/catalonian-independence-and-the-european-union/.

Weinstock, Daniel. "Toward a Proceduralist Theory of Secession." *Canadian Journal of Law and Jurisprudence* 13 (2000).

Weller, Marc. *Escaping the Self-Determination Trap.* Leiden, Netherlands: Martinus Nijhoff Publishers, 2008.

———. "The Legal Rules on Self-Determination Do Not Resolve Self-Determination Disputes." In *Settling Self-Determination Disputes,* edited by Mark Weller and Barbara Metzger. Leiden, Netherlands: Martinus Nijhoff Publishers, 2008.

Wellman, Christopher Heath. *A Theory of Secession.* Cambridge: Cambridge University Press, 2005.

Whelan, Anthony. "Wilsonian Self-Determination and the Versailles Settlement." *International and Comparative Law Quarterly* 43 (1994).

Wilson, Woodrow. "President Wilson's Fourteen Points." Speech to Joint Session of Congress. January 8, 1918. World War I Document Archive. https://wwi.lib.byu.edu/index .php/President_Wilson%27s_Fourteen_Points.

Wippman, David, ed. *International Law and Ethnic Conflict.* London: Cornell University Press, 1998.

Wong, Alan. "At Hong Kong Swearing-In, Some Lawmakers Pepper Their Oath with Jabs." *New York Times,* October 12, 2016.

World Atlas. "Countries of the World." (May 31, 2017). https://www.worldatlas.com/.

Žižek, Slavoj. *Welcome to the Desert of the Real!* London: Verso, 2002.

ACKNOWLEDGMENTS

This book has been an embarrassing number of years in the making. Had I bashed it out when I first thought of it, a great many secessions mentioned in it wouldn't be. I had the idea for this book long before I began writing it, or rather I began writing it in parts—reconnoitering the lower slopes of the argument in smaller articles, whose ideas now find their place and full expression in this book. Small sections of this manuscript draw from the following of my articles—in each case much altered and rewritten—with my thanks to these journals and publishers:

- "A World Elsewhere: Secession, Subsidiarity, and Self-Determination as European Values," *Revista d'Estudis Autonòmics i Federals* 23 (2016), 11–45.
- "For Freedom Alone: Secession after the Scottish Referendum," *Nationalities Papers* 44 (2016), 124–43. Copyright © Association for the Study of Nationalities, revised excerpts reprinted by permission of (Taylor & Francis Ltd, http://www.tandfonline .com) on behalf of Association for the Study of Nationalities.
- "The Spear Point and the Ground Beneath: Territorial Constraints on the Logic of Responsibility to Protect," *International Relations* 30(3), pp. 314–327. Copyright © 2016 by the Author. Revised excerpts reprinted by permission of SAGE Publications Ltd.
- "Taking the Measure of Nations: Testing the Global Norm of Territorial Integrity," *Wisconsin International Law Journal* 33 (2015), 563–86. Copyright © 2015 The Regents of the University of Wisconsin.
- "Shifting States: Secession and Self-Determination as Subsidiarity," *Percorsi costituzionali* 3 (2014), 751–64.
- " 'The Momentous Gravity of the State of Things Now Obtaining': Annoying Westphalian Objections to the Idea of Global Governance," *Indiana Journal of Global Legal Studies* 16 (2009), 25–58.
- "Assuming Bosnia: Taking the Polity Seriously in Ethnically Divided Societies." In *Deconstructing the Reconstruction: Human Rights and the Rule of Law in Postwar*

Bosnia and Herzegovina, edited by D. Haynes, 53–78. Burlington, VT: Ashgate, 2008.

- "The Blessing of Departure: Acceptable and Unacceptable State Support for Demographic Transformation—The Lieberman Plan to Exchange Populated Territories in Cisjordan," *Law & Ethics of Human Rights* 2 (2008), 221–85, by Berkeley Electronic Press. Revised excerpts reproduced with permission of Berkeley Electronic Press in the format Book via Copyright Clearance Center.
- "A Different Departure: A Reply to Shany's 'Redrawing Maps, Manipulating Demographics: On Exchange of Populated Territories and Self-Determination,'" *Law & Ethics of Human Rights* 2 (2008), 311–23, by Berkeley Electronic Press. Revised excerpts reproduced with permission of Berkeley Electronic Press in the format Book via Copyright Clearance Center.
- "Contemplating Failure and Creating Alternatives in the Balkans: Bosnia's Peoples, Democracy and the Shape of Self-Determination," *Yale Journal of International Law* 29 (2004), 423–75.
- "Indeterminate Claims: New Challenges to Self-Determination Doctrine in Yugoslavia," *SAIS Review of International Affairs* 20 (2000), 111–44.

All illustrations in this book have been drawn by myself or with data from sources indicated. For epigraphic quotations, I have received permission to use or confirmation of fair use from the following:

- "Fences: A Brexit Diary," by Zadie Smith. Published by *The New York Review of Books,* 2016. Copyright © Zadie Smith. Reproduced by permission of the author c/o Rogers, Coleridge & White Ltd, 20 Powis Mews, London W11 1JN.
- Lea Brilmayer, "Secession and Self-Determination: A Territorial Interpretation," *Yale Journal of International Law* 16 (1991), 177, 199.
- Giuseppe Tomasi di Lampedusa, *Il Gattopardo.* Giangiacomo Feltrinelli Editore, 1958.
- *Amadeus,* screenplay by Peter Schaffer, directed by Milos Forman. Saul Zaentz Company, 1984.
- "Principle of Proximity," by Jeremy Waldron (working paper), New York University Law School, 2011, by permission of the author.
- Donald Horowitz, "The Cracked Foundations of the Right to Secede," *Journal of Democracy* 14, 2003.
- E. J. Hobsbawm, *Nations and Nationalism since 1780, Programme, Myth, Reality* © E. J. Hobsbawm 1990, published by Cambridge University Press.
- Ivor Jennings, *The Approach to Self-Government* © Cambridge University Press, 1956.
- Rogers Brubaker, *Nationalism Reframed: Nationhood and the National Question in the New Europe* © Rogers Brubaker 1996, published by Cambridge University Press.
- Anthony L. Asiwaju, "Transfrontier Regionalism: The European Union Perspective on Postcolonial Africa, with Special Reference to Borgu," in *Holding the Line: Borders in a Global World,* edited by Heather N. Nicol and Ian Townsend-Gault. Vancouver: UBC Press, 2005, p. 133.

- Judith Resnik, "Law's Migration: American Exceptionalism, Silent Dialogues, and Federalism's Multiple Ports of Entry," *Yale Law Journal* 115 (2005–2006), 1564.
- Portions from the articles "At Hong Kong Swearing-In, Some Lawmakers Pepper Their Oath with Jabs," published on October 12, 2016, and "Young People Have Their Say about the Future of Hong Kong" published on June 30, 2007, originally appeared in *The New York Times* and are used here by permission. © *The New York Times.*
- Excerpt from "Psalm" from *VIEW WITH A GRAIN OF SAND: Selected Poems* by Wisława Szymborska, translated from the Polish by Stanislaw Baranczak and Clare Cavanagh, Copyright © 1995 by Houghton Mifflin Harcourt Publishing Company. Copyright © 1976 Czytelnik, Warszawa. Reprinted by permission of Houghton Mifflin Harcourt Publishing Company. All rights reserved.

Many people and institutions have supported my work over the years—many more than I can name here—but I would like to say particular thanks to William Alford, David Armitage, James Boyd, Paul Brass, Hannah Buxbaum, Moshe Cohen-Eliya, Zsuzsa Csergő, Margaret Graves, Jeffrey Isaac, Robert Ivie, Timothy Lovelace, Timothy Lynch, Jody Madeira, Christiana Mauro, Marco Prelec, Yuval Shany, Sanford Levinson, Henry Steiner, Brittany Terwilliger, Armin von Bogdandy, and Carsten Wieland for specific comments, advice, or support; and to audiences at Indiana University, Hebrew University, the University of Illinois, the Association for the Study of Nationalities at Columbia University, Ludwig-Maximillians-Universität, Freie Universität, Max-Planck-Institut für ausländisches öffentliches Recht und Völkerrecht, Istanbul University Faculty of Law, Koç University, Sabancı University, the University of Wisconsin, Institut d'Estudis autonomics, ICON-S, European Consortium for Political Research, American University of Iraq—Sulaimani, University of Edinburgh, George Washington University, University of Missouri—Kansas City, Hertie School of Governance, and the University of Ljubljana.

My sincere thanks to the Alexander von Humboldt Stiftung, the Max-Planck-Institut für ausländisches öffentliches Recht und Völkerrecht, Harvard Law School—including its Human Rights Program, Reginald F. Lewis Fellowship, and East Asian Legal Studies Program—and Indiana University for generously supporting my work.

And finally, most special thanks to Rachel Guglielmo, who has read more, advised more, encouraged more, and listened more to my endless thoughts on secession than anyone should have to. Finally finished.

INDEX